ORDNANCE SURVEY MEMOIRS OF IRELAND

Volume Eleven

PARISHES OF COUNTY LONDONDERRY III
1831–5

Published 1991.
The Institute of Irish Studies,
The Queen's University of Belfast,
Belfast.
In association with
The Royal Irish Academy,
Dawson Street,
Dublin.

Grateful acknowledgement is made to the Economic and Social Research Council and
the Department of Education for Northern Ireland for their financial assistance at different
stages of this publication programme.

Paperback ISBN 0 85389 390 X
Hardback ISBN 0 85389 397 7

Printed by W. & G. Baird Ltd, Antrim.

Ordnance Survey Memoirs of Ireland

VOLUME ELEVEN

Parishes of County Londonderry III
1831–5

Roe Valley Lower

Edited by Angélique Day and Patrick McWilliams.

The Institute of Irish Studies
in association with
The Royal Irish Academy

CONTENTS

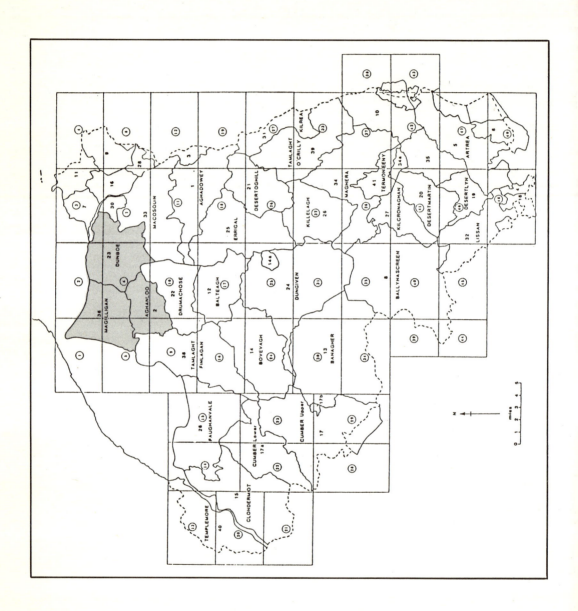

ACKNOWLEDGEMENTS

During the course of the transcription and publication project many have advised and encouraged us in this gigantic task. Thanks must first be given to the Royal Irish Academy, particularly former librarian Mrs Brigid Dolan and her staff, for making the original manuscripts available to us. Special thanks are due to Siobhán O'Rafferty for deciphering several passages in this volume.

We should like to acknowledge the following individuals for their special contributions. Dr Brian Trainor led the way with his edition of the Antrim memoir and provided vital help on the steering committee. Dr Ann Hamlin also provided valuable support, especially during the most trying stages of the project. Professor R.H. Buchanan's unfailing encouragement has been instrumental in the development of the project to the present. Without Dr Kieran Devine the initial stages of the transcription and the computerising work would never have been completed successfully: the project owes a great deal to his constant help and advice. Dr Kay Muhr's continuing contribution to the work of the transcription project is deeply appreciated. Mr W.C. Kerr's interest, as well as his own work on the Memoirs, gave inspiration. We thank him, also, for clarifying certain queries relating to this volume. Professor Anne Crookshank and Dr Edward McParland were most generous with practical help and advice concerning the drawings amongst the Memoir manuscripts. Finally, all students of the nineteenth century Ordnance Survey of Ireland owe a great deal to the pioneering work of Professor J.H. Andrews, and his kind help in the first days of the project is gratefully recorded.

The essential task of inputting the texts from audio tapes was done by Miss Eileen Kingan, Mrs Christine Robertson, Miss Eilis Smyth, Miss Lynn Murray, and, most importantly, Miss Maureen Carr.

We are grateful to the Linen Hall Library for lending us their copies of the first edition 6" Ordnance Survey Maps: also to Ms Maura Pringle of QUB Cartography Department for the index maps showing the parish boundaries. For providing financial assistance at crucial times for the maintenance of the project, we would like to take this opportunity of thanking the trustees of the Esme Mitchell trust and The Public Record Office of Northern Ireland.

Left:
Map of parishes of County Londonderry. The area described in this volume, the parishes of Roe valley lower, has been shaded to highlight its location. The square grids represent the 1830s 6" Ordnance Survey maps. The encircled numbers relate to the map numbers as presented in the bound volumes of maps for the county. The parishes have been numbered in all cases and named in full where possible, except those in the following list: Agivey 3, Arboe 4, Ballinderry 6, Ballyaghran 7, Ballyrashane 9, Ballyscullion 10, Ballywillin 11, Bovevagh 14a, Coleraine 16, Derryloran (no Memoir) 18, Kildollagh 28, Killowen 30, Maghera 34a, Magherafelt 35.

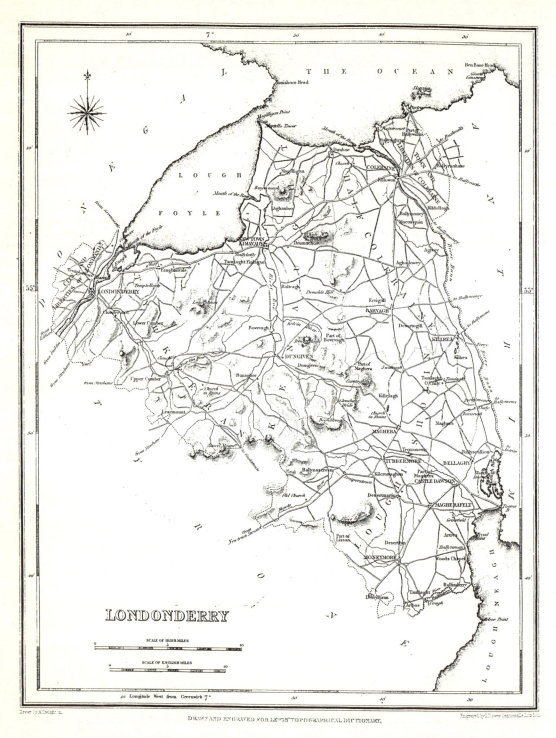

Map of County Londonderry, from Samuel Lewis' *Atlas of the counties of Ireland* (London, 1837)

INTRODUCTION AND GUIDE TO THE PUBLICATION OF
THE ORDNANCE SURVEY MEMOIRS

The following text of the Ordnance Survey Memoirs was first transcribed by a team working in the Institute of Irish Studies at The Queen's University of Belfast, on a computerised index of the material. For this publication programme the text has been further edited: spellings have been modernised in most cases, although where the original spelling was thought to be of any interest it has been retained and is indicated by angle brackets in the text. Variant spellings for townland and lesser place-names have been preserved, although parish and major place-names have been standardised and the original spelling given in angle brackets. Names of prominent people, for instance landlords, have been standardised where possible, but original spellings of names in lists of informants, emigration tables and on tombstones have been retained. Punctuation has been modernised and is the responsibility of the editors. Editorial additions are indicated by square brackets: a question mark before and after a word indicates a queried reading and tentatively inserted information respectively. Manuscript sections which have been underlined are indicated in italics, as are printed works. Original drawings are referred to in the text, and some have been reproduced. Manuscript page references have been omitted from this series. Because of the huge variation in size of Memoirs for different counties, the following editorial policy has been adopted: where there are numerous duplicating and overlapping accounts, the most complete and finished account, normally the Memoir proper, has been presented, with additional unique information from other accounts like the Fair Sheets entered into a separate section, clearly titled and identified; where the Memoir material is less, nothing has been omitted. To achieve standard volume size, parishes have been associated on the basis of propinquity.

There are considerable differences in the volume of information recorded for different areas: counties Antrim and Londonderry are exceptionally well covered, while the other counties do not have quite the same detail. This series is the first systematic publication of the parish Memoirs, although individual parishes have been published by pioneering local history societies. The entire transcriptions of the Memoirs made in the course of the indexing project can be consulted in the Public Record Office of Northern Ireland and the library at the Queen's University of Belfast. The manuscripts of the Ordnance Survey Memoirs are in the Royal Irish Academy, Dublin.

Brief history of the Irish Ordnance Survey in the nineteenth century and the writing of the Ordnance Survey Memoirs

In 1824 a House of Commons committee recommended a townland survey of Ireland with maps at the scale of 6", to facilitate a uniform valuation for local taxation. The Duke of Wellington, then prime minister, authorised this, the first Ordnance Survey of Ireland. The survey was directed by Colonel Thomas Colby, who had under his command officers of the Royal Engineers and three companies of sappers and miners. In addition to this, civil assistants were recruited to help with sketching, drawing and engraving of maps, and eventually, in the 1830s, the writing of the Memoirs.

The Memoirs were written descriptions intended to accompany the maps, containing information which could not be fitted on to them. Colonel Colby always considered additional information to be necessary to clarify place-names and other distinctive features of each parish; this was to be written up in reports by the officers. Much information about parishes resulted from research into place-names and was used in the writing of the Memoirs. The term "Memoir" comes from the abbreviation of the word "Aide-Memoire". It was also used in the 18th century to describe topographical descriptions accompanying maps.

In 1833 Colby's assistant, Lieutenant Thomas Larcom, developed the scope of the officers' reports by stipulating the headings or "Heads of Inquiry" under which information was to be reported, and including topics of social as well as economic interest. By this time civil assistants were writing some of the Memoirs under the supervision of the officers, as well as collecting information in the Fair Sheets.

The first "Memoirs" are officers' reports covering Antrim in 1830, and work continued on the Antrim parishes right through the decade, with special activity in 1838 and 1839. Counties Down and Tyrone were written up from 1833 to 1837, with both officers and civil assistants working on Memoirs. In Londonderry and Fermanagh research and writing started in 1834. Armagh was worked on in 1835, 1837 and 1838. Much labour was expended in the Londonderry parishes. The plans to publish the Memoirs commenced with the parish of Templemore, containing the city and liberties of Derry, which came out in 1837 after a great deal of expense and effort.

Between 1839 and 1840 the Memoir scheme collapsed. Sir Robert Peel's government could not countenance the expenditure of money and time on such an exercise; despite a parliamentary commission favouring the continuation of the writing of the Memoirs, the scheme was halted before the southern half of the country was covered. The manuscripts remained unpublished and most were removed to the Royal Irish Academy, Dublin.

The Memoirs are a uniquely detailed source for the history of the northern half of Ireland immediately before the Great Famine. They document the landscape and situation, buildings and antiquities, land-holdings and population, employment and livelihood of the parishes. They act as a nineteenth century Domesday book and are essential to the understanding of the cultural heritage of our communities. It is planned to produce a volume of evaluative essays to put the material in its full context, with information on other sources and on the writers of the Memoirs.

Definition of descriptive terms

Memoir (sometimes Statistical Memoir): An account of a parish written according to the prescribed form outlined in the instructions known as "Heads of Inquiry", and normally divided into three sections: Natural Features and History, Modern and Ancient Topography, Social and Productive Economy.

Fair Sheets: "information gathered for the Memoirs", an original title describing paragraphs of information following no particular order, often with marginal headings, signed and dated by the civil assistant responsible.

Statistical Remarks/Accounts: both titles are employed by the Engineer officers in their descriptions of the parish with marginal headings, often similar in layout to the Memoir.

Office Copies: These are copies of early drafts, generally officers' accounts and must have been made for office purposes.

Ordnance Survey Memoirs for County Londonderry

This volume, containing the memoirs for Magilligan, Dunboe and Aghanloo, three parishes in the lower Roe valley, is the third collection for the county and the eleventh volume in the present series. It describes the unique area around Magilligan with its great flat sandlands on the edge of Lough Foyle. This feature led to the parish being chosen as the site for the measurement of the baseline for the triangulation of the pioneering 19th century Irish Ordnance Survey. The economy of the area was very much influenced by this particular topography, and its farms, with warrens and bent grass manufacture, as well as the ordinary agricultural and fishing occupations, are described in great detail. This area, with Dunboe and Aghanloo, is rich in archaeological remains including early Christian churches and other later buildings, like the famous one-time episcopal palace of Downhill, Mussenden temple nearby and Hezlett House near Liffock. This fact, no doubt, and its location in the county Londonderry where most effort was directed into preparing material for publication in the mid-1830s, attracted the attentions of a great range of Memoir writers from various Engineer officers to the great Irish scholar John O'Donovan and antiquarian artist George Petrie, responsible for the research on place-names. Magilligan has the most extensive manuscript material, dating from 1831 until 1835, and is the most complicated with several sets of accounts as well as Fair Sheets. There is a main Memoir by Charles W. Ligar, an earlier Memoir account by O'Donovan and Petrie, who probably used material derived from George Downes and John Stokes as well as information from an early survey written by a local Presbyterian minister, the Reverend Samuel Butler. This report was given to the Memoir writers by the Reverend John Graham, the local Church of Ireland clergyman, whom the Memoir writer James Boyle drew on. Graham also supplied, in a most distinctive style, detailed information on natural history and local features. It is clear he (and Butler) had participated in an earlier survey undertaken in the 1820s by the North West Society, an agricultural improvement society. There is also information taken in the field by John Bleakly and Thomas Fagan, the Fair Sheets. These are brief, almost annotated in style but detailed in content and were used as primary sources by the Memoir writers. Thomas Larcom, the Assistant Director of the Survey, appears to have taken an early interest in the area: from 1831 there are notes about place-names and antiquities for Magilligan and Aghanloo. The latter follows much the same pattern as Magilligan, with several drafts and material dating from 1833 to 1835. Dunboe is fairly straightforward with a main account, Fair Sheets, and place-name material by John O'Donovan, all dated 1835; there is also a copy of an earlier officer's account. To assist the readers, the editors have rearranged the Fair Sheets to conform with subject headings in the Heads of Inquiry, with dates given where necessary; and where duplicate material has been removed, we have prefaced the Fair Sheet with the term "Extracts".

Drawings are listed below and are cross-referenced in the text; some are illustrated. The manuscript material is to be found in Boxes 29, 38, 39 and 45 of the Royal Irish Academy's collection of Ordnance Survey Memoirs, and section references are given beside each parish below.

Aghanloo: Box 29 II 1, 3–4, 6a and 6b, 7, 10–11, parts of 2, 5, 8a and 13.

Dunboe: Box 39 I 1, 2, 3.

Magilligan: Box 45 II (in full or in part) 1–13, 15–18, 21–3, with additions from Box 38 II 2.

Drawings

Aghanloo [section 3, all by C.W. Ligar]:

Aghanloo old church and churchyard, ground plan and section with dimensions.

Castle of Ballycastle, ground plan with annotations and dimensions.

Remains of Ballycastle, ground plan with annotations and dimensions.

Plan and view of 2 standing stones in Stradreagh townland.

Stradreagh Fort, ground plan and section with dimensions.

King's Chair in Largantea townland, view of entrance to burial chamber with dimensions [illustrated].

Kiln Pot in Stradreagh townland, ground plan and section with dimensions.

Cairn or mound in Ballyhanna townland, ground plan and section.

Chamber in mound in Ballyhanna townland, ground plan and section with dimensions.

Dunboe [sections 2 and 3]:

Stone tablet in old church of Dunboe, with inscription.

Dunboe old church, ground plan with dimensions; style of masonry inside east gable; view from south east showing monument in graveyard [illustrated].

Iron arrow found in moat of Big Glebe Fort, with dimensions.

Coin found in moat of Big Glebe Fort, obverse and reverse sides.

Big Glebe Fort, ground plan and section with annotations and dimensions, showing ramp and remains of stone gate posts.

Fort in Ballyhacket Lisawilling townland, ground plan and section with annotations and dimensions.

Fort in Dunalis Upper townland, ground plan with dimensions showing situation of Chief's Chair.

Chief's Chair in Dunalis Upper townland, with dimensions.

Bankish Hill Cove, ground plan with longitudinal section showing entrance and end called sewer or airhole, with dimensions; also 3 vertical sections with dimensions and notes.

Cove in Dunalis townland, ground plan with 2 longitudinal and 1 vertical section of cove with 2 branches, and dimensions.

Plan and section of proposed improvement to road between Coleraine and Articlave, with dimensions [all the above by C.W. Ligar]

Ballyveety Fort, outline with dimensions.

Deer's antler from Liffock, marginal drawing.

Church at Articlave, outline with dimensions.

Cave in Artidillan townland, ground plan.

Entrance to cave in Fermullen townland.

Cave in Farnlester townland, ground plan.

Natural cave in strand near parish boundary with Magilligan, ground plan.

Large cave near White Cave, ground plan.

Small cave near White Cave, ground plan.

Gull Cove, ground plan.

Temple Cave, ground plan.

Permir Cave, ground plan.

Pigeon Cave, ground plan.

Natural cave, ground plan [all the above by J. Bleakly].

Magilligan [sections 1, 5, 6, 8, 10, 13, 16, 17]:

Plan of Magilligan parish showing present and former boundary of the sea.

Deer's antler in Drummons townland, with dimensions.

Inscription from Catholic chapel in Tamlaght townland.

Old parish church, ground plan with annotations and dimensions.

Grave of Bishop Aidan, showing windows in wall of old church in background, with dimensions.

Doorway of old parish church, showing interior with forms and baptismal font [illustrated].

Magilligan or Tamlaght old church, east gable and Bishop Aidan's pulpit in the distance.

Communion cup with inscription and lid, and dimensions [illustrated].

Duncrun abbey and burying ground, ground plan and section.

Gravestone with double cross in Duncrun abbey.

Mound south of Duncrun abbey, ground plan and section.

Duncrun and neighbourhood, ground plan showing buildings, mound and antiquities [illustrated].

Stone weight found in remains of castle in Duncrun townland.

Witch hill in Gortmore townland, ground plan and section with dimensions of different stones.

Dun Patrick Fort, Duncrun townland, ground plan and section.

Cave at the base of Binevenagh, ground plan and section.

Natural cave about 30 feet above the base of Binevenagh.

Coin found in Magilligan, view of both faces [illustrated]. [All the above by C.W. Ligar]

Craigbolie Fort and rock of Binevenagh.

Ancient triangular enclosure on hill behind Castle Lecky, with dimensions [last two by J. Stokes].

Coins from Lower Drummons townland, marginal drawing.

Drag with claws for pulling top off rough land, marginal diagram.

Draining tile from Bellerena townland, marginal diagram [last three by J. Bleakly].

Rabbit burrows: ground plans of 5 types of burrows; longhandled burrowing spade; water table in lowlands, section; druims and misks, section.

Diagram showing shape of Crookdooish by Captain M. Waters.

Parish of Aghanloo, County Londonderry

Draft Memoir by C.W. Ligar, July 1835, with
one addition by J. Stokes

MEMOIR WRITING

Memoir Writing

Read 3 September 1835, very good [initialled]
RKD [Dawson].

NATURAL FEATURES

Hills

The highest points of land are Binevenagh
<Benyevenagh> 1,260 feet, Ballybrissell 1,147
feet, Stradreagh 1,072 feet, Ballyhanna 1,020
feet, Grange North 1,157 feet and Grange East
955 feet above the level of the sea, all of which
form the south part of the mountain generally
known under the name Binevenagh, which is the
last of the basaltic chain which extends through
the country. The part embraced by the parish
presents a steep slope to the south west for a
distance of half a mile, but then the slope becomes
much more gradual and forms the fertile portion
of the parish. A small stream divides it into 2
parts, distinguished by the names of Stradreagh
and Ballyhanna mountains; and through the path
thus formed the road from Newtown Limavady to
Downhill, made by the late Lord Bristol, ascends
to the summit of the mountain.

Lakes and Rivers

Lakes: there are none in the parish.

Rivers: the River Roe is connected with this
parish for 4 and a half miles, dividing it from
Tamlaght Finlagan for the first 2 and a half miles
[and] from Magilligan for 350 yards near the
latter part of its course. Its direction, although
very crooked and winding, is on the whole from
south to north and averages 100 feet in breadth.
The lowest part of it when connected with the
parish is 1 and one-eighth of a mile from its mouth
and it is slightly affected by the tide as far as it is
embraced by the parish. It is only navigable for
small boats except as far as Wooden bridge at
Bellarena, where the stone piers have collected a
quantity of sand so that nothing can pass unless at
high tides assisted by floods in the river. None are
employed in the part of the river within the limits
of the parish. [Insert footnote: The only boats
employed on the river at any part of it are 2 flat-
bottom boats belonging to Conolly Gage Esquire

which carry shells and mud for manure from
Lough Foyle. These are connected with the parish
of Magilligan as they do not go up so far as this
parish].

Although possessing a great body of water, this
river cannot be made useful for water power
owing to its having scarcely any fall through
the parish. It is subject to large floods which
are sometimes increased by the wind from the
north west and high tides which keep back the
water and prevent its discharge into Lough Foyle.
The largest floods generally take place from
the 1st November to the 1st January. Those
which occur about the month of August do much
injury to the crops and the others destroy fences
and carry away the productive soil where the
current of the water passes over, but in the places
where the water remains without motion, it deposits earth and fine sand which benefit the land.
From its very crooked course and flowing through
a level valley, it has a tendency to change its
direction, which it has sometimes done and often
tears away portions of its banks. It impedes the
communication between the parish and
Ballymacran in the parish of Tamlaght Finlagan,
where shells for manure are to be procured, but it
is in contemplation to erect a bridge at Carbullion
which would be of much importance to this parish. The bed of the river is composed of sand and
gravel.

There are some small streams in the parish,
tributaries to the Roe: the largest of them is the
Curly, which rises in the mountains of this parish
at a distance of 6 and a half miles from its junction
with the Roe. The parish is abundantly supplied
with water from these streams and from excellent
springs and wells.

Bogs

Nearly the half of the north part of the parish is
covered with bog which varies from 1,100 feet to
700 feet above the level of the sea. With the
exception of a few fir roots in the townland of
Largentea, no timber has been found embedded in
it. The depth of the bog is very unequal, being
spread over the inequalities of the ground. It is in
hollows, sometimes 10 feet deep, but in general it
is from 2 to 8 feet in depth. The substratum is
gravel and rock.

Woods

There is no natural wood in the parish or extensive plantation. The Glebe House has a small portion of ornamental planting and most of the farmhouses are supplied with a few trees and in many cases they are surrounded by orchards of considerable extent. Much advantage could be derived by planting the rough and, at present, unprofitable sides of mountains, a course which has been attended with success by Conolly Gage Esquire in the parish of Magilligan. [Insert note: More might be said of Mr Gage's plantation, its extent, the kinds of trees planted].

Coast

None.

Climate

The air of the parish is considered to be very healthy and is mild, being situated at a moderate elevation above the level of the sea. The following is the time at which the different crops are sown and are ripe. Seasons in which the crops are put down and become ripe: wheat put down from 15th October and is ripe from 10th August. Barley put down from 20th April and is ripe from 1st August. Oats put down from 1st March and is ripe from 10th August. Flax put down from 25th April and is ripe from 1st August. Potatoes put down from 1st May and is ripe from 1st October.

MODERN TOPOGRAPHY

Towns and Public Buildings

Towns: there is no town in the parish.

The public buildings consist of the parish church and schoolhouse. The church was commenced 12th August 1823 and finished 25th March 1825 and cost 900 pounds, which sum was furnished by the Board of First Fruits. The parish also paid 37 pounds for enclosing the churchyard. It is of a rectangular form, measuring 55 feet by 24 and a half feet on the inside and will accommodate 238 persons. It is substantially built and has a tower which tapers towards the top and is ornamented by 4 minarets. The church is lighted by 4 Gothic windows, 3 on one side and 1 in the gable, the inside finished in the plainest manner.

Schoolhouse

An excellent schoolhouse is in progress of erection by the Marquis of Waterford in the townland of Artikelly, near the side of the road leading to the parish of Magilligan. It is to consist of 4 rooms, 2 of which are to be 18 feet by 20 feet, and the other 2 20 feet by 8 and a half feet.

Gentlemen's Seats

The Glebe is the only gentlemen's residence but there are numerous good farmhouses throughout the parish. The Glebe House was built about the year 1789. It is a good family residence, is ornamented with a small quantity of young planting and is pleasantly situated on a slightly swelling hill at the base of the mountain.

Bleach Greens, Manufactories and Mills

There are no mills or bleach greens within the parish. There are brickfields in the townlands of Tullyarmon, Magheraskeagh, Carbullion and Artikelly.

Churning Machine

There is a small churning machine in the townland of Largentea of very simple construction, worked by a breast water wheel 6 feet 2 inches in diameter and 16 and a half inches broad across the rim, with a fall of water of 5 feet. The stream which supplies it proceeds from a very fine spring about 50 yards distant. The expense of the house and machinery was 5 pounds.

The construction of the machinery is as follows: to the axle of the water wheel is attached a cog wheel of metal, 8 inches in diameter. This cog wheel acts on another of half its diameter. To the latter is attached an iron crank 1 foot long which moves up and down a horizontal lever, to the opposite end of which is attached by an iron pin the handle of the churn. The horizontal lever which is formed of wood is balanced by an iron pin passing freely through it at a height of 6 feet from the ground. The lever passes through an upright piece of timber fixed in the ground and fastened at top to a beam. [Insert note: It would be desirable to know the produce of this mill].

Communications

The mail coach road from Newtown Limavady to Coleraine was formerly through this parish and the road is still kept in good repair although not used for a direct communication except by the parishioners. It ascends 2 steep hills on each side of Stradreagh mountain, but these might be avoided by keeping more to the south and near the Curly stream. The road is 21 feet broad clear of ditches and fences.

At half a mile from the first junction of this road with the parish on the side next to Newtown Limavady there is a road leaves it, which pursues a northern direction to the parish of Magilligan for a distance of 3 miles. It is kept in excellent repair and is 21 feet broad clear of ditches and fences; and at 1 mile from the point where this road branches off, there is also another road branching off to Downhill called the Bishop's Road, which takes a north east direction and was made by the late Lord Bristol (Bishop of Derry) about 52 years ago. 2 and a half miles of it is within this parish and is repaired by the county, but since his death the part of it on the summit of the mountain has become impassable.

Branching off from the Bishop's Road there is one called the Black Road, which was also commenced by Lord Bristol after the other was finished, but that part of it on the top of the mountain has never been gravelled and is therefore impassable. One mile of it only is contained within this parish.

There are also numerous other by-roads throughout the parish, all of which are in good repair.

Bridges

There are several small bridges over the streams which the above roads cross, which are generally in a good state of repair. It is in contemplation to erect a bridge across the Roe at Carbullion to form a communication between the parish of Tamlaght Finlagan and Aghanloo.

General Appearance and Scenery

The farmhouses scattered over the parish are adorned with a few trees and many of them with rich orchards. These and the highly cultivated fields combine well as a foreground to the beautiful scenery around. Near the church from the road to Magilligan the view is very fine: Lough Foyle appears as a long and narrow sheet of water over the planting surrounding several houses in Myroe, with the mountains in the county of Donegal in the distance. The profile view of the precipitous face of Binevenagh can be seen to great advantage from all parts of this parish, particularly so near the entrance of the Glebe House. From Artikelly the plantations at Fruit Hill and Streeve are seen, clothing a long slope which gradually descends on the right hand. Over this fine group of trees the basaltic headlands Donald's hill, Benbradagh and the White mountain are seen, and on the right of them the mountains of Banagher, presenting outlines of a round and different form and softened by the distance.

ANCIENT TOPOGRAPHY

Old Church of Aghanloo

The old church of Aghanloo is situated in the townland of Rathfard. It was taken down in 1812 and little more than the foundations at present remain, except at the south where the side wall is 8 and a half feet high. The building lies east and west and measures 65 and a half feet long and 23 and a half feet broad in the inside. The walls are 3 feet 8 inches broad. In the churchyard, which has become elevated with graves above the floor of the interior of the building, are interred the remains of the Reverend George V. Sampson, formerly rector of the parish of Errigal and author of the *Statistical survey of the county of Derry*, who died 10th day March 1827 in the 65th year of his age. [Plan and section drawing of Aghanloo old church and churchyard, showing situation and road, dimensions of church 65 and half feet by 23 and half feet on the inside, walls 3 feet 8 inches thick, depth of foundations 5 feet and 8 feet 8 inches, scale 40 feet to 1 inch, by C.W. Ligar].

Holy Wells

Near the old church on the north side there is an ancient well called Mecrin's Well; and in an orchard adjoining the churchyard on the south there is another called Tobar Tiggy. It is said that the children who were not thriving were cured by washing them in this well. In the townland of Ballymoney there is a spring called the Holy Well.

Castle in Ballycastle

There are in the townland of Ballycastle and holding of John Dunlop the traces of an old bawn or castle. It appears to have consisted of a dwelling house 46 feet long and 29 and a half feet broad, surrounded by a wall enclosing a rectangular courtyard 131 feet long and 100 feet broad. It is said that 4 flanking towers formerly stood, one at each end of the angles of the courtyard, 2 sides of which only remain. One serves as the back wall of the dwelling house of John Dunlop and to the other is attached his office houses. The cellar is all that remains of the dwelling house of the castle, the walls of which are 3 and a half feet in breadth. The castle is surrounded on the north west and north east by a natural bank 30 feet in height and on the other 2 sides by a fosse, the traces of which are at present but indistinct. At the base of the natural bank the ground is low and marshy and is overflowed by the floods of the River Roe. In it, it is said that an anchor and 4 silver dishes were found, and in 1834 there were 2 oars dug up from a depth of 8 feet under the surface near the place where the anchor was before discovered.

[Insert addition by J. Stokes: The foundations of the keep only are to be discerned, surmounted by a farmer's dunghill. Not more than 9 inches of their height remains and they form an oblong of 51 feet 10 inches in length and 34 and a half feet in breadth, including the thicknesses of the walls, 3 feet. The interior of the castle is occupied by manure and pools of putrid water. At the distance of 30 feet from the western end of the oblong part of what was once the surrounding court wall, it has been converted into the back wall of the farmer's house. The castle stood up on the summit of the steep bank which was evidently once the shore of the sea. In digging a ditch in the flat ground which now extends up to it, a boat and an anchor were found about 20 years ago not far from it].

[Ground plan with annotations showing modern dwelling house with courtyard, thickness of wall 3 feet 2 inches, outlying wall 5 feet 6 inches thick; another dwelling house, dimensions 46 feet by 29 feet 6 inches]. Plan of the remains of Ballycastle. It is said that there were 4 flanking towers, one at each angle of the building, scale of 40 feet to 1 inch. This [west] corner has not been rebuilt owing to a prevalent belief that it would be thrown down by a ghost called Stilty if attempted. The part in red is modern. This [south west] turret was standing in 1803 and was thrown down by Jacob Forsythe, nothing at present remains of it (Jacob Forsythe was the occupying tenant at that time). [Wall bounding courtyard]: this fell in 1834. This part was seen by John Dunlop in 1804, after it had fallen. The foundation of a building, supposed to have been one of the flanking flanking towers, was seen here [east corner] in 1803 by John Dunlop but has since been removed.

Remains of Ballycastle: [plan and section drawing of site, dimensions of courtyard wall 131 and a half feet long, scale 80 feet to an inch]. Overflowed when there is a flood in the River Roe. [Signed] Charles W. Ligar, 16th July 1835.

Castle

[Insert marginal query: Ballycastle ?] This castle is mentioned in *The history of the Presbyterian church in Ireland* by James S. Reid, published in Edinburgh 1834, as will be seen from the follow-

ing copy of part of a letter written by an officer of the Lagan forces in 1642. "From Strabane we marched upon the O'Cahan's country on the other side of Lough Foyle, and coming over against Londonderry 4 companies of the Derry joined with us to relieve Lymavady Castle and Ballycastle which had been, 10 weeks before, strongly beleaguered by great forces and yet had sallied forth and killed many hundreds of the enemy being commanded by a resolute young gentleman, Captain Thomas Philips, his elder brother, Mr Dudley Philips, being gone about with 3 boats to bring provisions from Derry. That night we were welcome guests to the 2 castles who despaired of all succour. Next morning we advanced our march to the enemy's country, where at Magilligan we encountered the enemy: the O'Cahans, the Magilligans, the O'Hagans and the O'Neals. We killed upwards of 500 of them and scattered the rest." [Insert footnote: Colonel Audley Mervyn's *Exact relations*].

Pagan Remains: Standing Stones

There are in the townland of Largentea large upright stones standing amidst a confused heap of smaller ones (which measures 40 feet in length, 6 feet broad and in some parts 2 feet high). The 2 standing stones are 5 feet 10 inches by 5 feet and occupy a direction with respect to each other from north west to south east. On the south east near the standing stones there is a small tract of ground which has never been tilled and is covered with stones of different sizes, some of which are sunk into the ground. This tract of ground measures 50 feet in length and 30 feet in breadth.

There is but one other standing stone in this parish [insert addition: called Murphy's Stone], which is situated in the townland of Stradreagh and mountain grazing of Samuel Moore. It stands in a sloping posture and measures 5 feet in height, 8 feet in length and 2 and a half feet in thickness.

Plan of 2 upright stones [A and B] standing amidst a heap of small ones and also of a tract of land near them which has remained untilled and studded with large stones, scale 40 feet to an inch. North east view of 2 standing stones which are shaded in the plan and of the group on the west, with dimensions: [A] 5 feet 10 inches high, 2 feet 10 inches broad, 2 feet 6 inches thick; [B] 5 feet tall, 3 feet 2 inches broad, 2 feet 9 inches thick. 21st July 1835.

Forts

There are 12 forts in this parish, many of which have, however, been destroyed viz. Stradreagh

Fort, 2 forts in Lisnagrib, 2 forts in Largentea, 4 forts in Ballycastle, Killybready Fort, Dirtagh Fort and fort in Freehall or Moneyvennon.

The fort in the townland of Stradreagh is in a more perfect state of preservation than any of the other forts in the parish. It is formed of earth, 72 feet in diameter and in the interior there are the foundations of a rectangular building 36 feet long and 24 feet broad.

[Plan and section drawing of Stradreagh Fort, scale 80 feet to 1 inch, with dimensions: diameter of inner circumference 70 feet, depth of moat 4 feet, ramp 9 feet high, depth of ditches inside banks from 5 to 10 feet].

Forts

2 forts in the townland of Lisnagrib: these 2 forts have been levelled and are under crops. One of them, the traces of which are visible, was of a circular form, 36 yards in diameter. They were both built of earth. The diameter of the other is 50 yards. It was also circular.

2 forts in the townland of Largentea: the parapets of these 2 forts are formed of stones. One of them has been removed except a very small portion. It measures 46 yards in diameter. The other, which is more perfect, is 48 yards in diameter; both are of a circular form.

4 forts in the townland of Ballycastle: the 4 forts which formerly existed in this townland have been all destroyed.

Killybready Fort: this fort measures 40 yards in diameter and is of a circular form. It is now nearly all destroyed and is under crop. It was composed of earth and stones but principally of the former.

Dirtagh Fort: part of this fort is now occupied as a garden, part as the site of a dwelling and of the parapet, a lime kiln has been built. It was of a circular form and measured 45 yards in diameter.

Fort in Freehall or Moneyvennon: this fort is of a circular form, 37 yards in diameter. The parapet is made of earth and stones.

Caves

Cave in the townland of Largentea: this cave is on Alexander Hopkin's farm. The mouth is on a level with the ground, is 1 foot high and 1 and a half feet broad. Its extent cannot at present be ascertained as it is choked up with stones, but its architecture is exactly similar to all others in this country, the side walls being formed of stones without cement and covered with long flags stretched across them. See description and drawings of the cove in Bankish hill in the parish of Dunboe.

Cave in the townland of Lisnagrib: this cave is under the dwelling house of William Johnston. From the descriptions given of this cave from persons who have been in it, it appears to be similar to all others in the country. It has now been closed for the last 10 years. An old wooden dish was found in it, quite rotten.

Cave in Stradreagh: the cave in this townland has been closed for 50 years.

Cave in the townland of Drumalief: this cave is described as being about 15 yards long and 4 feet wide at the mouth by the persons who have visited it, who also state that they were prevented from going farther by the stones of the building which had fallen in. The mouth has been closed for 5 years and is now covered with soil which is bearing a crop. An old wooden dish was also found in it.

Cairn or Mound in Ballyhanna

There is, on the summit of the mountain in this townland, a very strong and carefully constructed mound formed of stones. It is of conical form and rises to the height of 9 feet, with a base 48 feet in diameter. On the summit there is a small chamber or cavity enclosed by stones sunk on their edges. The cavity measures 4 feet 3 inches long, 2 and a half feet broad and 2 feet deep. [Plan and section drawing of mound of stones, showing chamber marked C, height of mound 9 feet, scale 40 feet to an inch. 21st July 1835].

[Plan and section drawing of stone chamber in the mound in Ballyhanna, one stone measuring 2 feet, scale 2 feet to an inch].

Ancient Building: Kiln Pot

In the townland of Stradreagh there are the ruins of an ancient building. The interior measures 37 and a half feet by 26 and a half feet and the walls, which are composed of stones without mortar, are from 4 feet to 7 feet thick. The whole is now grown over with grass and the inhabitants in the neighbourhood are not able to say what it was originally intended for but many think it was a place of worship or a Danish fortress. It is known by the name of the Kiln Pot. [Plan and section of an ancient building called Kiln Pot, showing modern fence with dimensions 26 feet 6 inches by 37 feet 6 inches, stone (A) 3 feet 10 inches by 1 foot 10 inches by 1 foot; (B) 3 feet by 2 feet by 2 feet 2 inches, scale 80 feet to 2 inches]. 13th July 1835.

Cairn on Stradreagh Mountain

On the summit of Stradreagh mountain there is a

large cairn of stones which has been taken as one of the trigonometrical stations for the Ordnance Survey. It is composed of stones which vary in size from 2 feet downwards. It is of a conical form, 5 feet high with a base of 54 feet.

King's Chair

In the townland of Largantea, on the north side of the old road between Newtown Limavady and Coleraine, there is a natural recess or cavity in a small ridge of rocks called the King's Chair. The only part of it which appears to have been made by art is a canopy stone which covers the recess. The breadth of the seat is 18 inches and height of the recess 4 feet 8 inches, the whole forming but an indifferent seat as to comfort for a man of moderate bulk, the breadth being scarcely 18 inches at the point where the shoulders would come into contact.

[King's Chair, view of entrance to burial chamber with dimensions: from (a) to (b) is 5 feet, (B) to (B) is 2 feet, breadth of seat 1 foot 6 inches. 21st July 1835].

Decorated Stones

In 1833 Andrew Moore of Stradreagh found in his field, about 150 yards from the building called the Kiln Pot, 2 circular stones of about 3 inches in diameter and about half an inch thick each. One of these stones had engraven on its surface the figure of a male and female, with a small circular hole through its centre. The other had a number of letters marked on it. There were also a number of amber bead stones found in the same place.

Finn Macuill's Finger Stone

There is in the townland of Stradreagh, by the side of the mountain, a large stone called Finn Macuill's Finger Stone. It measures 6 and a half feet in height, 6 feet broad and 4 feet long. Tradition says that Finn Macuill cast this stone from Keady mountain to the place where it at present stands, a distance of about 2 miles.

Ree Hill

In the same townland there is a small hill called the Ree. It is considered to be a very gentle place [insert footnote: that is, much frequented by the fairies or gentry as they are called] and believed to have been formed by the Danes. At a former period there was a large quantity of stones round its base and on its surface, but the greater part of them have been removed. It measures 28 yards long and 24 yards broad.

Parish of . Tyhanloo

King's Chair in Largantea

Draft Memoir by George Petrie, with
sections by J. Stokes

Name of Parish

In the *Valor beneficiorum* of James I, Bishop
Downham's visitation book and other authorities,
the name of this parish is written Aghlowe. This
conveys pretty nearly the sound of its Irish name
Ath-lugha, which would be pronounced Ah-
loo[longstress]a[short stress] and unquestionably
signifies "Lugh's or Loui's ford." For the true
etymology of the name, we have the older authority of the *Life of Saint Columba*, compiled from
more ancient authorities by Magnus O'Donnell,
chieftain of Tirconnell, in the commencement of
the 16th century. In that life mention is made of a
holy and humble man named Teca who dwelt at
a place called Ath-Luga, in the same tract in
which the shrine of Saint Columba was situated
(see Magilligan). This in itself points out its
locality, but it is also stated that the church of Teca
was situated near a river as the church of Aghanloo
is, on the east bank of the River Roe, and the
visitation book of Archbishop King calls this
church "ecclesia Sancti Tagai" or "the church of
Saint Teca." Hence it appears certain that the
name of this parish like most others in Londonderry is not of ecclesiastical origin but anterior to
the foundation of the parish church.

NATURAL FEATURES

General Appearance and Scenery

The parish of Aghanloo is bounded on the north
by the parish of Tamlaghtard or Magilligan, on
the east by Dunboe, on the south by Drumachose
and on the west by Tamlaght Finlagan. The general appearance of this parish, like all those contiguous to the mouth of the River Roe, is remarkable for its picturesque and diversified beauty.
The bold basaltic range of Binevenagh
<Benevenagh> separates the arable from the pas-
ture lands and rises abruptly from the plains to the
height of 1,259 feet, on a base of little more than
an English mile. The precipices of this mountain
at its junction with Magilligan parish are singularly grand, being not less than 200 feet in height
and having their bases covered with immense
subsidences of the mountain. [Insert note by R.K.
Dawson: 200 feet hardly warrants "singularly
grand"]. The lower parts of the parish present the
agreeable contrast of a green and fertile level

affording pleasing indications of the industry and
wealth of its inhabitants.

Mountains

Binevenagh, the north western point of the basaltic formation of the north of Ireland, occupies the
north eastern portion of the parish. Ballyhanna
and Stradreagh mountains, parts of the same
range, stretch to the south and spread themselves
over the eastern limits.

Rivers

The River Roe forms the western boundary of the
parish. There are also several rivulets flowing
from the mountains yielding the most excellent
water. [Insert addition by J. Stokes: Many little
picturesque waterfalls occur on the sides [crossed
out: of the mountain] among the numerous streams
that flow from it].

Woods

There are neither natural woods nor plantations
worthy of notice; but money might be made by
planting the rough and at present unproductive
slopes of Binevanagh, a course which has been
pursued with signal success by Connolly Gage
Esquire in similar situations in Magilligan. Turf
occurs only on the top of the mountain. It is
becoming scarce and much labour is expended in
procuring it.

Spa Water

[J. Stokes] The natural history of this parish will
be included in that of Magilligan. There was a spa
water in Dowland which has been ploughed over
and carried away by covered drains.

PRODUCTIVE ECONOMY

Brickfields

There are 2 brickfields. These as well as many
others in the adjoining parishes supply the consumption of Newtown Limavady. They will be
more properly included in the description of that
town.

MODERN TOPOGRAPHY

Communications

There are 5 statute miles and 4 furlongs of the road
to Coleraine and 4 miles and a furlong of the road
to Magilligan <McGilligan>. They cross many
small rivulets, which are admitted under the road

by gulleys <gullets>. On the parish boundary, in the townland of Killybready, there is a broken bridge on a by-road. It is said that Lord Bristol measured the whole road from Londonderry to his palace at Downhill and erected posts at each mile. Owing, however, to their being made of wood, they have long since mouldered away.

Buildings

[G. Petrie] There is no town or village in Aghanloo, and with the exception of the church, the Seceding meeting house and rectory, each of which are on a very limited scale, there are no buildings worthy of notice. There are 2 water mills, one for corn, the other for flax.

Roads

The leading roads are from Newtown Limavady to Magilligan and Coleraine. The former is in excellent repair but the latter, no longer being the mail line, is now neglected. A fine road leading through the parish from Newtown Limavady to Downhill was made by Lord Bristol, Bishop of Londonderry, but is now quite impassable for spring carriages.

ANCIENT TOPOGRAPHY

Antiquities

The parish is unusually wanting in remains of antiquity. There are no sepulchral monuments of pagan times and only 4 or 5 earthen forts which are worthy of distinct notice. Of the ancient parish church or Kill-Teca, the foundations only remain. It was founded by Saint Teca in the 6th century. After the plantation of Ulster this church was allowed to fall into ruin, in which state it remained for several years until repairs by the Haberdashers' Company. It was again, as Archbishop King states, "much defaced in the troubles" and again re-edified, from which period it continued to be used as the parish church till the commencement of the present century, when it was entirely taken down and a new church erected on a different site. The graveyard is still used. It contains many monuments of old as well as modern date, but none worthy of particular mention except the tomb of the Reverend George Vaughan Sampson, the able topographer of the county who was for many [years] rector of this parish. To the celebrity which he justly obtained in the reading world for his learning and scientific acquirements, he added

the higher distinction of being beloved by all classes within the immediate sphere of his private life, for his profession of the various virtues which should adorn the character of a Christian minister. His tomb is thus inscribed: [insert] (monumental inscription here).

Castle of the O'Cahans

Previous to the Plantation there was a castle of the O'Cahan's in this parish, situated in the townland of Ballycastle on the east bank of the Roe. This apart, which was anciently called Ath-na-long or the "ford of the ships", [it] was chosen by the Haberdashers' Company as the seat or hall of their proportion and the castle was either repaired or wholly rebuilt by the company's farmer, Sir Robert MacLellan, by whom it was inhabited. There are no remains of it now to be found nor of the little town which had grown up around its walls.

Plans for a Port

The project of making Ballycastle a port was entertained by the Haberdashers' Company at a remote time. From the records of the Irish Society we find that so far back as 1729 "the town of Ballycastle being projected to be made a port, the society opposed the measure as likely to become detrimental to their interests"; and we also find that the project being still entertained in 1730: a memorial or representation of the society relating to Ballycastle was ordered to be presented by the governor to the court of common council, which was done. No further notice of the affair occurs, and it is probable that upon the sale of the Haberdashers' proportion to the Earl of Tyrone in the following year, all further notion of [projecting?] the matter was finally abandoned.

ANCIENT TOPOGRAPHY AND PLACE-NAMES

Queries and Answers by Lieutenants Lancey and Larcom

Aghanloo: Aghalow in Down Survey. Is probably Achad-lughaidh (pronounced Looe[long stress]). There is an old church. Is this is name? [Answer] I do not know any other name for this.

  Lughaidh is a common name of saints, abbots in old history and achad is sometimes prefixed to lands or churches named after them. [Signed] T.A. Larcom, 23rd June 1831. [Answer] Templepatrick, Templemoyle, Templecairn: here the church is named first. [Signed] William Lancey, 27th June.

Memoir Sections by G. Downes and J. Stokes, 1835

General Appearance and Scenery

The scenery of Aghanloo appears tame after the rocks and precipices of Magilligan. The attention of the stranger who walks through from Newtown is entirely directed to picturesque objects outside the parish: to the rock of Binevenagh <Benyevenagh> or the features of Lough Foyle. The district itself may be described as fields formed by the bend of a connecting ridge between the mountains of Binevenagh in Magilligan and that of Keady in Drumachose. The bottom is a plain bounded by the windings of the River Roe. The parish has the general appearance of a long-settled and cultivated district.

SOCIAL ECONOMY

Early Improvements

The foundation of the present state and condition of Aghanloo may be said to be first the settlement of Ulster and secondly the rebellion of 1641. English names are frequent. The present rector has contributed to its agricultural improvements by introducing the practice of green feeding into the district immediately around him. He is also advantageous as the sole resident gentleman and as the person to whom the majority of the paupers of the parish look up [to] for occasional assistance in their wants. He has contributed to its ornaments by ploughing and improving the glebe after the example of his predecessor the Reverend [blank] Robinson. The appointment by the Marquis of Waterford of the present agent to his estate has been highly beneficial to the tenantry, and they are now recovering from the injurious effects of the former agent the Reverend James Meara. They are treated with kindness and attention and receive a premium every year of an iron plough or the price of one to the best ploughman on the property.

Obstructions to Improvement

The legal disputes about rights which obstruct improvement are at present unknown. There was a dispute about the parochial boundary where it had joined Benjamin Lane's property in Magilligan, but it is now settled. The ancient customs of continually subdividing farms and gavelkind <gabelkind> do continue and are much discouraged by the Marquis of Waterford, who does not wish to let farms under 20 acres. He is enlarging them by allowing insolvent tenants to sell their farms to the best advantage and by throwing the smaller holdings together at the expiration of leases.

Local Government

There are no resident magistrates in Aghanloo. The revenue police are in number none. For the number of the present constabulary, see Drumachose in which they reside, at Newtown Limavady. Respecting peculiar jurisdictions, there are none. There are no police within the parish and none nearer than Newtown Limavady. The petty sessions are held at Newtown Limavady by [blank] magistrates. The number of outrages committed within the last [J. Stokes continues]: no outrages have occurred within the last 5 years. As usual, petty disputes and quarrels are on the decrease and the perpetrators have always been vigorously punished. These offences, outrages have been committed with reference to neither commerce, agriculture or manufactures and were resorted to by misguided persons to satisfy anger only, intoxication or litigious disputes being their general cause. Party spirit latterly produced 2 outrages, the last of which was in November 1828.

Combinations exist to no extent. Illicit distillation is trifling in Aghanloo and the smuggling of goods trifling also. Respecting insurance, there is [crossed out: nothing to be said but] that the Glebe House is the only insured house in the parish.

Poor

The only provision for the poor, aged and infirm is the profession of begging. There is no alms house, endowment, no house of industry nor mendicity. As there is no certain employment for the labourers during more than 3 months in the year, most of them must become paupers for the remainder. There are no poor shops.

The average amount of the church collection is [blank]. There was a bequest made by Robert Henry Church Esquire in the year 1824 of 1 pound 2d 9d Irish currency per annum, to be paid forever to the poor of Rathfad, Shanvey and Drumbane. It is now lapsed and there are 10 guineas Irish currency with the interest due.

Dispensary

The health of the people has become improved by resorting to the dispensary of Newtown Limavady.

This is and was evinced by the absence of the following diseases: epidemic fever, Asiatic cholera. [Insert note: The absence of fever in Aghanloo is attributed to the locality and air]. The former was always in part checked by its existence and the latter was greatly mitigated by the exertions of its members at the time when it was prevalent in the country (refer to Drumachose).

Schools

The introduction of schools has led to a perceptible improvement in moral and religious feeling. As to the parishioners, they are anxious for an improvement in this particular, in some degree. This is obvious in all sects and the cause may be attributed to the establishment of the Sunday schools, the increased exertions of the clergy and the diminution of the hedge schools.

Religion

The people are of the Protestant, Presbyterian, Roman Catholic and Dissenting persuasions, in the proportion of 1, 3 and two-thirds, 5 and a half. The first number represents the Episcopalians, the second is Dissenting of all classes, the third the Catholics. There are also a few Methodists, about 16, and some individuals belonging to the Seceding and Reformed Synods. Their respective congregations are attached to the parish of Drumchose. The clergy are thus supported: the income of Protestant, Reverend William Smiley, tithe 315 pounds, glebe and house 50 pounds [total] 365 pounds; Presbyterian (of the Orthodox sect), Reverend George Steen, who receives 75 pounds regium donum, stipend 75 pounds; Roman Catholic (Reverend Edward O'Hagan, parish priest, 100 pounds from sundry sources and Reverend William McDonagh P.C.C., 60 pounds from sundry sources). There are a few members of the Remonstrant Synod. These attend Reverend William Porter at Newtown Limavady, as also do Mr Steen's congregation. Mr O'Hagan's parochial district includes Drumachose, a part of Aghanloo, part of Balteagh and a part of Tamlaght Finlagan.

Query on the Reverend G.V. Sampson

Query: in Tamlaght Finlagan, the Reverend G.V. Sampson is stated to have died in 1828, in Aghanloo in 1827. Is not the latter correct? [J. Stokes] The latter is correct.

Habits of the People

The Irish and Scotch population differ or agree as follows: in style, comfort etc. of cottages. It is to be observed, however, that among the farmers the Scotch considerably exceed the Irish population in numbers. The latter are chiefly in about the churchland. The style and comfort of the Scotch cottages is the best; all differences between the exterior of the houses.

Food

The principal diet of the poor is potatoes and herrings. The latter, owing to poverty, are principally used when in season; when out of season their food is altogether potatoes and milk.

Fuel and Dress

The fuel is very good but at an inconvenient distance from that part of the parish adjacent to Newtown Limavady.

The dress of the Scotch is the best quality and respectability. That of the Irish is inferior owing to their greater poverty.

The costume of the Scotch settlers is respectable. They all strive to have a suit of black. A brown cloth top coat called a "slip on" is usual and that of the Irish is generally simple, being coarse grey cloth or frieze with trousers of very strong, coarse linen or union linen. Those who dress the worst seem to be weavers and labourers. The use of bonnets and shoes among the Irish or Roman Catholic females is on the increase.

Longevity, Family, Marriage

Respecting longevity there is one living instance: Robert Biggam of Killybready is about 100 years and in perfect health. Samuel McLaughlin of Granagh lived to the age of 100. [Insert note by J. Stokes: I am unable to state anything generally about longevity].

The usual number in a family is a little more than 5. The earliest age for marriage is 16. There has been an instance of a girl named Devlin who lived at Carbullion and was married at 12.

Amusements and Customs

Their amusements are not very varied. The following are the chief: hurling and playing, dancing, singing, with ball playing occasionally. These recreations are of the ordinary kind but they seem to be very fond of fiddle playing. They resort also to the fair on the Wooden bridge at Bellarena in Magilligan (see that parish). But they have not so much time for amusements as they formerly had, owing to various causes. This, however, although they complain of it, should be reckoned an improvement rather than a disadvantage. Respecting patrons' days and traditions concerning them, it may be stated that there are not any patrons' days in Aghanloo. There are some of the usual superstitious feelings about fairies, forts and bad and ill-luck, but not to the same extent as in Magilligan owing to the greater proportion of Scotch. The corrupt phrase used here of costnent or "without diet" is still, it is said, used in the neighbourhood of Galloway in Scotland. This idiomatic expression is in frequent use amongst them.

The local customs most prevalent are the same as what are prevalent among all the Scottish inhabitants of the country. On Christmas Day and New Year's Day they assemble and exercise themselves at shooting at marks. The customary prize is a goose or duck, or perhaps a pair of rabbits, which is awarded to the best marksman in a certain number of rounds. The old churchyard is the favourite place.

Meetings

Social meetings among the Dissenters are customary. At these, the Scriptures are read and doctrinal points discussed among the company.

Games and Music

The games of card playing, cock-fights at Easter, Christmas and All Hallow Eve with hurling are diminishing from the gradual increase of seriousness in the general character of the parishioners. Respecting recitation and music, it may be observed that there are singing schools beginning to be introduced among the Presbyterians. These are held in rotation among the farmers' houses and after music, both sacred and profane, a dance generally concludes.

Emigration

The extent of emigration to America last year (1834) has been to the number of 30. The favourite season and place is from the beginning of spring to the end of summer and to St John's, New Brunswick with those that are very poor, that passage being said to be the cheapest. The proportion of those that return has been about one-sixth in the last year (1834). The number that occasionally go in search of harvest or other work is about one-third of the cottiers, and the countries in which they seek it are England and Scotland. They take their wives and families with them and

for winter support they either sow potatoes or beg. The remaining two-thirds usually go to distant parishes as running beggars. However, many support themselves by gathering sea manure on the mud banks of the lough, retailing whiskey and following other small trades.

Remarkable Events

The most remarkable person born in this parish was the father of George Berriman, who is said to have had 49 children.

The following are the most remarkable circumstances on record: in 1818 George Berriman was murdered at a dance in a barn in Artikelly. In 1828, as James Williamson was returning from the market at Newtown Limavady, he was beaten by a party of Irish from Ballycarton. These 2 outrages arose from party spirit; now decreasing, see Local Government.

ANCIENT TOPOGRAPHY

Ancient Remains

In addition to the church and castle already noticed in the report, there are a great number of ruins and forts in the townlands of Dirtagh, Stradreagh, and that part of Largantea towards Lady O'Cahan's bridge. Perhaps some of these are worth noticing.

Notes by J. Stokes [1833]

PRODUCTIVE ECONOMY

Owners and Size of Holdings

The parish belongs to the Marquis of Waterford, except the townland of Freehall which belongs to Mr McCausland. The size of the farms in Aghanloo is generally from 20 to 30 acres. The average rent per acre of the best land is said to be 1 pound 10s an acre, middling 1 pound, worst 15s. Tithe amounts to about 2s and county cess half a crown to each acre.

Manures and Implements

The manures are lime or shells. Burnt lime may be obtained at 9d per barrel, shells for not less than 1s per barrel. The latter is mixed with the scourings of the ditches. The soil is generally a mixture of clay and sand, the good soil being not more than a foot deep. The implements of husbandry are harrows, shovels, spades and three-pronged pitchforks.

Principal Crops

The principal crops are potatoes, oats, wheat, barley and flax. The quantity of oats sown for each acre of Irish plantation measure is 7 bushels, of wheat 4 bushels, barley 3 and a half bushels, flax 3 bushels, potatoes about 26 bushels. Wheat, when grown, is worth about 9 pounds per acre, barley 8 pounds per acre, flax 7 pounds per acre, potatoes 14 pounds per acre. Blanter oats and English wheat are sown here. Of the potatoes, there are cups, red Downs and English reds. The average market price of oats is 7d per stone, wheat 1 pound 2s 6d per barrel, barley 8d ha'penny per stone, potatoes 2d ha'penny per stone. There are some good meadows in the parish. These are frequently irrigated. The hills are used as pasture but are very thinly stocked. The butter made from the milk of an Aghanloo cow is a firkin containing 72 lbs.

Wages

Farm servants receive at an average 5 pounds a year for males and 2 pounds 10s a year for females. There are neither sheep nor any regularly-stocked farms.

Turf Cutting and Springs

The charge for turf cutting is 1s for 4 days.
    In Binevenagh there are 3 springs called Clear Holes.

Fish

Whitefish have been caught in the Roe weighing 4 lbs. The principal food of the poor of the parish is potatoes and herrings.

Manufactures

There are no manufactures in this parish. Females are employed in spinning and sometimes knitting for their own use. The yarn is generally spun to 3 hanks yarn for the warp and 5 for the weft, which they sell to weavers for 1s 8d a spangle. The spangle contains 4 hanks.

ANCIENT TOPOGRAPHY

Bog Butter

In the townland adjacent to Dineady a crock was found in the bog, having bones as well as ashes. In the neighbourhood of Straw there was found in the bog, many years ago, a very large urn containing 14 lbs of a peculiar substance intermediate between tallow and spermaceti. Quantities of it have been obtained from time to time by the country people who use it for culinary purposes, cast it into candles etc. They are generally found unenveloped by any covering, but the marks and impressions of the cloth which formerly contained it were always visible. In the spring of this year a cottier in Menai, near Straw, was cutting turf when he struck his spade upon a wooden urn which, on taking up, he found to be filled with this peculiar tallow. I have obtained half a lb of it. [Insert footnote: This memorandum by Mr Stokes forwarded with a sketch to Lieutenant Larcom, 9th January 1834, [signed] R.K. Dawson].

Fair Sheets by J. Bleakly, December 1834 to December 1835

NATURAL STATE

Valuation of Land

In the parish of Aghanloo there are 8,240 acres 1 rood 16 perches: value of the land 3,310 pounds 3s 7d at 8s per acre, value of houses 167 pounds 9s, total value 3,477 pounds 12s 7d.

Boundaries and River Roe

The reason why the parish of Aghanloo extends to the other side of the Roe is because of the change of the course of the river, which originally was more crooked.

SOCIAL ECONOMY

Legal Disputes about Boundaries

About the year 1831 a dispute took place between Benjamin Lane Esquire of Ballymacarton and Connolly Gage Esquire of Magilligan, about the boundaries between the mountainous parts of Ballymacarton and the mountain part of Magilligan. A number of the oldest inhabitants were called upon to show the boundary.

Captain Church's Land

The townlands which belong to Robert Henry Church Esquire are Drumbane, Rathfad, Shanvey and Ballybrissel, which are all churchlands.

Respectable Farmers

Respectable farmers are Mr and Mrs Church, Drumban; Matthew Turbitt, Ballymoney; John Jackson, Artikelly; John Dunlap, Ballycastle;

Samuel Murtland, Tullyarmon; and William Shannon, Largantea, according to the indispensable conditions. 19th December 1834.

Subdividing Farms

The ancient custom of subdividing farms is much discouraged by the Marquis of Waterford, who does not wish to let farms under 20 acres. In order to do away with this custom, the Marquis of Waterford has adopted the following plan. If a man holds a small farm and is unable to pay the rent, he is permitted to dispose of his farm to the best advantage, or at the expiration of the lease the small farms are put into one and let [to] a solvent tenant. The disposal of these small farms is generally left to the decision of an arbitration of men who understand the valuation of land: the occupying tenant to choose one and the person who is about to purchase to chose another. If they do not come to a decision, a third person is brought.

Enlarging of Farms

The Marquis of Waterford is enlarging the farms in order to enable the tenants to pass a vote. Information obtained from James Stewart, Samuel Olliver, Robert Henry Church Esquire, Joseph Olliver and William Bacon. 19th December 1834.

Marquis of Waterford's Tenants

The Marquis of Waterford's tenants are improving their houses but not ornamenting them. Could be much more improved, ornamented as forest, fruit and other trees are given by the agent to all the tenants who may apply for them. The tenants say they have not time for ornamental improvements from striving to make the rent and taxes.

Rents

Many of the tenants on the Marquis of Waterford's estate in this parish (when the Reverend [blank] Meara <Marrah> was agent) were unable to pay as their rents were very high. Some were in arrears <erears> and left their farms and others were ejected. The tenants were very much oppressed till Barre Beresford became agent and reduced the rents. Driving or seizing cattle for rent is not much practised: when tenants are in arrears, they are ejected. The rent of the best land before the present tenants occupied their holdings was about 2 pounds 10s per acre. The rent of the best land at present is about 2 pounds per acre, middling 1 pound and worst about 10s per acre. It was much easier to make money at the time when

lands were let at 2 pounds 10s per acre than it is at present to pay 15s per acre. The best lands in the parish are Ballycastle, Tirbullion, Ballyhenry, Clooney, Rathfad and Cressycrib. Information obtained from James Stewart, William Beacon, John Jackson. 15th and 16th December 1834.

Land Agents

The Reverend James Meara and his son John were both agents to the Marquis of Waterford; and were accounted very severe on the tenantry.

Dress

The dress of the Scotch is generally respectable. The better sort of farmers of the male sex have each a suit of black cloth which they wear on Sundays. Their working dress is of coarse cloth or frieze <frize>. Coats and corduroy trousers <trowsers> or breeches, waistcoats of some coarse pattern, some of striped <stript> drugget. Among the poorer sort, linen trousers also a top coat, commonly called a slip-on, of brown cloth. The Presbyterians wear broader leaf'd hats than the Protestants or Roman Catholics.

The females' dress is also respectable. Farmers' wives and daughters of the better sort have each a suit of black silk or brown, sometimes white or stained muslin in summer, leghorned bonnets with a green or black veil with boots or sateen shoes. Their working dress consists of a plain cotton or stuff gown with shoes and stockings. The Irish not so respectable as they are much poorer and have no taste for neatness: if the females can, have a cotton or stuff gown for going to mass or to market, with a cloth or cotton shawl and cap of thick muslin with red, pink or blue ribbons. Those who can afford it wear a brown, blue or grey cloak. Bonnets, cloaks and shoes are worn more than usual, an increasing in number. When going to markets they often walk barefoot, and when near the towns wash their feet in a pond or stream and put on their stockings and shoes. Males [wear] coarse grey or frieze or corduroy breeches, waistcoats, a cheap pattern or grey cloth, with shoes and a coarse wool hat. Information obtained from John Jackson, John Dunlop, Benjamin Lane Esquire and James Stewart. 26th December 1835.

Shoemakers

It is a general custom among the farmers who have large families, for economy's <oeconomy's> sake to purchase leather and bring shoemakers to the house to make strong shoes for the family. The fine shoes are bought in the shops. The shoemakers who go to the farmer's houses charge 1s per pair for making men's shoes; the same price is charged for women's shoes at the farmers' houses. The shoemaker's own house: 2s 6d a pair for men's shoes and 2s 6d per pair for women's shoes.

Longevity

Robert Biggam is the oldest man in the parish: is now about 97 years of age, lives in the townland of Killybready. James McLaughlin of Carbullion lived to be 100 years old; is now dead.

Early Marriage

One remarkable instance of early marriage is that of Alice Douglass, maiden name Devlin: was married at the early age of 14 years, lived in the townland of Carbullion. Sometimes a contract in marriage is effected and unequal matches made in order to secure property. Such was the case with Mrs Douglass. Information obtained from James Stewart, Samuel Olliver and Samuel Moore, farmers. 26th December 1834.

Knitting

The men and boys of the lower order are employed in wet weather in knitting coarse, woollen stockings and socks, grey colour; the long stockings at 1s per pair, short stockings at 6d per pair.

Militia Volunteers

It is about 53 years since the volunteers were reviewed by Colonel Carey in the townland of Artikelly in this parish.

Exhumation of Bodies

To prevent this practice, a night watch is kept in the old church of Magilligan until the body is decayed.

Social Meetings

There are about 7 social meetings in the parish of Aghanloo. There are 2 meetings each week of the Methodists in Artikelly.

Wooden Bridge and Fairs

The Wooden bridge was erected in 1800 and cost 500 pounds, 300 pounds of which was taken off the county, the other 200 pounds granted by

Connolly Gage of Bellarena. The county still keeps this bridge in repair.

The fair on the Wooden bridge commenced in 1800 and still continues. It originated from a fiddler named McNamara who assembled a few persons on the road near Mr Graham's house on the 14th July, whence they adjourned to the Wooden bridge, the best place for dancing. Now they spend the day dancing, drinking whiskey, eating cakes, fruit and dulse <dillisk>. Tents are erected for the people to sit and drink in.

On the 13th July a fair is held at the Back Strand. None resort thither but respectable people who come for sea bathing; principally Protestants at the Back Strand. At the Wooden bridge Roman Catholics spend a whole night in dancing. Generally the young men who dance pay the fiddler 1d per dance for self and, partner. From Benjamin Lane Esquire, C. Gage Esquire, Henry Abraham and John Dunlop. 24th December 1835.

Amusements

Other amusements are dancing, drinking whiskey, playing cards, playing commons, shooting at a mark for a prize. Many of the young men assemble (who are convenient) at the old churchyard of Aghanloo at Christmas, Easter and other state days and shoot at a mark, principally for poultry.

Singing school among the Presbyterians: a master is employed (at present at Myroe) who teaches sacred and profane music, vocal and instrumental; goes from house to house with his pupils by night. During the winter quarter charges 1s a month for males, 6d for females; concludes each night with a dance. From John Dunlap, Thomas Stevenson, Benjamin Lane Esquire. 25th December 1834.

Income of the Clergy

There are Episcopalians, Reverend William Smiley, 365 pounds [annual income]; Presbyterians, Reverend George Steen, 146 pounds; Remonstrant Synod, Reverend William Porter, 150 pounds; Reformed Synod, Reverend Arthur Fullerton, 40 pounds; Roman Catholics, Reverend Edward O'Hagan and the Reverend William McDonagh, 100 pounds and 60 pounds; Seceding Synod, David Lynch, 44 pounds; Methodists, John Armstrong, paid according to the number of his family. Information obtained from John Dunlop, William Beacon and the Reverend George Steene, James Chambers, clerk of the markets. 22nd and 23rd December 1834.

Support of the Poor

The poor at present are supported wholly by casual charity. In the year 1831 the Reverend William Smiley proposed that persons should be appointed to collect food and dress for the poor. 4 persons went voluntarily to collect through the parish money, flax, yarn.

Bequest

In the townland of Drumbane lived Paul Church Esquire, who died in 1824 and bequeathed to the poor of the following townlands: Drumbane, Shanvey, Rathfad and Ballybrissel, the sum of 1 pound 2s 9d to be distributed on every Easter Tuesday for ever by his heirs and successors. The late Paul Church Esquire was then proprietor of the above churchland. Information obtained from the Reverend William Smiley, James Williamson and John Dunlap. 3rd January 1835.

Schools

Granagh, James Trainer, teacher, a Roman Catholic. Pay school, annual income of the teacher is about 10 pounds per annum. The schoolhouse is a poor cabin, built of stone, thatched, cost about 2 pounds. Of the Established [Church] there are none, Presbyterians 5, Roman Catholics 15, total 20, males 15, females 5, total 20. Connected with no society, supported by the parents of the children.

Granagh, James Mullan, Roman Catholic; pay school, annual income 4 pounds 6s. A room in a thatched cabin, cost about 5 pounds. Of the Established Church there are 1, Presbyterians 4, Roman Catholics 15, males 15, females 5, total 20; supported by the children. A poor blind man is the teacher, assisted by his 2 daughters.

The Marquis of Waterford is building an excellent schoolhouse in the townland of Artikelly for the instruction and the use of both sexes. The house was ready for the roof when the late storm, 7th November 1834, tossed it nearly to the ground.

SOCIAL AND PRODUCTIVE ECONOMY

Duty Work

This system is only practised by Mr Gage of Bellarena <Ballyrena> and Mrs Church of Drumbane. If the rent is not paid up to the day, Mr Gage makes the tenants pay discount, and duty work is also required and must be paid in proportion to the number of acres held by the tenant. For instance John Donald holds 60 acres: must give 6 days of a man reaping, a horse, cart and man one day in each quarter. Previous to Mr Gage's coming to Bellarena, poultry were given: 2 hens or 1 pullet for every 10 acres. If Mr Gage should be absent and poultry not required, at his return 1s per hen or duck was demanded. The tenants were bound in their lease to pay this duty work.

Duty Work on Churchlands

The churchland property of Aghanloo: Drumbane, Shanvey, Rathfad and Ballybrissel was bequeathed to Robert Henry Church by his late uncle, Paul Church, who also bequeathed the sum of 1 pound 2s 9d to the poor of the above townlands, and is now in the hands of Robert Henry Church Esquire of Drumbane. P.C. bequeathed to his wife, Jane Church of Drumbane, the house and land she now occupies, with the duty work of the above townlands which is paid in dry turf and poultry, in proportion to the size of the farms. James Williamson holds 50 acres, must give 20 loads of dry turf and 8 hens exclusive of rent. Information obtained from John McClary, James McDonald, Allen Sherra, Alexander Wilson and James Williamson, farmers. 6th January 1835.

No bog to the churchlands: the tenants cut turf on the Marquis of Waterford's property and pay 2s 6d for 4 days' cutting of turf. Dated 6th January 1835.

Local Taxes

The local taxes are tithes and county cess; amount to about 6s per acre, Irish plantation measure.

Weights and Measures

The weights in the grocers' shops are from a quarter of a ounce to 1 stone of 14 lbs. The measures in whiskey shops are from a jonney (which is a measure containing half a glass, price 1d) to a quart. Their weights and measures are British and Irish as both are called for. Jonneys are called for in general more than any other measure, particularly on market and fair days.

PRODUCTIVE ECONOMY

Lime Kiln

There are 9 lime kilns in the parish of Aghanloo: one of these in the townland of Tircorran, built by the Marquis of Waterford in 1831 for the use of the tenantry. This kiln is sufficient to burn 140 barrels at a time. Each tenant on application to the agent may receive a permit to burn 120 barrels, the other 20 barrels free. 2s 6d is paid to the agent for this permit, 2s 6d to the owner of the land for trespass and 15s 6d to the man who is appointed to quarry and lift the stones, making a total of 1 pound 6d for a permit, trespass, quarrying and lifting. Lime kilns, if possible, are built convenient to a quarry and bog. In those kilns prepared for burning roach lime, the stones are put in large and placed vertically, formed into an arch in order to admit of the air. The turf is put under the arch so that the ashes do not mix with the lime. 48 hours is sufficient to burn a kiln of this description.

Lime kilns in general belong to the occupying tenant, except 2 which have been erected by the Marquis of Waterford for the benefit of the tenants. Each tenant may have the burning of 1 kiln of lime containing about 6 score barrels, by paying 2s 6d to the bailiff for a permit; and if a road does not lead to the quarry or kiln, 2s 6d is paid for trespass. Out tenants pay 5s for a permit. If the tenants do not put the lime on their own farm, they must also pay 5s additional for a permit. 2 men are appointed by the agent to take care of the quarry and raise the stones for those who may employ them. The common cost of raising or quarrying a kiln is 1 pound. The stones are put into the kiln about 70 lbs weight and will burn very well. The lime kiln in Tircorran will turn out about 120 barrels of lime. The tenants on Lord Waterford's property who wish to sell lime must pay for a permit 5s. The fees and duties attendant on lime quarries and kilns are paid to the agents, who pay the persons appointed to take care of quarries and kilns. From Reverend William Smiley, Robert H. Church Esquire, Joseph and Samuel Olliver. 13th, 15th and 16th December 1834.

Spinning Wheels

Some years ago spinning wheels were given out to the tenants by the Marquis of Waterford. Since the failure in the linen trade none has been given out, nor any abdications made. Yarn from 3 to 6 hanks yarn of flax, tow 1 to 1 and a half hanks; 8 hundred linen is made of tow. Information obtained from Wilson, John Jackson, James Maginnis, farmers, and J.M. Black, smith. 31st December 1834.

Charcoal

Charcoal is made from turf and used by smiths. The following is the process: good black turf is cut, and when perfectly dry, are put into pits made in the earth about 2 feet deep. Fires are put into these pits and about 3 or 4 inches deep of earth is strewn over the pits. One day's cutting of one man with 2 men to attend will cut turf sufficient to make 1 ton of charcoal. Total expense when at home will be about 10s.

Sheepskins

Sieves are made of sheepskins and are prepared by spreading lime on the fleshy side of the skin and folding it up for 2 or 3 days; then the wool will be easily taken off. The skin is put into water for 2 or 3 days, then rolled round a hoop about 3 inches in depth and when perfectly dry, holes are punched into the skin. Rees are also made of sheepskins, holes much wider. Information obtained from John Dunlap, Thomas Stevenson and John Donald, farmers. 24th December 1834.

Linen Trade

Quality of the yarn of Aghanloo: flax yarn from 3 to 6 hanks, tow yarn generally 1 hank out of the lb, 3 hank yarn for warp and 5 hank yarn for weft, makes a 13 hundred web. 52 yards by 28 inches wide may be put into the loom and woven in 1 clear month for 31 days. 8 hundred linen is made from tow yarn. A good weaver will weave 6 yards of 8 hundred linen each day, at 3d per yard. Since the failure in the linen trade, the weavers were compelled to quit weaving and go out to work at the farm. Very little wool is manufactured in the parish. A little frieze is made for home use and worn by the inhabitants at work. Information obtained from John Quinn, James Moffitt and John Wilson. 5th January 1835.

Flax and Market Price

The produce of an acre of flax of the best [kind ?] is about 4 and a half cwt rough, of the [remainder blank]. The present market price of flax is about 3 pounds 10s per cwt rough. From the Reverend George Steen, Robert Henry Church Esquire, John Dunlop. 23rd December 1834.

Fuel

The fuel in Aghanloo is very good: cut turf and bog fir. The fir is collected in summer and harvest and put up for the winter on a loft or place prepared near the fire in the kitchen to be dry. In winter the men are employed by night in splitting the fir for fuel and candlelight. About 18 years ago the parishioners (from want of weather to dry the turf) were compelled, those who could afford to, to purchase coals at Londonderry. Bog fir is sold at Newtown Limavady at 5s per cartload. Information obtained from James Stewart, Clarke Stewart and James Williamson, farmers. 25th December 1835.

Imported Timber

The timber used in the parish is American fir and Baltic timber. Fir is most used as it is cheapest. Baltic is best but not much used as it is much dearer; generally purchased in Newtown Limavady, Coleraine and Londonderry.

Farm Buildings

The farm buildings are erected and kept in repair by the occupying tenant who, when building a new house or putting on a new roof, may, on application to the agent, receive slates free of expense except carriage. From John Jackson, James Stewart, James Chambers. 22nd, 23rd December 1834.

Implements of Husbandry

The implements of husbandry are iron and wooden ploughs, box carts, long-wheeled cars, wheel and hand barrows, rollers, a few drill harrows, spades, shovels, grapes, pitchforks, winnowing <whinnowing> machines, rakes, sythes, reaping hooks, common harrows, turf spades or slanes, sieves and riddles, flails for threshing, corn screens, shears <sheers> for clipping sheep, shears for clipping hedges, 1 threshing machine, the property of Benjamin Lane Esquire of Ballycarton. B.L. pays tithes to Aghanloo and county cess to Magilligan. William Shannon of Largantea has a machine for churning milk, wrought by water. William Beacon of Artikelly has 2 winnowing machines which he lets at 1s each per day. Break harrows, moulding ploughs, a floughter or scraw spade for cleaning the surface of the bog, a turnip harrow for sowing turnips; seed for this harrow is for the use of the tenantry, granted by the agent.

Ploughing Match

The Marquis of Waterford gives a premium every year of an iron plough or the price of one, to the best ploughman.

Green Feeding

The green feeding of Aghanloo: turnips, clover, beans and some vetches. About 20 acres of turnips in the parish this year; about 7 years ago not 1 acre. The increase in the growth of turnips this year is chiefly owing to the failure in the potato crop last season. The farmer whose potato crops failed sowed turnips instead. Information obtained from William Beacon, Reverend William Smiley and Henry Abraham. 16th and 17th December 1834.

Nearly all the potato crops of Samuel Moore of Artikelly failed, and [he] sowed turnips in their stead. The Reverend William Smiley was the first person to introduce green feeding into this parish. Samuel Moore has the largest field of turnips in the parish. Horses are fed on half-boiled turnips given whole, with a little oatmeal or bruised corn. Carrots are good feeding for horses. William Wilson of Gortnamoney had the largest field of beans in the parish.

Meadow

The meadow in Aghanloo is not plenty. The cattle and horses are fed mostly straw; chopped whin <whine> for the horses, boiled potatoes and chaff are given to the cows. The inhabitants of Newtown Limavady buy fodder (hay) in Aghanloo. The people sell the hay and do not half feed the cows. Information obtained from James Trainer, John Dunlop and John Jackson. 21st January 1835.

Grasses

Perennial <per annual> rye grass is the most common. The culture of improved and artifial grasses is not common. Information obtained from the Reverend William Smiley, Robert Henry Church Esquire, John Dunlop. 22nd and 23rd December 1834.

Preventative against Murrain

When geese are fed on the same pasture with cows, the cows never take the murrain, as the geese eat a herb which gives cattle this disease.

Drainage

All mountain bog, does not require much draining. When required, is performed by those who cut turf; by cutting the turf drains are made and the water carried off. Information obtained from John and James Biggam, William Shannon, Alexander Hopkins, Samuel Moore, Matthew Turbitt, Samuel Huston and James Moffitt, farmers. 8th January 1835.

Soil and Drainage

The soil on the upper part of the parish is a stiff, red clay; sandy loam on the lower or flat part.

Common drainage: open drains in the flat or marshy part about 8 feet wide and 4 feet deep; and French drains, a few on the middle with open, narrow drains. In some wet places the French or covered drains: the stones are placed angular. Drainage not common.

Inundations of the River Roe

The townlands which suffered by the late inundation of the River Roe are Ballycastle, Ballyhenry, Shanvey, Carbullion, Gortnamoney, Granagh, Clooney, Artikelly, Drumbane, Rathfad, Ballymaglin, Tullyarmon and Ballycarton. A large quantity of potatoes were carried off by the floods. Some of Mr Church's tenants have lost 100 barrels and a great quantity were rotten from the water remaining in them so long. A quantity of hay was also taken off. Many ditches were thrown down and large heaps of sand were cast upon the fields which will take a great deal of labour to remove. Houses have been tossed by this flood, which took place on the 7th November 1834.

Manures

Compost of sand, shells, moss and stable manure or clay; shells and sand with stable or cow house manure for the loamy soil. The sand is left to sour in a pool at the door of the house; sometimes mixed with the scourings of ditches. Information obtained from John Dunlop, Samuel Olliver, Robert Olliver, farmers. 2nd January 1835.

Marl and Burning the Ground

No marl in the parish of Aghanloo. Burning the ground for manure is not practised as other manures are so plenty. The manures are farmyard, compost of lime and clay, sometimes moss. Shells are generally put on by themselves.

Plantations

None in the parish except a little for shelter and ornament. The Reverend William Smiley has planted some Scotch fir, larch, alder and beech. The trees are thriving pretty well, are from the age of 14 to 4 years old, situated to the east of the church in the townland of Glebe. Glebe House is about 25 chains east of the church and south west aspect. Nature of the soil a red, gravelly clay.

The north wind is most injurious to trees of all kinds; all trees inclined to the south.

Transport and Markets for Crops

The expense of bringing crops to Coleraine is 5d per cwt per mile. The markets to which produce is carried from the parish of Aghanloo is Newtown Limavady, Dungiven and Coleraine.

Exports

Much more exported produce goes from Londonderry than from Coleraine.

Oxen used

Robert Henry Church Esquire uses oxen because it was the custom in India where he (Mr C.) resided for many years. After Mr Church's return from India, he used 6 oxen in a team and attempted to make 1 ox draw 2 carts laden with turf from the mountain.

Price of Oats

Good oats are sold on the ground at from 5 to 6 pounds per acre, Irish plantation measure; about 6 bushels to sell an acre, Cunningham measure. All contracts between man and man are made in Cunningham measure, leases all Irish plantation measure. Present market price of oats 8d ha'penny per stone. From James Stewart, Samuel Moore and Samuel Olliver, farmers. 31st January 1835.

The average crop of oats is from 3 to 4 boles of 12 bushels each bole, market price at Newtown Limavady from 8d to 9d per stone.

Wheat

A man will lash about 6 stalks of wheat a day; method by taking as much of the wheat in stalks as a man can hold in his 2 hands and beating out the grain against the side of a barrel in a creel afterwards. The straw is threshed with a flail in order to take out any grain that may have remained in. The growth of wheat is much increased this year: chiefly the golden Essex <Esex> which does best in this parish; produce of an acre from 6 to 12 barrels; barley from 6 to 10 barrels of 18 stone per barrel.

Field Beans

About 4 bushels to sow an acre, Cunningham measure. John Wilson of Gortnamoney last year (1833) sold the produce of an acre (88 stone) of field beans in Liverpool and received in the clear 12 pounds; all sent for export. Sort sown are the Norfolk Highland <Hiland> and Goland beans.

Field Peas

About 2 bushels to sow an acre, produce about 30 bushels. Those who have not a great quantity generally sell in Newtown Limavady or Coleraine at from 8d ha'penny to 9d per stone for 14 lbs, peas at 1s 3d per peck. The peas when ground and mixed with oatmeal make coarse bread. The bread is baked on a griddle afterwards hardened before the fire. A brose <browse> is sometimes made of it by pouring boiling water on a small quantity in a bowl, used with salt. Pea meal makes very bad stirabout, does not thicken.

Potato Washers

None in the parish. Riddles are sometimes used and are of the usual shape (circular) and materials. The hoop of ash about 3 inches deep, the bottom of tough, split ash and are used to riddle grain of every description. Some riddle potatoes with them.

General Remarks on Agriculture

The market price of potatoes at present in Newtown Limavady is from 10d to 1s per bushel of 5 stone. There are 7 grazing or stock farms in Aghanloo.

Irrigation of meadows: in the townland of Largantea, Alexander Hopkins, James Hopkins, Mark Hopkins and William Shannon, James Stewart of Ballymaglin.

Not much conacres let: George Dunlop of Ballycastle let some at 8 pounds per acre.

The Irish breed of black cattle is most common and does best in the parish: yet there are English and Scottish breeds of horses, Devon and Ayrshire cows, Dutch and Berkshire pigs, a few Poland geese and Friesland cows.

TOWNLAND DIVISIONS

Townlands

Carbullion: no looms; 20 pigs, 2 sheep, 23 head of black cattle, 10 horses, 15 geese, 20 ducks, 18 hens; 1 farm above 20 acres, 5 farms above 10 acres.

Granagh: there are 3 looms; 19 pigs, 22 head of black cattle, 14 horses, 12 geese, 36 ducks, 36 hens, 6 goats. Some of the geese are called swan geese from the colour of their bill, which resembles that of a swan. Their bodies are of a dim colour with black feet. One farm above 20 acres, the rest under 10 acres. Inhabitants extremely poor, houses mere cabins, chiefly built of mud and sods, gables are very dirty. Samuel Scott has a good house. Information obtained from Samuel Scott, Arthur Sandford and James Mullan, farmers. Dated 1st January 1835.

Gortnamoney: only 1 farmer and 2 cottiers; 4 horses, 11 head of black cattle, 6 pigs, 6 turkeys,

18 ducks, 20 hens, all Irish breeds of cattle and poultry. William Wilson, proprietor of the townland, has the greatest quantity of field beans in the parish. Information obtained from William and John Wilson and John Jackson, farmer. 23rd December 1834.

Ballymaglin: 24 sheep, 9 pigs, 28 head of black cattle, 13 horses, 1 loom, 1 lime kiln, 12 geese, 4 turkeys, 24 ducks, 24 hens; all Irish breed except 1 Ayrshire cow; 1 limestone quarry. Rotation of crops: first potatoes, second barley, third wheat, fourth flax, fifth oats, sometimes potatoes after wheat. One farm above 100 acres, only 1 farmer and 3 cattle in the townland.

Rathfad: 2 looms, 8 horses, 6 pigs, 16 head of black cattle, 1 farm above 50 acres, 1 farm above 20 acres and 1 farm above 10 acres; 20 geese, 5 turkeys, 18 ducks and 18 hens.

Townlands

Ballycastle: 1 loom, 1 farm above 20 acres and 6 farms above 10 acres. John Dunlap of this townland has had the earliest crop of potatoes in the parish (mosscheepers), so early as the 13th June. The different sorts of potatoes are American whites, American reds, golden dwarfs; red Downs are the general crop; posies, Miller's thumbs, bangers, Killimankies, seedlmeys, cups, blacks. There were 3 remarkable floods in the River Roe about 40 years ago which swept away Alexander's bridge. The second flood took place about the 21st November 1831, the last the 8th November 1834. 30 pigs, 23 horses, 36 head of black cattle, 1 sheep, 46 geese, 8 turkeys, 18 ducks and 20 hens. When fodder is scarce, if the produce of an acre of oats is good, the straw is sold for about 30s. Those who purchase an acre of the ground of good oats pay from 5 to 6 pounds per acre and generally calculate upon getting the straw for reaping, threshing and making into oatmeal. Rotation of crops: [1st version] first potatoes, second barley, third wheat, fourth flax, fifth oats; [2nd version] first potatoes, second barley, third barley and clover, fourth wheat or oats.

Drumbane: there are 3 looms, 12 horses, 27 head of black cattle, 3 sheep, 12 turkeys, 30 geese, 29 ducks and 40 hens, with a great many pigeons, English, Irish and Scotch breed. Order of crops: first wheat, second potatoes, third barley or wheat, fourth flax laid down with clover and grass seed. Mr Smiley has a Newfoundland dog which has killed all his poultry and ate the belly out of his broad sow.

Drumaderry: 6 looms, 14 horses, 9 pigs, 40

head of black cattle, 10 sheep, 8 geese, 5 turkeys, 9 ducks, 18 acres, all Irish breed. Rotation of crops: first potatoes, second barley, third wheat, fourth flax, fifth oats laid down with clover and grass seed.

Freehall: 6 looms, 3 farmers, 5 cottiers, 10 horses, 30 head of black cattle, 4 pigs, 9 geese, 29 ducks, 44 hens, 3 farms above 10 acres, 1 lime kiln, roads in very bad repair.

Townlands

Cressycrib: 6 looms, 11 horses, 45 head of black cattle, 8 sheep, 16 pigs, 18 geese, 2 turkeys, 36 ducks, 40 hens, some half-bred pheasants. Order of crops: first potatoes, second barley, third oats, fourth flax laid down with clover and grass seed; sometimes wheat after barley. 1 farm above 20 acres and 5 farms above 10 acres.

Dirtagh: 3 looms, 1 lime kiln, 22 horses, 30 head of black cattle, 5 sheep, 12 pigs, 2 geese, 30 ducks and 40 hens, 1 farm above 20 acres, 2 farms above 10 acres; all Irish breed.

Stradreagh: 17 looms, 3 lime kilns. Rotation of crops: first potatoes, second corn which is sown in April, third flax. One farm above 200 acres. Greater part of the townland mountain, rest small [farms]. There are 20 pigs, 1 sheep. The sheep are taken away in winter as they are generally grazing sheep. 40 geese, 42 hens, 10 turkeys, 40 ducks. Plenty of mountain bog. Scotch and Irish breed of black cattle with Alexander Hopkins. Inhabitants very poor and numerous. When weavers are numerous in a townland, it is a sign of poverty as agriculture is generally neglected. Information obtained from Alexander Hopkins, John McIlmoyle and Alexander Moore, farmers. 6th January 1835.

Killybready: there are 2 looms, 3 lime kilns, no sheep, 1 ass, 3 lime kilns, 1 for burning roach lime. In roach lime kilns the stones are put in large lumps and a place made for the turf where the ashes do not mix with the lime. This lime is quite free from dirt and best adapted for stucco work. In other kilns the stones are broken into small pieces and layers of turf and stones put in alternately. This is used for land manure. There are 2 farms above 20 acres and 5 farms above 10 acres. The largest farm in the townland is 34 acres. There are 11 horses, 28 head of black cattle, 12 pigs, 24 geese, 36 ducks and 40 hens. Rotation of crops: first potatoes, second oats, third flax, fourth oats again and let out for pasture. 8th January 1835.

Townlands

Largantea: no looms, 1 farm above 100 acres, 1 farm above 50 acres, 1 farm above 20 acres and 1 farm above 10 acres. There are 19 horses, 100 head of black cattle, 20 sheep, 6 pigs, 10 turkeys, 40 geese, 16 ducks, 8 hens. The horses are Scotch and Irish breed, the black cattle all Irish breed. There are 2 limestone quarries and 1 fort. Rotation of crops: first potatoes, second oats, third flax and some turnips sowed in July. William Shannon of this townland has erected an excellent cheap and useful machine for churning milk. Diameter of water wheel 6 feet, water comes on wheel, a breast, metal cog wheel 9 inches, small wheel 5 inches. Erected in 1832, cost of whole house, machine etc, only 4 pounds. Not one horse power, fed by a spring about 10 perches from the house: a great saving of manual labour.

Grange Park: 1 loom; no sheep at present, 11 horses, 3 head of black cattle. At present all the stock except a few which belong to Samuel Moore and James [?] Grimley are grazing cattle and are brought home at winter. As the land is mountainous and no shelter, little or no crops in the townland, all grazing. The herd has 1 pig, 2 geese, 6 hens, 6 ducks. The horses belong to Samuel Moore of Tullyarmon and are all Irish breed.

Ballymoney: no looms, 5 horses, 11 head of black cattle, no sheep, 5 pigs, 4 geese, no turkeys, 12 ducks and 11 hens. 1 farm above 20 acres and 1 farm above 10 acres. Only 2 farmers in the townland. Rotation of crops: first oats, second flax, third potatoes with manure. After this crop wheat is sown. Flax is laid down with clover and grass. The cattle are all Irish breed. One first-rate house, the property of Matthew Turbitt. Information obtained from Matthew Turbitt and Samuel Moore, farmers.

Tircorran: 1 lime kiln, 1 limestone quarry, 1 farm above 50 acres, 1 farm above 20 acres, 2 farms above 10 acres; no sheep, 4 horses, 45 head of black cattle, 5 goats, 12 ducks, 30 hens, Scotch and Irish breed of black cattle. Rotation of crops: first potatoes, second barley, third oats for 3 or 4 years in succession. After this crop peas are sown, which enrich the land by the slime etc. which falls from the stalk. Peas are a preventative against weeds. By this method the ground is manured for corn again. If the ground is poor, 2 heaped bushels of peas will be sufficient to sow an acre. If rich, 2 sleeked bushels will be sufficient; produce 24 bushels per acre. James Hughy sold the peas in his own barn for 4s per bushel. 13 stone of barley to sow an acre produces 8 barrels, market price at Newtown Limavady 8d per stone. Potatoes is the first-rate crop, barley second, oats third and oats or peas in the upper part as clay land is best for peas. Information obtained from John Hughy, Samuel Moore, Matthew Turbitt and John Piper, farmers. 12th January 1835.

Townlands

Tullyarnon: 7 looms, 4 sheep, 70 head of black cattle, 23 horses, 18 pigs, 32 geese, 80 hens and 50 ducks. 1 farm above 30 acres, 2 farms above 20 acres, 2 farms above 10 acres. Rotation of crops: first 2 crops of oats on lea ground after ploughing, third manured for potatoes, fourth barley laid down with red clover, cut 1 year and then let out 2 years for grazing.

Maghraskeagh: 2 looms, 5 farmers in the townland, all under 10 acres. 10 horses, 15 head of black cattle, 11 pigs, 12 geese, 26 ducks, 29 hens. Rotation of crops: first potatoes, second barley, third wheat, fourth flax, fifth oats.

Artikelly: 2 looms, no yarn consumed at home but tow yarn, 1 hank out of the lb, which [is] made into 8 hundred linen for coarse shirts, home bleached at the Curley burn. Rotation of crops: first potatoes, second barley, third wheat, fourth flax, fifth oats. 30 pigs, 12 horses, 36 head of black cattle, all Irish breed, 6 turkeys, 24 geese, 48 ducks, 46 hens, all Irish breed of poultry. Jackson's and Ashe's are the only good houses in the townland, rest very dirty and in bad repair. The window and bed curtains in Mrs Jackson's of Artikelly are of striped drugget (red and white), home manufactured. Information obtained from John Jackson, Henry Abraham and William Beacon. 13th January 1835.

Clooney: 9 horses, 18 head of black cattle, 8 pigs, 10 geese, 24 ducks, 20 hens, no turkeys. Rotation of crops: first potatoes, second barley, third wheat or flax, fourth oats. Small farms and poor houses, dirty and in bad repair, could be much improved as lime is plenty in the parish.

Ballyhenry: in this townland there are 2 looms, 18 farmers, 2 above 20 acres, rest from 20 to 30 acres; 14 horses, 30 head of black cattle, 40 pigs, no sheep, 1 turkey, 80 ducks, no hens. Rotation of crops: first potatoes, second barley, third oats or wheat, fourth flax. The most prevailing crop is oats, potatoes next; a dark, loamy soil. The farmer gained this year by selling the produce of an acre of good, clean, scutched flax. Drainage is performed by cutting a drain 4 feet wide and 3 and a half feet deep, which makes the mearings between each man's farm; part a subsoil of sea sand. Suffered much by the late flood. 2 goats. Rent is paid for the River Roe.

Townlands

Ballyhanna: 10 pigs, 9 horses, 25 head of black cattle, 18 sheep, 3 goats, 20 geese, 2 turkeys, 20 hens, 6 ducks. Rotation of crops: first barley, second oats, third potatoes, then let out for pasture 3 years; soil is stiff clay. 2 farms above 20 acres, 4 farms above 10 acres. Average crop of oats about 3 boles, each bole 3 bushels of 3 stone per bushel. Market price in Newtown Limavady 8d ha'penny per stone. Information obtained from John Wilson, John Jackson, William Connell, Matthew Thompson. 14th January 1835.

Drumalief: there are 3 looms, 2 sheep, 6 pigs, 10 horses, 30 head of black cattle, 40 geese, 4 turkeys, 50 hens, 40 ducks.

Ballybrissel: 20 sheep, 9 horses mixed Scotch and Irish breed, 12 head of black cattle, 6 pigs, 12 geese, 12 ducks, 13 hens, 7 goats, 1 loom.

Shanvey: no looms, 10 horses, 16 head of black cattle, 7 sheep, 6 pigs, 3 goats, 17 geese, 1 turkey, 6 ducks, 25 hens. 3 farms above 20 acres and rest under 10 acres, only 5 farms in the townland. Inhabitants very poor, suffered much from the late flood.

Ballycarton: 2 looms, 1 small lime kiln. Rotation of crops: first potatoes, second barley, third wheat or oats; sometimes barley is laid down with clover, and as the manure is plenty they seldom take more than 3 crops without manure. Potatoes are often planted on stubble ground if the farm is small. Beans and peas with some vetches. 20 sheep, 21 horses, 36 head of black cattle, 22 geese, 12 turkeys, 50 ducks, 100 hens, 26 pigs. 1 threshing machine, 2 horsepower, diameter of horizontal wheel 3 feet. 1 farm above 50 acres, 2 farms above 20 acres, tenure of Mr Jones' farm lives renewable forever. Information from Benjamin Lane Esquire, Miles Sweeny, Alexander Olliver, Reverend David Lynch and Matthew Turbitt. 19th January 1835.

MODERN TOPOGRAPHY

Cost of Aghanloo Church

The cost of building Aghanloo new church is about 900 pounds.

ANCIENT TOPOGRAPHY

Antiquities

In the townland of Ballycastle, in the farmyard of John Dunlap, are to be seen the remains of an old turret and ruins of an old castle.

List of Informants

Information obtained for the whole parish from the Reverend William Smiley, John B. Cavanagh, Robert Henry Church Esquire, Robert Ross, the Reverend George Steen, Reverend Edward O'Hagan, parish priest, John Dunlop, John Jackson, James Stewart, Thomas Stevenson, William Beacon, Joseph Olliver, Matthew Turbit, Dr Dill, Samuel Olliver, John Wilson, Thomas Martin, James Chambers, clerk of markets, Matthew Pollock and Charles Jackson, Captain Nesbitt C.G.P. Information obtained from James Mullan, teacher and John B. Cavanagh, surveyor to the marquis [of Waterford]. 18th December 1834.

Fair Sheets by T. Fagan and J. Bleakly, April to July 1835

NATURAL FEATURES AND SOCIAL ECONOMY

Floods

High floods on the Roe and seasons of the year they generally occur: the largest floods take place in the Roe from 1st November to 1st January. There was a high flood in the Roe 21st November 1831. It sunk pools in the townland of Granagh and holding of John Piper, 20 feet deep and 40 feet long. It took much labour of men and horses to fill up these pools.

There was a high flood in the Roe on 8th November 1834 that done great injury to potatoes and other crops. Along the holmes of the Roe it sunk a pool in the townland of Ballycastle and holding of John Dunlop, 130 feet long, 80 feet broad and from 15 to 20 feet deep. Informants John Dunlop and John Piper.

Lammas Floods in the Roe

The Lammas <Lammis> floods in the Roe does great injury to crops of every description along the Roe. These floods are partly occasioned <occationed> by the high tides which occur at that season following the changes of the moon. Lammas means first of August and floods often occur in the month of August. The floods inundating the holmes in the townland of Granagh must rise from 8 to 12 feet in the river, distance from the mouth of the Roe along the line of the river 7 miles. Where the floods make a breach in the banking at its outgoing, it carries with it a quantity

of the brows and occasions pools of large size and injures the soil to a great extent.

Retention of Floods on Roe

The floods remain on the holmes along the Roe from 12 hours to 3 weeks. The lava or glar and sand left on the holmes along the Roe by the floods is so beneficial to the soil that 3 floods will produce a fair crop of oats. Informants Israel Moody and many others. 6th July 1835.

Areas Flooded

Distance covered by the floods along the Roe. The following are the distances from the Roe that the floods cover the holmes of the undernamed townlands: in the townland of Granagh 60 yards; in some parts of Carbullion 1,120 yards; in some parts of Ballycastle 1,120 yards; in Shanvey 1,680 yards [insert note by C.W. Ligar: incorrect viz. might be feet instead of yards]; in Ballymaglin, in some parts 100 yards.

Shanvey, Rathfad, Drumbane are the townlands that suffer most by the floods of the Roe. When a high flood takes place in the Roe, 2 others most commonly succeeds it. The ordinary tide rises 4 feet in the Roe opposite Ballycastle and is known to force back the fresh water at Ardnargle and in the high tide up to the Roe bridge at Newtown Limavady. Informants Dennis McFaull and John Dunlop.

Shells and Shell Boats coming up the Roe

The Marquis of Waterford at some former period allowed one half acre of ground in the townland of Ballymaglin for a shell stead to accommodate his own tenants. There has been no shells left on this ground since the Wooden bridge was built at Magilligan. The ground is now laboured. The reason locally assigned for the boating of shells up the Roe being discontinued since the erection of the aforesaid bridge is, that the only time the shell boats came up the Roe was with the tides and that boats could not pass under the bridge, and the procuring of boats with falling masts was too expensive for persons hitherto driving shells up the Roe; secondly, the arches of the bridge are too low for heavy boats to venture through at high tides. Informants John Dunlop, Dennis McFaull and others.

Waterfall

A waterfall is also in Stradreagh above the fort, the water of which forms into a small river called the Lynn. [Insert query by C.W. Ligar: This doubtful: is not the fall called Lynn and not the river].

Exchange of Land

There are 7 and a half acres on the east of the Roe, in Mr Gage's demesne, that formerly belonged to the parish of Tamlaght Finlagan [insert addition: but there was an exchange made by the clergymen]. It belongs at present to the parish of Aghanloo and is a subdivision of Ballyhenry East. Informant Charles Begley, rent agent. 9th July 1835, [signed] Thomas Fagan.

MODERN TOPOGRAPHY

Church of Aghanloo

The church of Aghanloo was commenced to be built on the 12th August 1823 and finished 25th March 1826. The expense of erecting this church was defrayed by the Board of First Fruits, amount 900 pounds. Expense paid by the parish for enclosing the churchyard 37 pounds. Informants John Leech, sexton, and John Dunlop, farmer. 8th July 1835.

Glebe House: the Glebe House of Aghanloo was erected about 1789.

Artikelly Pound

There is a pound in the townland of Artikelly, built by the Marquis of Waterford for the use of the tenants on the manor of Freemore. The pound is on the eastern side of the old road leading to Coleraine by the Long Causey and about 100 yards from the crossroads leading to Aghanloo church. The pound is 15 yards by 12 yards. The wall is 7 feet high and 20 inches thick, part of which is in bad repair.

The road at the pound is 23 feet broad in the clear, made and repaired at the expense of the county.

Schoolhouse in Artikelly

An excellent schoolhouse has been (partly built) in the townland of Artikelly by the Marquis of Waterford. It is on his estate. The house is 10 yards from the side of the road leading to the church and has 4 apartments. 2 of the rooms are each 18 feet by 20 feet, the other rooms are each 8 and a half by 20 feet. The walls are brick.

Road leading to Turf Bog

This is an accommodation road for the use of the Marquis of Waterford's tenants leading to Stradreagh bog, and is 22 feet in the clear and in good repair at the expense of the county.

Lisnagrib Bridge

Lisnagrib bridge has 1 arch 3 and a half feet wide and 4 feet high, built of stone and lime, in good repair, the wall being 28 feet long and 2 feet 4 inches high and 18 inches thick; and the roadway is 20 feet broad. This bridge divides Dirtagh from Lisnagrib.

Dirtagh Bridge and Road

Dirtagh bridge has 1 arch 16 feet wide. The wall is 62 feet long, 2 feet high and 18 inches thick. The bridge is 18 feet wide on the top. This bridge is on the old leading road from Newtown Limavady to Coleraine <Colerane> called the Long Causey. The road between Lisnagrib bridge and this is 26 feet wide in the clear. Another by-road leading from this road to the mills at Bolea, called the Mill Road, is 20 feet broad in the clear. The above mentioned roads and bridges are made and kept in repair by the expense of the county and are all in good repair.

New Line of Road leading from Artikelly to Granagh

A new line of road which commences at Artikelly and passes through the townlands of Clooney and Gortnamoney is only finished as far as the townland of Granagh, but will extend to the townland of Ballycastle. This is an accommodation road for the use of the tenants on this part of the Marquis of Waterford's estate and is 24 feet wide in the clear. What is made is not in good repair, as there is not a sufficiency of stones and gravel put on a soft, clay bottom. Made at the expense of the county. Information obtained from Israel Moody and Daniel Murtland, farmers. 7th May 1835.

Roads

The Bishop's Road is made about 52 years and was made by the late Bishop Hervey. A line of road branching off the Bishop's Road and locally called the Black Road was also first purposed by Bishop Hervey but at a later period than the road above mentioned. Informants John Moody and others.

Bridge at Dowland

This bridge divides the townland of Ballycastle

from Dowland and has 1 arch 18 feet wide. The wall is 2 and a half feet high, 18 inches thick and 30 yards long on the east side. The bridge is of this [shape: small plan, dimensions 2 by 22 feet] broad on the top. 15 years ago the old part being only 18 feet wide; since that time the new part was built which breadth [is] 22 feet, made at the expense of the county. From John Dunlop. 12th May 1835.

Contemplated Bridge across the Roe

There is a bridge about to be put across the Roe at Carbullion to form a communication between the parish of Tamlaght Finlagan and the parish of Aghanloo, and also to enable the farmers of different parishes on the east of the Roe to procure shell manure on the shores of Ballykelly and Ballymacran. The expense of erecting the bridge is partly to be defrayed by the Marquis of Water-ford and his tenantry. If this bridge was erected, it would be found of the highest advantage to many parts of the counties of Derry and Antrim as it would open a communication from the east to the south west of the Roe and enable the resident landholders in the neighbourhood of Coleraine, Garvagh, Kilrea <Kilreagh> and other parts to procure shells and many other useful commodi-ties from the south west of the Roe. Informants John Dunlop and others.

PRODUCTIVE ECONOMY

Churning Machine in Largantea Townland

This machine is the property of William Shannon. The water wheel is a breast and 6 feet 2 inches in diameter and 16 and a half inches broad across the rim. The fall of water is 5 feet. Total cost of house and machine is 5 pounds and is wrought by a stream proceeding from an excellent spring called Well Glass, situated about 50 yards above the machine. This is the best and largest spring in this part of the country.

Seasons for Sowing and Harvesting Crops

[1st informant] Wheat is put down from 1st No-vember, barley is put down from 1st May, oats are put down from 1st March, flax seed is put down from 1st May, potatoes are put down from 1st May. Wheat is ripe and cut down from 5th Au-gust, barley is ripe and cut down from 5th August, oats are ripe and cut down from 12th August, flax is ripe from 1st August, potatoes are ripe for putting into pits from 1st of October. Informant Israel Moody, farmer.

[2nd informant] Wheat is put down from 1st October, barley is put down from 15th April, oats are put down from 1st March, flax seed is put down from 20th April, clover and hay seed is put down from 15th April, turnips are put down from 10th June, field peas are put down from 1st March, vetches are put down from 1st March, beans are put down from 1st March. Wheat is ripe and cut down from 15th August, barley is ripe and cut down from 1st August, oats are ripe and cut down from 10th August, flax is ripe for putting out from 1st August, clover and hay are fit to be cut down.

For green feeding second year, 10th June, turnips are given cattle from 1st November, field peas are ripe for use from 10th August, vetches are ripe for cutting from 10th August, beans are ripe for use from 10th August. Informants John Dunlop and others.

ANCIENT TOPOGRAPHY

Gawdy's Well

This is an excellent spring in the townland of Artikelly and about 100 yards from the pound. This well takes its name from a man called Robert A.Gawdy, who discovered the well.

Freehall and Moneyvennon Fort

This fort is of earth in the centre, the parapet is of stones and earth and is 37 yards in diameter. The south west side of the parapet is of stones, the earth being drawn off by James Moffit, the propri-etor, for manure. The fort is sown with corn and is on the estate of Anderson McCausland Esquire of Culmore Point.

Cave at Lisnagrib

There is a cave at William Johnston's back door in the townland of Lisnagrib. The mouth (which is now 15 years closed) when open would admit a man standing upright and 3 men could stand in a line across the cave inside. Thomas Johnston went into the cave about 10 yards, but could proceed no further from the stones which had fallen in and stopped the passage. The stones of the cave were regularly laid and appeared as if other apartments were inside. It is supposed to extend in a straight line about 20 yards, with rooms which the inhabitants suppos to extend under the dwelling house. An old dish of wood with a turned stick were found quite rotten inside the cave. From William Johnston, proprietor.

Lisnagrib Fort

This fort is of earth, 36 yards in diameter but all destroyed and planted with potatoes, and is on William Miller's farm and about 50 yards from the Bishop's Road leading from Newtown Limavady to Downhill. Information obtained from William Miller. 6th May 1835.

Discoveries in Townland of Granagh

About 10 years ago the bones of a man of extraordinary size were discovered (by Israel Moody and on his farm in the townland of Granagh) in the bottom of an old ditch and a foot under the surface. The bones appeared undisturbed since interment, the skull retaining its natural shape except a crush occasioned by the spade coming in contact with it when in the act of digging. Convenient to the place where the bones where discovered was also found a piece of old coin with a button, the shell of which remains in the house of Israel Moody. The piece of coin was larger than a shilling, the following inscription on one side: "P.S. Vivers"; and on the other side was the shape of a crown, 2 faces and the number 15 underneath. [Insert marginal note by C.W. Ligar: This inscription was from the memory of the person who found it]. On the shell of the button which appeared to be copper-plated was a vulture's head and a serpent's tail. The Reverend Samuel Butler of Magilligan has the coin. The bones were deposited in the place where they were found, which is on a bank near the proprietor's house and 20 yards from the edge of the River Roe.

Discoveries in Clooney

The bones of a man of unusual size were discovered 12 years ago, 2 feet under the surface and on a hill about 100 yards from Daniel Murtland's house and on his farm in the townland of Clooney. These bones were found by Daniel Murtland 12 years ago and were put down by him in the same place where they were found. Information obtained from Israel Moody and Daniel Murtland, farmers. 7th May 1835.

Discoveries in Carbullion

About 50 years ago in the townland of Carbullion and in the barn of George Douglass, was discovered by his (G.D.'s) father (in the digging up of the barn floor) the entire bones of a large man apparently on his side. These bones were deposited in the place from whence they were taken. From George Douglass, farmer.

Butter or Tallow from Carbullion

Last summer (1834) in a clay field covered with rushes and which had never been tilled, was discovered about 20 inches under the surface by John Piper and on his farm, a quantity of butter or tallow in a vessel of wood (see specimen obtained by J.B. and labelled). From John Piper, farmer.

Killybready Fort

Killybready Fort is on John Biggins' farm and was originally 40 yards in diameter [insert addition: made of earth] and is now nearly all destroyed and sown with corn.

Standing Stone

This stone is called Murphy's Stone and is situated in the bog part of Stradreagh.

Ruins of Old Castle

Nothing remains of this old castle but the foundation of the walls which are 55 by 34 feet and 3 and a half feet thick. The walls in one end are 10 feet deep and 6 feet in the other. David Graham has seen the foundations of 4 turrets <turrits>, 3 of which are destroyed. The only remaining one is at the south corner of John Dunlop's dwelling house, and is of a square form and is 6 and a half feet high and 2 feet 9 inches on each side. The walls which originally surrounded the old castle now form part of the walls of John Dunlop's dwelling and office houses. It is said a ghost in the form of a man walking on stilts is seen by night walking round the old castle. No servant maid will consent to live with Dunlop for fear of the ghost "Stilty" [insert marginal note: a name the ghost goes by]. It is also said that a man was shot on Drumbane white hill by a cannonball from the inhabitants of this castle. The inhabitants of this castle are not now known in the parish.

Forts and Superstition in Ballycastle

There were originally 4 forts in the townland of Ballycastle but are now all destroyed.

James McLaughlin was the most superstitious man ever lived in Ballycastle and used to cure cattle of elfshot by salt and water poured off money.

Fairy Bushes in Drumbane

There are 4 fairy bushes in the townland of Drumbane and which were seen on fire by night in winter by David Graham, who also heard bagpipes playing at those bushes. Information obtained from John Dunlap and David Graham, farmers. 12th May 1835.

Old Church in Drumbane

The old church was taken down by an act of vestry in 1812, after which divine service was performed in the present Glebe House by the Reverend George Vaughan Sampson. [Crossed out: The old church was without a steeple and was supposed to have been a Roman Catholic chapel. The roof was of Glenwood oak, the couples 2 feet asunder with boards nailed to the couples, on which the slates were added, nailed without laths].

Wells

Tubbertiggy Well: this is a good spring in the townland of Drumbane, and it is said that children who were not thriving were cured by washing them in this well.

Tubberduell Well is a good spring in the townland of Ballymaglin. Information obtained from William Beacon, John Dunlop and David Graham. 13th May 1835.

Old Castle

Lady Maxwell was a branch of the McClelland family whom, it is supposed, were the founders of the old castle at Ballycastle in the parish of Aghanloo. The McClellands came over from Scotland at the time of Cromwell's war. Lord McClelland was a general in Cromwell's army, built the house now occupied by John Dunlop and lived in it for some time after the war. Sir Thomas Maxwell was husband to Lady Maxwell and claimed 7 townlands in the manor of Freemore. It is supposed that General McClelland, for his faithful services in Cromwell's war, obtained from Cromwell by charter the manor of Freemore, which the Beresford family obtained by purchase and marriage with the Maxwell family. Cromwell rewarded all those who fought at his service, from the general down to the private. Tradition says the old castle was destroyed during the time William III was in the country. 15th May 1835.

Mary's Well

In the townland of Ballymoney, in Matthew Turbit's field and about 20 yards from Turbit's house, is a spring called the Holy Well or Mary's Well, and is so called from an old woman named Mary Galbraith who used to frequent this well for

water and washing and was in the act of washing yarn in heavy rain at this well, which is near the edge of the river, when a great flood came down the river and which had nearly carried her off.

Carn on Stradreagh Mountain

On the summit of Stradreagh mountain, at the trigonometrical station, a carn of stones, the base of which presents the appearance of a fort and is 54 feet in diameter [insert marginal note: largest stones 2 feet long and vary down to 6 inches in length]. From Samuel Moore. 11th May 1835.

Superstitions of the People

It is a bad omen to miss the sowing of a piece of a ridge of corn or other grain. The person who does, will die or lose some of family by death before that time 12 months.

If a cock crow on roost at an unusual hour and his legs feel cold, it is also a bad omen as some of the family will die before the expiration of 12 months; but if warm, they will not die but will be removed to the direction or point in which the cock's head is turned before 12 months. It is also a bad omen for a hen to crow at any time.

When going on a journey it is not lucky to meet a woman (when first going out) with red hair.

In the townland of Tullyarmon about 20 years ago, on the farm of Matthew Turbit was a fairy bush of hawthorn which, from a scarcity of fire [wood], was cut down by John Farran, a workman to Matthew Turbit, notwithstanding (J.F.) being warned by many of his superstitious neighbours against cutting this gentle bush, as all ancient trees of this description and forts are called. The evil of cutting this bush was felt by John Farran, whose wife and child in consequence thereof lost the power of their limbs and himself reduced to extreme poverty.

A horse nail is put into the horn of the cow to prevent an ill-eye or witching. A petrified urchin shell (called an elfstone) is suspended over the cow house door to prevent the cattle from injury by elf shooting. A gentleman who served with his majesty's service as an officer in the army resided in this parish, was suspected and believed by the absurd inhabitants of Aghanloo to have what is called an evil eye (that is, a covetous disposition), so that whatever cattle looked upon if he went out fishing <fashing> in the morning, they were seized with a disease and died. This misfortune, as it was thought, was known to himself. Information obtained from Matthew Irwin. 15th May 1835.

Dirtagh Fort

Dirtagh Fort is now a garden, the property of William Blaney, part of his house being built on the fort, and a lime kiln on the parapet which is on the side of the road. This fort is circular and is 45 yards in diameter and was all fenced with black sallow.

A fairy tree is also in this townland, at the edge of Dirtagh burn, and is of hawthorn.

Fort and Cave in Stradreagh

This is a most beautiful fort of earth, situated near the mountain part of Stradreagh. This fort is circular and 72 feet in diameter. The entrance is on the south east side and is 12 feet wide. The wall or parapet is 4 feet broad on the top and about 12 feet high above a beautiful trench which is outside the fort. A small part is inside and 36 by 24 feet.

A cave was also in this townland, but is now 50 years closed. From Alexander Hopkin and William Fisher, farmers. 5th May 1835.

Cave in Drumalief

The cave in Drumalief on John Dysart's farm is about 15 yards long and 4 feet wide at the mouth. Those who ventured in were prevented by the stones which had fallen in and stopped the passage. An old wooden dish was also found in this cave. The mouth of the cave is 5 years closed and now planted over with potatoes.

Curious Stone: The Millstone

A stone called the Millstone from which a field in John Dysart's farm takes its name: this stone is of a millstone nature and is sunk under the surface of the earth and is 5 feet in diameter, John Dysart having dug 5 feet round this stone but could not come near the bottom and was still growing longer as he sunk near the bottom. Information from John Dysart, proprietor of the above. 6th May 1835.

Largantea Fort

Largantea Fort is on William Shannon's farm and 100 yards from the house. This fort is of stone, as is the wall, and is 48 feet in diameter and very rough.

Cave in Largantea

This cave is on Alexander Hopkins' farm and about a furlong from the churning machine and Lady O'Kane's bridge. The mouth of the cave is 1 foot high by 1 and a half feet wide. The only person known to enter this cave is the daughter of Alexander Hopkin, who said she could stand upright when inside. 29th April 1835.

Fort in Lisnagrib

This is a fort of earth in the townland of Lisnagrib that is now all destroyed and sown with oats. Information obtained from John Jackson and John Biggan, farmers. 6th May 1835.

Ballycastle Ancient Castle

[Thomas Fagan] Description of the ruins of Ballycastle ancient castle: there stands at present in the townland of Ballycastle and holding of John Dunlop the ruins of an ancient building locally called a castle. There is several feet in height <highth> and length of the walls of the castle cellars or underground apartments and also of the parapet protection walls that surrounded the castle and castle yard still undisturbed on the premises. Dimensions of the cellar: cellar walls and other walls still undisturbed on the premises are as follows: length of the cellar in the clear 46 feet, breadth of cellar in the clear 29 feet, breadth of the cellar walls now seen to be above the surface of the ground on which they stand is 41 inches. From the top of these walls to the cellar floor is said to be 10 feet in depth. Those walls are also said to be 6 feet broad at the foundations.

This extensive cellar is occupied as a dungpit. There is 53 feet of one of the castle's side walls still standing and serving as the front wall of a barn and other office houses. This wall is 2 and a half feet thick at present and varies from 7 to 9 feet in height. There is 131 and a half feet of the parapet or protection wall that surrounded the castle yard still standing and serving as the back side wall of a barn and other office houses. This wall is 3 and a half feet thick and varies in height from 1 to 10 feet. The aforesaid range of office houses is 31 feet broad from out to out. The dwelling house, garden walls and several other fences with some office houses all enclosing a large farmyard is built with the stones of the ancient castle. The front wall of the dwelling house is 34 inches thick. The site of the above ruins, farmhouse and farmyard is surrounded on all sides by extensive orchards and vegetable gardens. There is still to be seen on the premises the stone on which the ancient gate hung. This stone is 16 inches long, 11 inches broad and 7 inches thick. The bed for the iron crank that fastened the gate is 12 inches long and 4 inches broad. 21st May 1835.

Haunted Room and Ghost called Stilty

There stands at present at the south west end of John Dunlop's dwelling house in Ballycastle, and on the ruins of some of the ancient buildings belonging to the old castle, a domestic apartment that stood 21 feet long and 21 feet broad from out to out. Tradition says that this apartment could not be kept standing though it was often rebuilt <reabuilt>. The reason locally assigned for the repeated falling down of the above apartment is that it has always been haunted by a ghost <gost> called Stilty; and that this ghost not only tumbled the aforesaid room whenever it was rebuilt but also annoyed and intimidated any or all persons about the dwelling house when business required them to go outside into the yard or garden after night. In short, the dread <dred> of meeting with the Stilty ghost renders it very difficult for any farmer occupying the above premises to get male or female servants to remain any length of time in their employment. The aforesaid apartment is at present totally dilapidated, nor would the occupying tenant attempt to rebuild it. Informant John Dunlop.

Antiquities from Ballycastle

Tradition says that there was discovered at some former period, north and within 140 yards of the ruins of Ballycastle ancient castle under the surface, the anchor of a ship and 4 silver table dishes. In 1834 there was 2 oars discovered 8 feet under the surface and near the same spot that the aforesaid anchor and silver dishes was got in. [Crossed out: It seemed from the situation that the oars lay in when discovered that the persons using them were rowing to Londonderry]. Those oars fell in fragments as soon as they were removed from beneath the surface. Informant John Dunlop. 21st May 1835.

Old Church of Aghanloo

The ruins of the ancient church of Aghanloo <Aughenloo> stands 50 feet long in the clear and 23 feet 8 inches broad in the clear, height of that part of the side wall now standing is 8 feet 8 inches, breadth of wall at the bottom 44 inches. The bank or surface of the above wall is 4 and a half feet higher than the level of the floor of the above old church.

Ancient Wells: Mecrin's and Tubbertiggy

There stands north and within a few yards of the old church an ancient well locally called Mecrin's

Wells, both; and in an orchard joining the old burial ground there stands an ancient well locally called Tobar Tiggy. The road is 21 feet wide clear of all drains and fences at the new church of Aghanloo.

Inscription on Tombstone

Part copied off a tombstone: The Reverend George V. Sampson, formerly rector of the parish of Errigal <Errigle>, died on the 10th day of March 1827 in the 45th year of his age.

Ancient Mound in Ballyhanna

There stands at present on the summit of the mountain in the townland of Ballyhanna and holding of William McLaughlin, a circular mound raised with stones and at present nearly grown over with soil. The base of this mound is set round with a row of stones sunk in the ground and many of them 1 foot higher than the soil. This mound is convex <covex> on the top and the summit from 7 to 9 feet higher than the level of the field on which it stood. It is 48 feet in diameter. On the summit and the centre of this mound there is an enclosure or building much resembling a vault or grave, enclosed by stones sunk on their ends in the ground. This vault is 4 feet 3 inches long, 2 and a half feet broad and 2 feet deep. I have inspected the above mound 1st July 1835, [signed] Thomas Fagan.

Murchy's Stone in Stradreagh

Murchy's Stone is a standing stone in the townland of Stradreagh and mountain grazing of Samuel Moore and Company. This stone stands in a sloping <sloaping> position and measures 5 feet in height, 8 feet in length and 2 and a half feet in thickness. I have inspected the above stone, 25th June 1835.

Unusual Tenure

The late John Biggan of Killybrady, the middle landlord at some former period of Stradreagh, wishing to get a renewal of his lease of the last mentioned townland from Lord Waterford, the terms of a penny renewal to be as long as the above Murchy's Stone would stand. This singular request Lord Waterford declined to comply with but inserted Biggan and sons' lives in the lease. Informant Thomas Harken.

Standing Stones (Cromlech) in Largantea

There stands at present in the townland of

Largantea and holding of William Shannon 2 curious-shaped standing stones. They stand within a few feet of each other in the ruins of stone wall. This wall is 40 feet long, 6 feet broad and parts of it 2 feet high. The standing stone on the north west is 5 feet 10 inches high above the ground, 2 feet 10 inches broad and 2 feet 6 inches thick. There appear small holes on its top and surface like the print of fingers. The standing stone south east is 5 feet high, 3 feet 2 inches broad and 2 feet 9 inches thick.

South east of the above standing stones stands a small tract of ground which has never been laboured. This ground seems to have been an ancient burial ground. The surface is partially studded with stones of different sizes, many of them sunk in the ground. There are also sunk graves or crevices appear on its surface together with a scrag of sloe bushes, briars etc. This ground measures 70 feet in length and 30 feet in breadth. I have inspected the above column's ground. 25th June 1835.

Crock of Money in Danish Fort

[Crossed out: Tradition says that one of the late Alixanders of Newtown Limavady found an earthen crock full of money in the Danish fort now standing in Stradreagh and that the enclosure from which the crock was taken can still be seen in the east side of the above fort. Informant Joseph Grumley].

King's Chair in Largantea

The King's Chair in Largantea and holding of Robert Dunn is a void space or cave formed between 2 large and lofty stones in the face of a rising brae <bray>. The canopy is composed of flags covered with soil. There is a small seat in the interior formed of small stones and soil. The void or cave where the king sat is 4 feet 8 inches high, 4 feet 8 inches long and 18 inches broad. The 2 stones forming the cave are as follows: one of them is 5 feet high, 4 feet 8 inches broad and 3 feet thick. The second of those stones is 6 feet high, 4 feet 8 inches broad and 4 feet 6 inches thick. There are other large stones on a line with the front base. There are some appearance of this chair having been formed by art as one of the large stones is supported by small stones put in at the base. This chair looks to the Cady.

Finn Macuill's Finger Stone in Stradreagh

There stands at present in the townland of Stradreagh and in the mountain grazing of Alixander Hopkins and Company a large whinstone locally called Finn Macuill's Finger Stone. This stone measures 6 and a half feet high, 6 and a half feet broad and 7 feet long. It is rough on the surface. Tradition says that Finn Macuill cast the above stone from the Keady hill to the spot where it at present stands. Informant James Lynch. I have inspected the above stone. 27th June 1835.

Danish Fort in Largantea

There stands in the townland of Largantee and holding of Robert Dunn the ruins of a Danish fort. The parapet is totally demolished and nothing of it remains at present on the premises but 3 moderate-sized stones that formerly stood in the parapet. The remains of this fort is in grazing. This fort was circular, 46 yards in diameter. I have inspected the above ruins. 27th June 1835.

Ree Hill in Stradreagh

There stands at present in the townland of Stradreagh and holding of James Grumley a small hill locally called the Ree. It is considered a very gentle place. It is also believed to have been formed by the Danes at some former period. There was a large quantity of stones round its base and on its surface but the greater part of those stones has been removed from time to time to build houses, walls. This hill measures 28 yards by 24 yards.

Kiln Pot in Stradreagh

South east and about 40 yards from the above Ree there stands the ruins of some ancient building of an oblong form. The interior of this building is 38 by 27 feet. The ruins of the walls, which are composed of stones, stands from 2 to 4 feet high and from 3 to 5 feet broad and grown over with soil in many parts. The local inhabitants are not able to say what the building had been originally designed for but many think that it was either a house of worship or a Danish fortress. This building is locally called the Kiln Pot. [Crossed out: I have inspected the above ruins]. 27th June 1835.

Discoveries in Stradreagh

In 1823, Andrew Moore of Stradreagh discovered 18 inches under the surface of a clay soil in his farm at about 150 yards from the former building mentioned above and called the Kiln Pot, 2 circular stones about 3 inches in diameter and half an inch thick each. One of those stones had engraven on its surface the images <immages> of a male and female and a small circular hole through its centre. The second of those stones had engraved on its surface a number of letters. There was also a number of amber bead stones got in the same place at various times. Informant Andrew Moore.

Ancient Grave in Largantea

There stands at present in Largantea and holding of William Shannon an ancient grave 7 and a half feet long, 5 feet 9 inches broad and about 1 foot high. There is a stone sunk at the head of the grave 53 inches (4 feet 5 inches long), 34 inches high and 6 inches thick. There are 2 other stones of inferior size sunk along the side of the top, covered with small stones and now grown over with soil. The above grave stands about 60 yards south of a Danish fort in the same farm.

Giant's Graves in Ballyhanna

There stands at present in the townland of Ballyhanna and in the holding of Samuel Huston 2 long graves locally called giant's graves. Those graves are raised of soil and small stones, some of which stones appear on the surface. They lie east and west and near the base of Ballyhanna mountain, one 125 yards north of the other. Those graves were explored in 2 different places in 1806 and also at a later period by some persons in hopes of getting hidden treasure, but nothing of interest found.

In a direct line west and within 80 yards of one of the above giant's graves there stands another ancient grave raised with soil and stones. This grave is 18 feet long, 12 feet broad and from 1 to 2 feet higher than the level of the field on which it stands. At some former period there was a large quantity of stones on the top and round the base of this last mentioned grave. Those stones have been removed from time to time for building fences etc. I have inspected the above giant's graves. 1st July 1835, [signed] Thomas Fagan.

Fair Sheets by J. Bleakly and J. Stokes, December 1834

SOCIAL ECONOMY

Manor Court and Petty Sessions

There is no manor court in this parish.

Petty sessions: not more than 30 persons have come before the petty sessions from the whole district during the last 12 months, and least of all

from Aghanloo. The general character of the parishioners with respect to orderly conduct and disposition is very good.

Offences Against the Law

Offences against the law are considerably on the decrease. Intoxication has been the occasion of any offences that were committed in the parish for many years past, as the people were in the habit of drinking whiskey at fairs and markets and on their way home at whiskey shops on the road, where potteen is sold. Drinking whiskey is very much on the decrease as the people have not money to spare.

Illicit Distillation

There are no combinations, very little illicit distillation or smuggling in the parish since the reduction.

Revenue and Constabulary Police

Newtown Limavady has always been the station for a party of revenue police until the year 1832, when they were removed from the town. There are at present in Newtown Limavady a party of constabulary consisting of 8 police and a chief constable. Information obtained from the Reverend William Smiley, John B. Cavanagh, James Stewart and Captain Nesbitt G.C.P.

Insured Houses

The Glebe House is the only insured house in the parish.

Health

The parishioners are generally very healthy (tho' not very clean), chiefly owing to the locality and wholesome atmosphere. Information obtained from Robert Ross, clerk of petty sessions, Fredrick Steele, Doctor Dill and Doctor Wark. Dated 10th and 11th December 1834.

Religion

The parishioners of every sect are in some degree religiously disposed and very attentive to their respective places of worship. The cause may be attributed chiefly to the exertions of the clergy and the establishment of Sunday schools and social meetings.

Party Spirit

On Monday night the 17th November 1828, as

James Williamson was returning from the market of Newtown Limavady, he was attacked by a party supposed to have come from the townland of Ballycarton. 17 of the men were accused, and were examined and aquitted. Williamson lived in the townland of Rathfad, was supposed to have been an Orangeman, was in a state of intoxication coming home from the rabble fair on Galloping Monday. Williamson had a wife and 4 children. The wife is since married to another Williamson. The children are still living with their mother in the townland of Rathfad.

Another outrage originating from a party spirit: about the year 1818, George Berriman was murdered at a dance in a barn at Artikelly; was a Protestant about 20 years old, had no wife. Berriman's father was a remarkable character: had double fingers and double toes on each hand and foot and had 49 children, twins at each birth, by different women, was in the capacity of a herd in the townland of Ballyhanna. Information obtained from Robert Ross, postmaster, Robert Henry Church Esquire and John Jackson. 11th and 12th December 1834.

Remarkable Events

About the year 1754 a contest arose between Maxwell Close and John Gordon Esquire, concerning the proprietorship of the following 6 townlands: Ballycastle, Carbullion, Drumalief, Lisleen and Dowland. During this contest the tenants paid no rent as they did not know to whom they should pay rent, as both parties claimed the property. A division among the tenants took place to see whom they would chose for their landlord. The tenants were ordered to receive all papers that would come to them, when a man named Simpson of Carbullion deceived them by telling them to take no papers that might come to them. The tenants would neither give up their houses nor pay rent. Shortly after this the army was sent and consumed their houses. Maxwell Close Esquire was the right heir, Harras was agent to Maxwell Close.

Fair in Artikelly

Originally there were fairs held in Artikelly. Only 2 were held until the patent was taken and the fair removed to Newtown Limavady, in consequence of a fight which took place at the first fair at which a tinker was killed. There were only 2 fairs held in the year in this town, the one at May and the other at November. There was also one market held in Newtown Limavady, one each week. Informa-

tion obtained from James Stewart, William Beacon and John Jackson. 15th December 1834.

Table of Schools by J. Stokes

[Table contains the following headings: townland in which situated, date established, religion of teacher, number of pupils by sex, remarks as to how supported]. [Insert covering note: Must be replaced by one on the parliamentary form].

Dirtagh, established 1800, 1 Protestant teacher, 40 males, 25 females, total 65 pupils; at present wholly supported by the peasantry. It was formerly under the Kildare Street Society. It was originally a hedge school.

Stradreagh, established 1834, 1 Protestant teacher, 23 males, 17 females, total 40 pupils; supported wholly by the peasantry.

Ballycarten, established 1832, 1 Protestant teacher, 71 males, 15 females, total 86 pupils; supported by the new Board of Education.

Ballycastle, established 1600: this school became extinct in 1833, the parents withdrawing their children on account of the incapacity of the schoolmaster. It had been latterly supported by the Kildare Street Society and the rector. It was not originally a hedge school. Its institution is supposed to have occurred more than 200 years ago. Further particulars are unknown. [Overall total number of pupils] 191.

The Marquis of Waterford is thinking of instituting a school.

Schools

Lisnagrib, James Forsythe, teacher, a Presbyterian. A pay school, total annual income of teacher 15 pounds. A small, thatched house built of stone and lime, cost 4 pounds. Of the Established Church 6, Presbyterians 44, Roman Catholics 10, Methodists 3, males 49, females 14, total 63. Connected with the London Hibernian Society who give books to the children; supported by the children. This school is just commencing under the London Hibernian Society.

Stradreagh, William Fleming, teacher, a Methodist. Pay school, total annual income of teacher 8 pounds, schoolhouse built of stone and lime, slated, cost about 10 pounds. It is 15 feet by 15 feet. Of the Established Church 3, Presbyterians 30, Roman Catholics 5, males 20, females 18, total 38. Schoolhouse built by subscriptions. Just commencing under the London Hibernian Society, school supported by the children.

Ballycastle, John Burns, teacher, a Roman Catholic. Pay school, total annual income of teacher 10 pounds; a farm car-house or small, thatched cabin, cost about 30 pounds. Of the Established Church 4, Presbyterians 20, Roman Catholics 10, males 12, females 22, total 34, connected with no society. Information obtained from James Forsythe, William Fleming and John Burns, teachers.

Ballycarton national school, established 1832, William Tate, teacher, a Roman Catholic. Both free and pay school, total annual income of teacher 13 pounds. Schoolhouse built of stone and lime, thatched, cost about 8 pounds. Of the Established Church 3, Presbyterians 11, Covenanters 1, Roman Catholics 50, males 48, females 17, total 65. Under the National Board, who pay the teacher 8 pounds per annum.

Drumbane working school for girls, 3 days in the week. Jane Johnston, teacher, a Presbyterian, free school. The teacher, who is a servant to Mrs Smiley, receives 1 guinea per annum additional wages from Mrs Smiley. The school is held in Mr Smiley's porter's lodge. Of the Established Church 8, Presbyterians 6, females 14, total 14. This school is supported by Mrs Smiley, who also teaches the girls housekeeping.

Magheraskeagh, Henry Abraham, teacher, a Protestant. Pay school, total annual income of teacher 3 pounds 15s. The kitchen of a dwelling house or thatched cabin; of the Established Church 7, Presbyterians 9, males 9, females 7, total 16. Just commencing, connected with no society, supported by the children. The teacher is the clerk of Aghanloo church. Information obtained from William Tate, the Reverend William Smiley and Henry Abraham. 11th, 12th, 13th and 16th December 1834.

Emigration

About 30 have emigrated to America during the last season and about 5 have returned; about 5 to England. All who go to England return. The decrease in emigration to England is chiefly owing to the thriving state of agriculture, as the labourers have employment at home; chiefly Roman Catholics.

State of the Poor by J. Stokes

There are nearly 200 cottiers, making with their families 1,000 individuals of that class in the parish. Almost every large farmer has a cottier under him: some 2 and some 3. In Rathfad there are 8 families and 60 individual cottiers; in Drumbane 12 families and 61 individual cottiers; in Ballycastle 24 families and 144 individual

cottiers; in Shanvey 3 families and 18 individual cottiers; in Ballymaglin 2 families and 14 individual cottiers; making in these 5 townlands 297 persons who are driven by the existing state of things frequently to support themselves by begging.

The holding of a cottier in Aghanloo is usually 26 perches of a garden and 25 feet in front of a house, for which they pay 25s a year. They act as labourers to the different farmers and the only certain employment that they can calculate upon in the year occurs in the following seasons: 6 weeks harvest, 10 days potato digging, 1 month turf cutting, setting potatoes with a few days for contingent employment. These are done by them for the farmers who give them 10d a day without diet for so doing. "Costmut" [crossed out: a corrupted Irish phrase], is the usual term for being without diet. [Insert correction by G. Downes: "costnent", phrase used at Aberdeen, Mr Stokes].

Thus the only certain employment for them is for 3 months in the year. In the remaining time they support themselves by chance. Those who can afford it, pay their passage to England and the remainder emigrate to the distant parishes as running beggars. Only 1 in 3, however, will amass the means of crossing the channel. Their wages of 10d a day is not always given: 5d a day is frequent. The present wages of spinning is 10d a week among them but 1 in 3 only are thus employed in some townlands. From the foregoing table of 5 townlands, it appears that the average number to a family among them is nearly 6 and one-eighth.

Notes and Queries on Productive Economy by G. Downes with sections by J. Stokes, December 1834

PRODUCTIVE ECONOMY

Manufactories

There are no mills or bleach greens within the parish. There are brickfields in the townlands of Tullyarmon, Magheraskeagh, Carbullion and Artikelly.

Manufacturing or Commercial

There are no manufactures. Females are employed in spinning for market or home consumption or knitting for their own use. Yarn is generally spun to 3 hank for the warp and 5 hank for the weft, which they sell to weavers for 1s 8d per spangle; the spangle contains 4 hanks. In addition to this, it may be stated that the spinning of flax has become so identified with the habits of the people that although the profit has become small in comparison to what it was, they are still attached to the employment and with almost no profit on small quantities. They will work merely for the sake of not being idle. All the linen worn by the parishioners is manufactured among themselves and bleached before their doors to a degree called "half bleaching." The present wages for spinning are 10d per week. [Insert footnote: "They have wages for spinning." Does "for their own use" apply merely to the "knitting" in the above sentence? [Answer]: It applies wholly to spinning and partly to the linen weaving].

Fairs and Markets

The several queries in the "Heads" respecting fairs may be chiefly answered thus: there are no fairs in the parish at present but there were originally 2 held in Artikelly. After the second, they were transferred to Newtown Limavady in consequence of a fight which had taken place at the first. The first was in May and the second in November. This occurred in [blank].

For markets: there are none.

Respecting weights and measures, they are statute.

Rural Economy

The whole parish belongs to the Marquis of Waterford and Captain Church, except Freehall which is Mr McCausland's. These proprietors are all resident but one, the marquis. The agent of the marquis is H.B. Beresford Esquire who resides at Brookhall, Londonderry, and he has a sub-agent, J. Given Esquire of Farlan. Both are paid by fixed salaries; agents are paid in money.

The holdings are generally from 20 to 30 acres [insert marginal note: it is elsewhere stated "from 5 to 80"]. The number above 100 acres is 4, above 50 acres is 4, above 20 acres is 28, above 10 acres is 66. The rest are below 10. The Marquis of Waterford is at present enlarging the smaller ones. They are generally held by lease and the usual tenure is 21 years and 1 life. They hold direct. The average acreable rent for the best land is 2 pounds, for middling 1 pound, for the worst 10s. [Insert marginal query: Is it really so? It is elsewhere stated "the rent varies from 1 pound to 2 pounds per acre"]. The rent is paid wholly in money. Before the agency of Mr Beresford, the best land was 2 pounds 10s per acre.

The number of respectable yeomen in the farming class is 6. This number is of those who exhibit in the exterior of their dwellings an attention to ornament as well as cleanliness. There are nearly 200 cottiers, of whom 2 or 3 are generally under some large farmer. The cottier's holding is generally of 26 perches of garden and 25 feet in front of the house, for which he pays 1 pound 5s a year. [Insert query and answer: Does this mean a house 25 feet from gable to gable in front of the garden, or a plot of 25 feet in front of the house, besides the garden in the rear? [Answer]: It means 25 feet from gable to gable in front of the garden]. The large farmers farm for the purpose of subsistence wholly. The quantity of land let in conacre is but small: John Dunlop of Ballycastle let some at 8 pounds per acre. The fields generally vary in size from 3 to 6 acres but sometimes contain 10. They are quadrangular and in parallelograms. The smaller have been generally made in wet situations. The fences are generally earthen.

Taxes

The immediate local taxes or cesses are county cess and church cesses. The latter are so small that the parishioners count them insignificant.

Farm Buildings and Model Farms

The farm buildings are good and commodious. They are erected and kept in repair by the tenantry who are, however, supplied with slates by the Marquis of Waterford on his estate. Captain Shadden's farm acted as a model farm whilst he resided in the parish, which was until a few years ago. He introduced the proper use of sea manure, which had before been used in a desultory and unsystematic manner. The soil is generally stiff in the highest parts, and in the low ground sandy. In Magheraskeagh the soil, or till, is very shallow, of not more than a spade in depth. Under it there occurs a hard, red gravel, and, finally, a bed of sea sand of unknown depth. It forms a comparatively unfertile ground. [Insert footnote: Does not this subsoil of sea sand occur in other townlands? Several are nearer the sea than this? Another statement is more general respecting the shallowness of the soil: "The soil is generally a mixture of clay and sand, the good soil being not more than a foot deep"]. The parishioners find that a subsoil of sea sand occurs in the townlands of Ballyhenry, Ballycastle, Ballycarton, Drumbane, Shanvey, Ballymaglin and Rathfad. They also find shells, particularly in Ballycastle.

Manures

The manures are lime or shells. Burnt lime may be obtained at 9d a barrel, shells at not less than 1s. The latter is mixed with the scourings of the ditches. [Insert footnote: elsewhere "The manure is usually a mixture of scrapings of ditches, sour bog, sea shells and table litter. Lime is not much used on account of the scarcity of turf and the distance of limestone. The cost of laying it on the ground is 11d a barrel, whereas the cost of drawing and laying down field manure is but 9d." This is the truest]. There is also a compost much used, of sand and shells, moss and stable manure. It may be stated generally that almost every variety of manure is used more or less in Aghanloo. The only material which they cannot conveniently procure is bog stuff.

Marl is not abundant: there is one lime kiln in full work belonging to the Marquis of Waterford in Tircorran, the rest belong to the tenantry. Burning the ground for manure prevails as far as it is necessary for the reclaiming of bog.

Lime kilns in general belong each to an occupying tenant. The marquis' large kiln contains 120 statute barrels and each tenant may have the content burned by paying 2s 6d for a permit, and if there is any trespass unavoidably committed by the carts either in coming to the kiln or to the quarry, it is customary to pay 2s 6d to the farmer to whom the ground happens to belong. Those who do not reside on the estate are charged 5s for a permit to burn. Those who do not lay the lime on their own ground are also charged 5s. 2 men are employed to take care of the quarry and raise the stones for those who may employ them. They receive 1 pound for quarrying the amount of 20 barrels of lime. The usual size of stones thrown in is 70 lbs. The marquis' bailiff superintends the kiln and the profits are believed to be applied to charitable purposes by the proprietor. This large kiln is useful from its size, which produces a saving of labour in the stone breaking which used not to be done to such a small degree as is necessary in the diminutive kilns of the parishioners, and also a saving of fuel from the superiority of its draught. The parishioners find by experience that it is a saving to procure their burnt lime from this kiln.

Implements of Husbandry

The implements of husbandry are of the Scotch and English kind and have been so this half century. The following is an enumeration of them: scythes, sickles, Scotch and English ploughs, drill harrows, rollers, box carts, winnowing machines, those being machines for weeding corn, and 1 churning machine. [Insert footnote: elsewhere "The implements of husbandry are harrows, shovels, spades and three-pronged pitchforks." This cannot be all]. The Irish implements still in use are long-wheeled cars and slide cars, wooden ploughs, heart-shaped shovels, grapes, pitchforks, comb hooks.

Oxen are used by Mr Church alone: he finds them advantageous. In a ploughing team 2 horses are used; in other teams, such as of oxen, Mr Church uses oxen partly because he was accustomed to them in India.

Crops

No particular rotation of crops is in general use amongst the parishioners, but those most common are the following: 1st potatoes, 2nd barley, 3rd wheat, 4th flax, 5th oats.

The principal crops are: potatoes, oats, wheat barley and flax. [Insert footnote: Can wheat be included among the principal crops? It is elsewhere stated "wheat is not often sown"]. Blanter oats and English wheat are sown. Of potatoes, cups, red Downs and English reds. Potatoes are put down at the rate of 24 and sometimes 30 bushels per acre. [Insert footnote: elsewhere "about 26 bushels"; however, the statements do not vary materially]. The produce of this varies from 150 to 350 bushels and depends on favourable seasons and proper cultivation. Potatoes are sold at 14 pounds an acre, in the market at 2d ha'penny per stone, on an average. [Insert footnote: elsewhere "at 8d a bushel"]. At present, December 1834, the market price of potatoes is in Newtown Limavady from 10d to 1s per bushel; the bushel containing 5 stone. Field beans are also frequently sown and exported to England and Scotland: 4 bushels statute are sown to an Irish plantation measure; 63 bushels is considered as a good crop. They are sold in England and Scotland. This is only the second time since the crop was introduced; in one instance 12 pounds per acre was cleared.

Oats are sown at the rate of from 6 to 7 bushels an acre. [Insert footnote: elsewhere "The quantity of oats sown for each acre of Irish plantation measure is 7 bushels"]. This produces from 30 to 50 bushels. At Newtown, oats are sold at 1s 6d a bushel. Oats are sold on the spot at from 5 pounds to 6 pounds. Oats are the principal grain crop. The growth of wheat is increasing. The crops of Aghanloo may be thus ranked in importance and extent: first potatoes, second oats, third flax, fourth wheat or barley, fifth beans or peas. There are numerous varieties of potatoes in use.

Wheat is sown at the rate of 4 bushels an acre. It produces from 6 to 12 barrels per acre. The acre is Irish plantation measure. Golden Essex is said to be second best: an average crop is worth on the spot about 9 pounds an acre; in the market it is sold at 1 pound 2s 6d a barrel. Field peas are sold in the neighbouring market towns at 1s 3d a peck. Barley is sown at the rate of 3 and a half bushels an acre. This produces from 6 to 10 barrels per acre, Irish plantation measure. An average crop is sold on the spot at 8 pounds an acre. At market the prices is 8d ha'penny a stone. Flax is sown at the rate of 3 bushels an acre; this produces 4 and a half cwt. An average crop is sold on the spot at 7 pounds an acre. At market the price is at present 3 pounds 10s per cwt. This is for December 1834.

Transport to Markets

The expense of carrying produce to market is 5d per cwt. To the Newtown market it is the value of a day's labour, which is about 3s at an average, varying according to the season of the year and the estimated importance of the [?] latter. The produce is exported to England from the parts of Londonderry and Coleraine. Very little has been sent this season, and the chief pressure on the farms at present is in the low price of their grain. The popular opinion is that it has been caused by the importation of foreign corn and that no demand for British exists in foreign countries.

Wages

Farm servants receive on an average 5 pounds a year males, 2 pounds 10s a year females. Labourers receive 10d a day without diet, or, according to a corrupt Irish phrase, "costmut" [costnent]. The only certain employment they can reckon on (with a few contingencies) are 6 weeks in harvest, 10 days of potato digging and 1 month of turf cutting, setting potatoes. Their regular wages are sometimes lowered to 5d. The charge for turf cutting is 1s for 4 days.

Grazing

7 of the farms are devoted almost exclusively to grazing. Some are partly laid down with the following of grasses: clover and trefoil, perennial rye grass. These are put down at the one time. The culture of improved and artificial grasses is in-

creasing, though not as common as could be wished. The grass most prevalent in the pastures is rye grass in the artificial pastures and various kinds on the natural i.e the mountains. There are some good meadows which are frequently irrigated and in the following manner: one of the numerous streams and rivulets to be met with are dammed up; a narrow trench is then cut to the meadow and the water let in to make its way back to the rivulet as best it can. For example, in the townland of Largantea and Ballymaglin, Alexander Hopkins, Mark Hopkins, James Hopkins, William Shannon and James Stewart find it frequently necessary to irrigate in the above manner. They are in a hilly, dry part of the parish. The operation is not required in the lowlands or near the Roe. The parish being generally dry, except in a few unimportant places, covered draining is not found necessary.

The tops of the hills are used as pasture but are very thinly stocked. [Insert query: all the hills? [Answer]: yes]. The stock is [blank] for there are no sheep. [Insert footnote: elsewhere "only 12 sheep or thereabouts"]. There are no regularly-stocked farms. The following are the preventive causes: first, small farms; second, bad fences; third, want of a remunerating profit price. Most probably the last; to be overcome, requires only to be combated.

Cattle

Of black cattle, the breed is chiefly Irish and the number 1,274. The breed of horses is English, Irish and Scottish and the number 344. The breed of pigs is Dutch and Berkshire and the number 216. The breed of poultry is Irish with a mixture of the pheasant and the number 2,363, including every kind. The breed of sheep is Irish and the number 145.

The following improved breeds have been introduced: cattle Devonshire and Ayrshire; horses English; pigs Dutch; poultry Poland; geese in Granagh and a few Friesland <Friezeland> hens.

Cattle Trading

There are no professed cattle dealers, and jobbers buy them up and drive them to the markets of [blank]. None of the parishioners support themselves exclusively by cattle dealing. There is apparently more dealing in pigs than in any other kind of livestock. On the spot they are sold for the usual Newtown Limavady market price. The cattle jobbing began in the year: [answer] time immemorial.

Green Feeding

Green feeding is extensively practised and with the following vegetables: turnips, vetches, clover, grass, horse beans. About 7 years ago turnips were unknown but they have increased this year in extent of cultivation according to the late partial failure of the potato crop. In all such instances, turnips were sown in their stead.

Uses made of the Bogs

The bogs are grazed at certain seasons such as spring and harvest when there is no turf cutting. The turf is not consumed wholly in the neighbourhood. It is carried to Newtown Limavady and sold at from 1s to 1s 6d for cartloads and from 8d to 1s for carloads. The people have no free right to turbary or grazing. As for mines and mineral deposits, there are none at present known. There is no flow bog properly so called in any part of the parish except a small spot near the Bishop's Road.

The bog wood is used for the following purposes: first fuel, second as a substitute for candle light, third roofing houses and for the rough work of cabins. Rope-making from bog wood does not appear to be understood here. The extent to which turf is made into charcoal for smiths' forges is increasing. All the smiths of the parish use it in preference to coal. Its cost on the spot is 10s per ton.

Drainage

As for draining the bogs, the attempts hitherto made have been confined to the tenantry, some of whom, however, have done it systematically. They only adhere to the custom of cutting their turf in lanes and passages most likely to produce that effect.

Planting

About planting, it may be observed in general that there is none in the parish except for what has been put down for shelter or ornament: the former of ash, sally and a little alder, the latter of fir, alder, beech and ash. The best thriving trees seem to be those of ash. All the ornamental planting to be seen in Aghanloo has been executed by the rectors: the Reverend W. Smiley and his predecessor the Reverend W. Robinson at the Glebe. The rest are sheltering groves, most numerous in

Ballymaglinn and Drumbane, both of which are in the northern part of the parish and adjacent to Magilligan. None of the proprietors have ever planted any waste tracts. There is no nursery for young trees. The trees at the Glebe are from 4 to 14 years old. The aspect of the ground on which they stand is south west and the soil a kind of stiffened clay. As to the success of the enterprise, it may be remarked that although in an unfavourable and exposed situation, these trees are at present healthy and thriving.

Respecting the growth of different kinds of timber under the different circumstances of soil, aspect, slope and expenses: there are also many orchards particularly in Drumbane, Ballymaglinn and Ballycastle. They are injured by the north winds.

The timber of the district is not sufficient for its consumption. As to the different circumstances of exportation and importation, all the wood necessary for the use of the carpenters of the parish is imported usually from the woods of Walworth or any of the demesnes of the neighbouring gentlemen in which the operation of thinning happens to be in execution. In building the better description of houses, the American fir timber is used, it being the cheapest.

Fishing

White fish of the following kinds have been caught in the Roe weighing 4 lbs. [Insert note: refer to Captain Portlock]. The other streams contain [blank].

SOCIAL AND PRODUCTIVE ECONOMY BY J. STOKES

Income of Roman Catholic Clergy

The Reverend William McDonagh is supported by about one-third of the total of the benefice. This is the general rule for the report of curates in the Catholic Church. The fees are from 2s 6d to 10s for marriages and funerals.

Lord Waterford's Premium and Boundaries of Parish

Lord Waterford gives a premium every year of a plough.

The reason why the parish of Aghanloo extends to the other side of the Roe is said to be because of the change of the course of the river which formerly ran more crooked. The Marquis of Waterford's tenants are improving their houses very much but not ornamenting them. They have every facility for doing so as forest, fruit and other trees are supplied gratis by the agent to all that ask for them.

Townlands belonging to Mr Church

The townlands which belong to Robert Henry Church Esquire are Drumbane, Rathfad, Shanvey and Ballybrissel, all churchland. The rents are paid in money to him but with the rents, duty work and duty hens are given.

Flood

On the 7th of November 1834, an inundation of the River Roe took place which greatly injured the townlands: Ballycastle, Ballyhenry, Shanvey, Carbullion, Gortnamoney, Granagh, Clooney, Artikelly, Drumbane, Rathfad, Ballymaglin, Tullyarmon and Ballycarton, by sweeping off hay and potatoes, throwing down houses, injuring fences. Some of Mr Church's tenants lost 100 barrels of potatoes.

Cattle Prices

The price of a good cow in Aghanloo is from 6 pounds to 6 pounds 10s, in Newtown Limavady the same. Cattle jobbers have sometimes bought a cow in Londonderry for 6 pounds 10s and sold her in Newtown Limavady for 7 pounds 5s. The prices of cattle are partly affected by the number that happens to be in the fair or market.

Spinning and Linen Trade

Some years ago, spinning wheels were given out to the tenantry by the Marquis of Waterford. Since the failure in the linen trade, no applications have been made.

Use of Field Beans

Norfolk, Highland and Goland beans are the sort most usually sown in the parish of Aghanloo. The produce of an acre of field beans in John Wilson's farm, Gortnamoney, of good land was about 88 bushels. 2 bushels of field peas are sown to an acre, Irish plantation measure. The produce is about 30 bushels. Those who have not a great quantity of beans or peas sell them in Newtown Limavady or Coleraine. The parishioners frequently grind their peas into meal, of which, when mixed with oatmeal, they make a coarse bread called by some mashlin bread. They also use peameal as stirabout which, however, is of bad quality as it is always thin. They sometimes make

a brose too by pouring hot water on a small quantity in a bowl and then using it with salt or sugar.

Itinerant Shoemakers

For the sake of economy, the farmers who have large families purchase leather and bring shoemakers to the house to make strong shoes. The fine shoes are always bought at shops. The tradesmen thus employed charge 1s per pair at the farmer's house for making men and women's shoes. At their own house they charge 2s per pair for men and 1s 6d for women.

The sieves are made of prepared sheepskin punched with holes.

Potatoes and Flooding

John Dunlap of Ballycastle has had mosscheaper potatoes as early as the 13th of June. The different varieties known are American whites, golden dwarfs, red Downs, posies, Miller's thumbs, Bangors, white Downs and Ballymankeys, seedlings, black cups and American reds.

There have been 3 remarkable floods in the River Roe: the first about 40 years ago, the second on the 21st November 1831, the third on the 8th November 1834.

Weaving and Poverty

In Aghanloo the greater the poverty of the townland, the more numerous are the weavers. This is universally the case.

Churning Machine

William Shannon of Largantea has erected an excellent [?] chop and useful machine for churning milk. The diameter of the wheel is 6 feet, the water falls abreast and the interior metal cog wheel is 9 inches with a small one of 5 inches. It was built in 1832 and the cost of the whole house and machine was 4 pounds. It is less than 1 horsepower and is fed by a spring about 10 perches distant.

Basket Making

Basket making is a branch of productive economy carried on to some extent in Aghanloo along the banks of the Curly and in the neighbourhood of Artikelly. One family in that village makes annually 24 dozen of baskets of various kinds, which are sold in Londonderry at from 5d to 1s 6d according to the size. These baskets made for home consumption are chiefly potato creels. There are 78 looms in this parish.

Mud Houses

There are many houses in Aghanloo entirely composed of mud or sods, particularly in the neighbourhood of the old church. Others are built partly with stone and lime and partly with gables of clay.

Distinctions between Townlands

It has been found that in the townland of Ballycarton there was the greatest number of poultry, in the townland of Stradreagh the greatest number of looms. Stradreagh is the poorest townland in the parish and in Ballycarton, Ballycastle and its neighbourhood there is the greatest number of small gardens and orchards. There are 24 goats in the parish. One ass only was found but probably there are a few in the mountains.

Rabbit Catching

The season for catching rabbits commences on the 1st of November and ends on the 12th of February. The carriers purchase them on the spot for 6d per couple or 3d each and sell them in Newtown Limavady at from 8d to 10d per couple, being 60% profit. They agree to return the skins to the farmers who then sell them to Coleraine dealers chiefly, who export them to various places. The warrens are becoming less productive owing chiefly to the number annually killed interfering with that which is necessary to continue the stock. Many of the rabbits are also eaten by the rats which attack them when caught in traps.

Making Mats of Bent Grass

When the bent grass of the warren is a year old, it is cut in the month of August. It is cut either above or at the joint and laid on the sand to dry like hay for 8 days. When that period is elapsed, it is fit for plaiting, a process performed by children. For coarse matting the bent is formed into strands of 7 strikes each, and sometimes 13 according to the breadth or thickness required. The piece, when complete, is from 30 to 31 yards long and of various breadths and is sold at the Coleraine, Belfast, Antrim and Londonderry markets at 1d per yard. It is sold in almost all parts of Ulster and some has been taken to Dublin but it could not compete with the rush mat. On the spot it sells at

an average for 22d per web of 30 and a half yards. When in season, a man can cut from 6 a.m. to 6 p.m. material for 6 webs, which is found to be equivalent to 24 sheaves or 2 stooks. [Crossed out: This day's labour is thus worth 11s. If he manufactures and sells it himself in the adjoining markets, it is worth 15s]. Mats for doors are made 2 and a half feet long and 2 feet broad. They sell for 3d each at the market and a man will make 8 of them in a day. Besoms and "bosses" or small footstools are also made. The former are sold at the adjoining market at from 3d to 4d each. The latter are seldom bespoke. The bent grass itself is sold on the spot at 6d per stook.

Conacres and Rents

The practice of setting conacre ground is diminishing from the frequency with which the crop is thrown back upon the farmer's hands if it is not found to be good.

The cottiers of Oughtymoyle generally pay 1 pound 17s 6d for a house and cow's grass and place for the manure. Some other cottier pays his rent by work.

Condition of Houses

The farmhouses of the Presbyterians are the most comfortable, the Protestants not so comfortable but the Roman Catholics in all parts very poor and their houses bad and dirty.

Cottiers

The townlands of Duncrun and Ballyleighery contain the greatest number of cottier tenantry. It is worthy of remark that few individuals of this class in Magilligan are without a horse, although they may be at the same time so poor as to be unable to keep either a cow or pig. They are accordingly half-starved and sometimes entirely so. An instance has been found of an old cottier who is in the constant habit of tying his horse to one side of his bed, his cow to the other and making a litter for his pig at the foot. The general habit of thus admitting the cattle into the dwelling house is, however, by no means uncommon.

In those parts of the parish that are without any stones, the houses are sometimes built entirely of sods and earth.

Farm Size

In Mr Gage's estate in this parish there are 3 farms above 100 acres, 8 farms above 50 acres, 14 farms above 20 acres and the rest under 20 acres.

Notes on Population by C.W. Ligar

SOCIAL ECONOMY

Answers by C.W. Ligar to Queries on Social Economy

What are the absolute numbers or relative proportions of the various religious denominations? [Answer]: See report of the census.

What proportion or number migrated annually for harvest work and whither? [Answer]: Not more than 5 or 6 annually.

What are the precuniary emoluments of all the Presbyterians and other Dissenting clergy who are not "Orthodox"? [Answer]: The Presbyterian minister's emolument is as follows: stipend 71 pounds and regium donum 75 pounds Irish.

Is there any illicit distillation at present? [Answer]: None at present.

Could a list of the cases from this parish treated at Newtown Limavady dispensary be procured for 1833 and 1834 or even totals? [Answer]: Sent with the memoir of Drumachose.

What was the amount of emigration in 1833 and 1834 and to what places, specifying which of the Canadas? [Answer]: See [emigration] table.

Emigration Table by J. Bleakly

Emigration

List of persons who have emigrated from the parish of Aghanloo during the years 1833 and 1834 [table gives name, age, year in which emigrated, townland of origin, religion, port emigrated to].

John Johnston, 28, Roman Catholic, 1834, from Shanvey to Philadelphia.

Bridget Johnston, 22, Roman Catholic, 1834, from Shanvey to Philadelphia.

Eliza Garven, 23, Roman Catholic, 1834, from Drumbane to Philadelphia.

John Hopkins, 30, Established Church, 1834, from Ballycastle to Quebec.

Eliza Hopkins, 25, Established Church, 1834, from Ballycastle to Quebec.

James Hopkins, 10, Established Church, 1834, from Ballycastle to Quebec.

John Hopkins Junior, 8, Established Church, 1834, from Ballycastle to Quebec.

Matilda Hopkins, 6, Established Church, 1834, from Ballycastle to Quebec.

William Hopkins, 4, Established Church, 1834, from Ballycastle to Quebec.

Eliza Hopkins Junior, 2, Established Church, 1834, from Ballycastle to Quebec.

Hugh Thompson, 20, Presbyterian, 1834, from Ballycastle to Quebec.

Samuel Ferguson, 22, Presbyterian, 1833, from Ballycastle to Quebec.

Richard Gallagher, 20, Roman Catholic, 1834, from Carbullion to Quebec.

John Gallagher, 18, Roman Catholic, 1834, from Carbullion to Quebec.

John Mortland, 20, Roman Catholic, 1834, from Granagh to Quebec.

David Moore, 35, Presbyterian, 1834, from Granagh to Quebec.

James Conaway, 30, Presbyterian, 1834, from Granagh to Quebec.

Mary Sandford, 35, Presbyterian, 1833, from Granagh to Philadelphia.

Mary Simeon, 23, Presbyterian, 1833, from Granagh to Philadelphia.

Jacob Thompson, 52, Established Church, 1834, from Tullyarmon to Quebec.

Jacob Thompson Junior, 16, Established Church, 1834, from Tullyarmon to Quebec.

Ann Thompson, 19, Established Church, 1834, from Tullyarmon to Quebec.

Mary Thompson, 45, Established Church, 1834, from Tullyarmon to Quebec.

William Henry, 52, Presbyterian, 1834, from Tullyarmon to Quebec.

Thomas Henry, 25, Presbyterian, 1834, from Tullyarmon to Quebec.

Ann Henry, 50, Presbyterian, 1834, from Tullyarmon to Quebec.

William Henry, 20, Presbyterian, 1833, from Tullyarmon to Quebec.

Mary Garven, 32, Roman Catholic, 1834, from Tullyarmon to Philadelphia.

Rachel Dysart, 24, Roman Catholic, 1834, from Tullyarmon to Philadelphia.

John McLaughlin, 28, Presbyterian, 1833, from Lisnagrib to Philadelphia.

Jane McLaughlin, 28, Presbyterian, 1833, from Lisnagrib to Philadelphia.

William Johnston, 25, Presbyterian, 1833, from Lisnagrib to Philadelphia.

John Johnston, 16, Presbyterian, 1833, from Lisnagrib to Philadelphia.

Mary Condle, 22, Presbyterian, 1833, from Ballyhenry to Philadelphia.

John Smith, 21, Presbyterian, 1833, from Ballyhenry to Philadelphia.

Elisabeth Smith, 20, Presbyterian, 1833, from Ballyhenry to Philadelphia.

James Mullan, 20, Roman Catholic, 1834, from Granagh to St John's.

Jane Johnston, 18, Presbyterian, 1834, from Lisnagrib to Quebec. 6th, 8th and 11th June 1835.

Statistics on Productive Economy

PRODUCTIVE ECONOMY

Tables of Productive Economy

[In these, 2 numbers are given with each crop: however, it is unclear to what these refer].

1, Artikelly, acreage: 252 acres 3 roods 34 perches; waste: 5.5%, 13 acres; tillage: 91.3%, 230 acres; value: 182 pounds 10s; rate per acre: 14.5; oats: number 30, 42.6; potatoes: number 18, 246.9; flax: number 19, 4.6.

2, Ballybrissel, acreage: 265 acres 3 roods 16 perches; waste: 89.5%, 237 acres; tillage: 9.4%, 24 acres; value: 29 pounds 15s; rate per acre: 2.2; oats: number 11, 38.7; potatoes: number 9, 209.8; flax: number 26, 4.3.

3, Ballyeaston, acreage: 463 acres 2 roods 24 perches; waste: 83.1%, 384 acres; tillage: 15.7%, 72 acres; value: 76 pounds 4s; rate per acre: 3.3; oats: number 19, 37.1; potatoes: number 10, 201.2; flax: number 11, 4.2.

4, Ballycastle, acreage: 292 acres 3 roods 1 perch; waste: 1.5%, 4 acres; tillage: 95%, 277 acres; value: 243 pounds 4s; rate per acre: 16.7; oats: number 10, 34.8; potatoes: number 13, 200.6; flax: number 6, 3.9.

5, Ballyhanidy, acreage: 432 acres 3 roods 37 perches; waste: 85.2%, 368 acres; tillage: 12.9%, 55 acres; value: 49 pounds 1s; rate per acre: 2.3; oats: number 4, 30.9; potatoes: number 16, 200.6; flax: number 16, 3.7.

6, Ballyhenry East, acreage: 282 acres 3 roods 18 perches; waste: 1.6%, 32 acres; tillage: 86.7%, 244 acres; value: 200 pounds 13s; rate per acre: 14.2%; oats: number 18, 30.8; potatoes: number 4, 191.3; flax: number 18, 3.7.

7, Ballymaglin, acreage: 365 acres 3 roods 29 perches; waste: 75.4%, 275 acres; tillage: 23.8%, 86 acres; value: 80 pounds 4s; rate per acre: 4.4; oats: number 9, 29.8; potatoes: number 27, 191.3; flax: number 22, 3.7.

8, Ballymoney, acreage: 89 acres 1 rood 17 perches; waste: 5.6%, 4 acres; tillage: 22.9%, 82 acres; value: 61 pounds 10s; rate per acre: 13.9; oats: number 7, 29.6; potatoes: number 31, 185.8; flax: number 30, 3.7.

9, Carbullion, acreage: 170 acres 3 roods 17 perches; waste: 10.5%, 17 acres; tillage: 86%, 146 acres; value: 129 pounds 4s; rate per acre: 15.2; oats: number 6, 29; potatoes: number 7, 185; flax: number 4, 3.4.

10, Clooney, acreage: 65 acres 1 rood 21 perches; waste: 2.2%, 1 acre; tillage: 96.3%, 62 acres; value: 52 pounds 7s; rate per acre: 16.1; oats: number 22, 28.9; potatoes: number 19, 178; flax: number 7, 3.4.

11, Cressycrib, acreage: 57 acres 2 roods 6 perches; waste: 12.3%, 7 acres; tillage: 56.8%, 49 acres; value: 57 pounds 5s; rate per acre: 20.1; oats: number 27, 28.8; potatoes: number 11, 178; flax: number 13, 3.3.

12, Dirtagh, acreage: 230 acres 2 roods 13 perches; waste: 5.3%, 16 acres; tillage: 92.2%, 295 acres; value: 190 pounds 2s; rate per acre: 11.10; oats: number 12, 28.5; potatoes: number 26, 172.8; flax: number 9, 3.2.

13, Dowland, acreage: 170 acres 39 perches; waste: 13.5%, 22 acres; tillage: 83.3%, 141 acres; value: 110.15; rate per acre: 13; oats: number 23, 28.4; potatoes: number 14, 166.6; flax: number 27, 3.2.

14, Drumaderry, acreage: 235 acres 1 rood 24 perches; waste: 8.6%, 120 acres; tillage: 89.8%, 211 acres; value: 168 pounds 1s; rate per acre: 14.3; oats: number 26, 27.8; potatoes: number 12, 160.5; flax: number 21, 3.1.

15, Drumalief, acreage: 191 acres; waste: 10.7%, 20 acres; tillage: 87.7%, 167 acres; value: 116 pounds 16s; rate per acre: 12.2; oats: number 16, 27.8; potatoes: number 23, 154.8; flax: number 23, 3.1.

16, Drumbane, acreage: 184 acres 39 perches; waste: 7%, 12 acres; tillage: 90.9% 167 acres; value: 120 pounds 12s; rate per acre: 13.1; oats: number 13, 27.8; potatoes: number 22, 151; flax: number 1, 2.8.

17, Freehall, acreage: 209 acres 1 rood 15 perches; waste: 28.6%, 39 acres; tillage: 69.3%, 144 acres; value: 87 pounds 3s; rate per acre: 8.4; oats: number 25, 27.3; potatoes: number 8, 148.1; flax: number 14, 2.8.

18, Glebe, acreage: 32 acres 1 rood 19 perches; waste: nil; tillage: 97.7%, 31 acres; value: 21 pounds 5s; rate per acre: 13.3; oats: number 1, 26; potatoes: number 1, 148; flax: number 25, 2.6.

19, Gortnamoney, acreage: 66 acres 3 roods 29 perches; waste: 1.95%, 1 acre; tillage: 95.1%, 62 acres; value: 56 pounds 5s; rate per acre: 17; oats: number 8, 26; potatoes: number 24, 148; flax: number 15, 2.5.

20, Grange Park, acreage: 1,076 acres 27 perches; waste: 83.8%, 901 acres; tillage: 15.6%, 167 acres; value: 38 pounds 18s; rate per acre: 0.8; oats: number 28, 25.5; potatoes: number 6, 143.3; flax: number 28, 2.4.

21, Grannagh, acreage: 125 acres 1 rood 17 perches; waste: 8.6%, 10 acres; tillage: 88.6%, 110 acres; value: 80 pounds 2s; rate per acre: 1.3; oats: number 20, 24.7; potatoes: number 28, 143.2; flax: number 29, 2.4.

22, Killybready, acreage: 202 acres 2 roods 6 perches; waste: 2.4%, 4 acres; tillage: 95.1%, 192 acres; value: 121 pounds 6s; rate per acre: 12; oats: number 29, 22.4; potatoes: number 15, 143; flax: number 20, 2.3.

23, Largantea, acreage: 698 acres 2 roods 8 perches; waste: 85%, 593 acres; tillage: 13.2%, 92 acres; value: 160 pounds 16s; rate per acre: 4.7; oats: number 3, 22.2; potatoes: number 25, 139.4; flax: number 24, 2.1.

24, Lisnagrib, acreage: 314 acres 3 roods 23 perches; waste: 33.6%, 105 acres; tillage: 62.9%, 197 acres; value: 148 pounds 10s; rate per acre: 9.5; oats: number 14, 22.2; potatoes: number 20, 134; flax: number 10, 0.4.

25, Maghraskeagh, acreage: 91 acres 2 roods 20 perches; waste: 6.8%, 6 acres; tillage: 89.9%, 81 acres; value: 59 pounds 19s; rate per acre: 13.2; oats: number 17, 22.2; potatoes: number 17, 139.6; flax: number 8, 0.3.

26, Rathfad, acreage: 166 acres; waste: 17.8%, 29 acres; tillage: 80.4%, 133 acres; value: 102 pounds 18s; rate per acre: 12.4; oats: number 21, 22.2; potatoes: number 24, 129.6; flax: number 12, 0.3.

27, Shanvey, acreage: 203 acres 3 roods 24 perches; waste: 38.6%, 78 acres; tillage: 60%, 121 acres; value: 111 pounds 8s; rate per acre: 10.11; oats: number 15, 21.6; potatoes: number 29, 126.5; flax: number 17, 0.3.

28, Stradreagh, acreage: 765 acres 1 rood 1 perch; waste: 69.4%, 530 acres; tillage: 29.1%, 222 acres; value: 181 pounds 18s; rate per acre: 4.9; oats: number 24, 26.6; potatoes: number 2, 123.4; flax: number 2.

29, Tircorran, acreage: 187 acres 30 perches; waste: 57.8%, 108 acres; tillage: 41.9%, 78 acres; value: 71 pounds 7s; rate per acre: 7.7; oats: number 2, 18.5; potatoes: number 3, 111; flax: number 3.

30, Tullyarmon, acreage: 268 acres 28 perches; waste: 10.5%, 28 acres; tillage: 87.6%, 234 acres; value: 205 pounds 17s; rate per acre: 1.5; oats: number 5, 18.5; potatoes: number 5, 111; flax: number 5.

Proportions and Cost of Compost and Dung

1, Artikelly, 32 tons of compost, cost 46s, rate 1s 5d per ton; 19 tons of dung, cost 15s 6d, 9d per ton.

2, Ballybrissel, 18 tons of dung, cost 17s 5d, rate 11d per ton; [other manure not specified]: 2, 20, 10.

3, Ballycarton, 35 tons of compost, cost 33s, rate 11d per ton; 19 tons of dung, cost 16s 7d, 10d per ton.

4, Ballycastle, 42 tons of compost, cost 56s, rate 1s 4d per ton; 23 tons of dung, cost 17s 8d, 9d per ton.

5, Ballyhanna, 20 tons of dung, cost 19s 4d, rate 1s 1d per ton.

6, Ballyhenry East, 55 tons of compost, cost 48s, rate 10d per ton; 29 tons of dung, cost 25s 4d, 1s per ton; [other manure not specified]: 5 and a fifth, 22s, 3.9.

7, Ballymaglin, 69 tons of compost, cost 53s, rate 9d per ton; 26 tons of dung, cost 20s, 9d per ton; [other manure not specified]: 9 and a fifth, 40s, 4.4.

8, Ballymoney, 42 tons of compost, cost 76s, rate 1s 9d per ton; 19 tons of dung, cost 15s 4d, 9d per ton; [other manure not specified]: 9 and a fifth, 40s, 4.4.

9. Carbullion, 22 tons of dung, cost 17s, rate 9d per ton; [other manure not specified]: 6 and a fifth, 19s, 3.

10, Clooney, 78 tons of compost, cost 95s, rate 1s 2d per ton; 28 tons of dung, cost 20s, 8d per ton; [other manure not specified]: 9 and seven-tenths, 52, 5.

11, Cressycrib, 56 tons of compost, cost 41s, rate 8d per ton; 27 tons of dung, cost 20s, 8s per ton.

12, Dirtagh, 47 tons of compost, cost 97s, rate 1s 1d per ton; 26 tons of dung, cost 18s, 8d per ton.

13, Dowland, 69 tons of compost, cost 114s, rate 1s 7d per ton; 22 tons of dung, cost 16s, 8d per ton; [other manure not specified]: 7 and seven-tenths, 20s, 3.

14, Drumaderry, 43 tons of compost, cost 56s, rate 1s 3d per ton; 20 tons of dung, cost 16s, 9d per ton; [other manure not specified]: 9 and an eighth, 37s, 4.

15, Drumalief, 22 tons of dung, cost 16s, rate 8d per ton; [other manure not specified]: 11, 45s, 4.1.

16, Drumbane, 45 tons of compost, cost 59s, rate 1s 2d per ton; 26 tons of dung, cost 20s 8d, 9d per ton.

17, Freehall, 23 tons of compost, cost 28s, rate 1s 2d per ton; 21 tons of dung, cost 19s, 10d per ton; [other manure not specified]: 9 and a fifth, 39s, 42.

18, Glebe, 49 tons of compost, cost 36s, rate 8d per ton; 25 tons of dung, cost 18s 4d, 8d per ton; [other manure not specified]: 9 and a fifth, 36s, 3.10.

19, Gortnamoney, 63 tons of compost, cost 64s, rate 1s per ton; 31 tons of dung, cost 22s, 8d per ton.

20, Grange Park, 22 tons of dung, cost 16s, rate 8d per ton.

21, Granagh, 42 tons of compost, cost 34s, rate 9d per ton; 22 tons of dung, cost 18s, 9d per ton.

22, Killybready, 71 tons of compost, cost 184s, rate 2s 7d per ton; 29 tons of dung, cost 22s, 9d per ton; [other manure not specified]: 3 and three-fifths, 41s, 11.

23, Largantea, 29 tons of dung, cost 25s, rate 10d per ton; [other manure not specified]: 2 and a tenth, 37s, 12.

24, Lisnagrib, 50 tons of compost, cost 74s, rate 1s 5d per ton; 25 tons of dung, cost 20s, 9d per ton.

25, Meagheraskeagh, 46 tons of compost, cost 33s, rate 8d per ton; 19 tons of dung, cost 13s, 8d per ton.

26, Rathfad, 22 tons of dung, cost 17s, rate 9d per ton; [other manure not specified]: 9 and a fifth, 34s.

27, Shanvey, 20 tons of dung, cost 14s 8d, rate 8d per ton; [other manure not specified]: 10 and four-fifths, 42s.

28, Stradreagh, 54 tons of compost, cost 46s, rate 10d per ton; 22 tons of dung, cost 19s, 10d per ton.

29, Tircorran, 51 tons of compost, cost 90s, rate 1s 8d per ton; 22 tons of dung, cost 16s, 8d per ton.

30, Tullyarmon, 47 tons of compost, cost 60s, rate 1s 3d per ton; 36 tons of dung, cost 25s, 8d per ton.

Cultivation, its Mode and Results.

[Table contains the following headings: name of townland, estate, farm, proprietor and tenant, acreage, soil and subsoil, drainage, manures, rotation of crops, quantity and price of seed and produce, times of sowing and harvest, woods, stock, markets].

Ballymaglin, Grocer's Company and Marquis of Waterford, soil depth 6 inches to 1 foot 6 inches, soil: loam and clay, subsoil: sea sand, drainage very bad; crop rotation: wheat 3, barley 2, oats 5, potatoes 1, flax 4; stock: 24 sheep, 9 pigs, 28 head of black cattle, 13 horses, 12 geese, 4 turkeys, 21 ducks, 24 hens.

Ballycastle, subsoil: sea sand and shells; crop rotation: wheat 3, barley 2, oats 5, potatoes 1 and sometimes 4, flax 4; second rotation: wheat 4, barley 2, oats 4, potatoes 1, barley and clover 3.

Drumbane, subsoil: sea sand; crop rotation: wheat 1, barley 3, potatoes 2, flax 4.

Drumaderry, manor of Freemore; crop rotation: wheat 3, barley 2, oats 5, potatoes 1, flax 4.

Cressycrib, crop rotation: barley 2, oats 3, potatoes 1, flax 4, laid down with clover and grasses.

Stradreagh, manor of Freemore; crop rotation: oats 2, potatoes 1, flax 3.

Killybready, manor of Freemore; crop rotation: oats 2 and 4, potatoes 1, flax 3.

Largantea, manor of Freemore; crop rotation: oats 2, potatoes 1, flax 3.

Tullyarmon, manor of Freemore; crop rotation: barley 4, oats 1 and 2, potatoes 3.

Tircorran, manor of Freemore; manures: stalks of the pea crop left on the ground once in 6 years; crop rotation: barley 2, oats 3 and 4 and 5, potatoes 1, peas 6.

Magheraskeagh, manor of Freemore; crop rotation: wheat 3, barley 2, oats 5, potatoes 1, flax 4.

Artikelly, manor of Freemore; crop rotation: wheat 3, barley 2, oats 5, potatoes 1, flax 4.

Clooney, manor of Freemore; crop rotation: wheat 3, barley 2, oats 4, potatoes 1, flax 3.

Ballyhenry, estate churchland, proprietor Mr Gage and Church; soil: dark loam, subsoil: sea sand; crop rotation: wheat 3, barley 2, oats 3, potatoes 1, flax 4.

Ballycarton, estate churchland, proprietor Benjamin Lane; crop rotation: wheat 3, barley 2, oats 3, potatoes 1.

Ballymoney, crop rotation: wheat 4, oats 1, potatoes 3, flax 2 and 5.

Parish of Dunboe, County Londonderry

Memoir by C.W. Ligar, with Sections by J.
Bleakly and J. Stokes, July, September and
November 1835

NATURAL FEATURES

Hills

[Dated] 16th November 1835. The surface of the
parish is in general a gentle and easy slope, being
the north east side of the range of basalt hills
which stretches through the county from south to
north. The highest part of the range within the
parish is 1,000 feet and the following are points of
less elevation: the Sconce hill, 797 feet, Altibrian,
823 feet, Ballinrees, 525 feet, and Ballystrone,
525 feet above the level of the sea.

Altibrian, the Sconce hill, Ballinrees and
Ballystrone form a secondary range to the larger
one above mentioned, and branches from it to the
west. It partakes of the character of the larger
range, being steep on the south west and sloping
gently on the opposite side. All the small undulations and hills of the parish have the same peculiarity.

Lakes and Rivers

There is no lake in the parish.

The River Bann before falling into the sea
divides this parish from Ballyaghran for 1 and a
half miles, during which its direction is from east
by south to west by north. Its breadth at high water
when first connected with the parish is 250 yards.
Before falling into the sea it becomes broader and
forms a bay 700 yards in breadth. Its mouth,
which is obstructed by a bar of sand, is 484 yards
at high water. (For description of the bar and the
navigation of the river, see Coleraine Memoir). In
high tides, during the time of flow when the wind
is north and north west, a few fields are flooded,
but only remain so till the ebb tide commences.

There are several small streams in the parish
from which, and numerous springs, it is abundantly supplied with water. The principal stream
is the Articlave burn, which rises in the mountains
of the parish and passes through it in a direction
from south west to north east.

Bogs

In the mountains there is a great extent of bog
from 550 feet to 950 feet above the sea, and
varying in depth from 1 to 8 feet. Fir and oak trees
have been found imbedded, the former predomi-

nating in quantity. The trees are all broken off at
about 2 feet above the roots which remain upright,
and the trees, it has been generally remarked, lie
in a direction from west to east.

A great quantity of fir and oak trees have been
found at a former period in the low grounds,
where the bog has at present nearly all been cut
away and reclaimed. They were found broken off
at about the same height from the roots and lying
in the same direction as those on the mountains.

Woods

There is at present no wood of a natural growth,
but the timber found imbedded in the bogs leave
evident traces of its former existence in the parish.
The situation of the parish from its exposure to the
north west wind passing over the sea is very
unfavourable to planting. Several attempts have
been made to plant about Downhill House but
without success. However, in a deep glen in the
vicinity there is a flourishing plantation of a
considerable extent. In the townland of Altibrian
<Artibrian>, the late Alexander Alexander Es-
quire planted to a small extent. The trees, which
consist principally of alders with a few Scotch,
larch and spruce firs, were put down in belts about
15 yards broad. From being planted in these
narrow belts the trees have not afforded each
other sufficient protection, and are in some parts,
where most exposed, not growing well. Some of
the alders and larch firs which have been down 9
years are 10 feet high, but the spruce and Scotch
firs are not doing so well. There are a few trees
surrounding some of the farmhouses which are
very much withered on the north west side and are
found to decay very soon. It is a common saying
that anything but trees will grow in the parish of
Dunboe.

Coast

The north side of the parish presents to the ocean
a line of cliffs nearly perpendicular, from 150 to
350 feet in height and extending from east to west
for 3 miles, slightly curved towards the north.
Towards each extreme of this line there is a sandy
beach between the rocks and the water, but in the
central part the water washes the base of the cliffs.
There is no creek or harbour, and boats do not

venture over the breakers except in fine weather during the summer. Along the line of coast 9 caves penetrate the rocks for a distance of from 16 to 170 feet. They are each known by some particular name, and one of them is called the Tory's (robber's) Cave from its having been formerly resorted to by Cushey Glenn, a notorious robber, and a gang of men of similar character.

Climate

The air of this parish is extremely healthful. The following are the periods at which the different crops are put down and become ripe: wheat put down from 20 October, ripe from 20 August; barley put down from 5 April, ripe from 10th August; oats put down from 1 March, ripe from 15 August; rye put down from 5 February, ripe from 10 August; flax put down from 15 April, ripe from 1 August; clover and hay seed put down from 20 March, ripe from 20 June, 2nd year; turnips put down from 1 June, ripe from 1 November; field peas put down from 21 March, ripe from 15 August; vetches put down from 10 March, ripe from 1 July; beans put down from 1 March, ripe from 20 August; red beet put down from 1 May, ripe from 1 November; potatoes put down from 20 April, ripe from 1 October. There is but very little difference in the sowing of the mountains and lowlands of this parish, but in ripening the mountains are, with few exceptions, 20 days later.

MODERN TOPOGRAPHY

Towns and Villages

Towns none.

The village of Articlave, situated on the road between Coleraine and Downhill at 4 miles from the former place and 2 from the latter, consists of one street with 57 houses. It contains also a mill and the following public buildings (which will be described in connection with the parish at large): the parish church, Presbyterian meeting house and schoolhouse. All the houses except 6 are but 1-storey high and thatched. Many of them are in bad repair and give a very indifferent appearance to the village. A good, 2-storey house has been lately built and is at present a public house, and a grocer and general dealer has also lately erected some office houses. Otherwise there is no appearance of improvement. A penny post was established on the 11th May 1832. The letters are carried by a foot post from Coleraine and arrive at Articlave at 50 minutes past 4 p.m. and are dispatched from Articlave at 15 minutes past 8 a.m.

See appendix for a list of the occupations and trades in the village.

Public Buildings

The parish church, Presbyterian meeting house and schoolhouse have before been stated to be in the village of Articlave. There is also a Seceding meeting house situated in the townland of Ballinrees.

Parish Church

The parish church was built in 1691, and is about to be repaired and the windows renewed and altered in their positions so as to give a thorough light, which is not the case at present as there are no windows on the north side. It is of a rectangular form, measuring 51 and a half feet by 20 and three-quarter feet on the inside. The west end is adorned with a square tower surmounted by 4 pinnacles, with a vane on each. There are 2 stoves in the church: the expenses attending their erection was defrayed by Sir James Bruce Bart and the archdeacon. The candles used in the evening service and the fuel for the stove are also supplied by the archdeacon. A gallery is required but it is thought will not be supplied for some time. The whole church is undergoing repair. The seats have been taken down.

Presbyterian Meeting House

Presbyterian meeting house is an unornamented building of a rectangular form and measuring 78 feet by 32 on the outside. The cost of its erection was defrayed by subscriptions from the congregation and a donation of 50 pounds from the late Lord Bristol, Bishop of Derry, and cost 350 pounds. The date of erection, 1785, is shown by the following inscription on a stone tablet in the side wall of the building: "This house was built AD 1785 under the care of our late worthy pastor the Revd William Knox, who after 37 years ministerial labours resigned his breath to God who gave it. 29th August 1801."

In 1830 the building was raised, the cost of which and some additional seats in the gallery amounted to 250 pounds. Towards this sum the Clothworkers' Company gave 50 pounds and Sir James Bruce Bart 20 pounds. There is accommodation with the aid of a gallery extending round 3 sides of the house for 368 persons, allowing 23 inches to each person. As the present house is too small for the increasing congregation, it is in contemplation to make an addition to it, the esti-

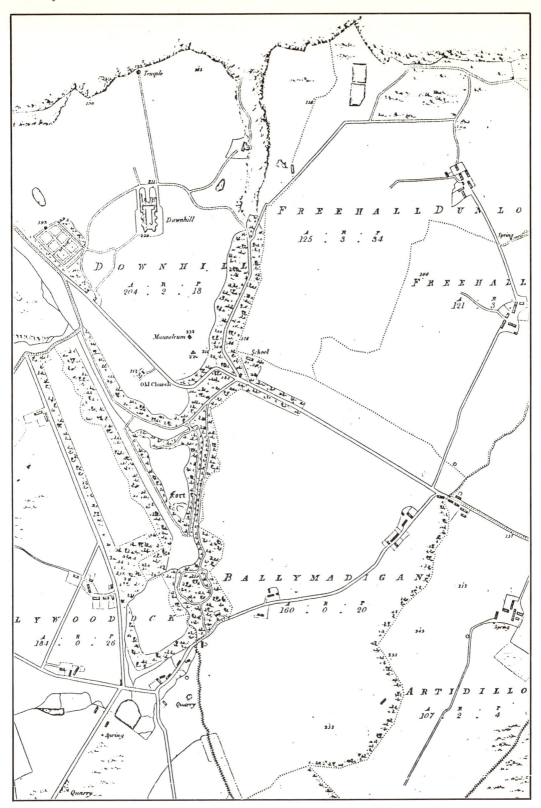

Map of Downhill and neighbourhood from the first 6" O.S. maps, 1830s

mated expense for which is 350 pounds. The pews in the lower part are in bad repair.

Schoolhouse

Articlave schoolhouse is situated within 30 yards of the church and contains 2 schoolrooms and apartments for the master. It is well built and slated, measuring 61 feet by 21. The cost of building was defrayed by a grant from the Kildare Street Society and Archdeacon Monsell.

Seceding Meeting House

Seceding meeting house is situated on the south side of the old line of road from Coleraine to Newtownlimavady and is locally called the Whin meeting house, from being surrounded by a number of furze bushes (which are known by the name of whins in this as well as in other parts of the county). It is of a rectangular form, 69 feet by 26 feet. The pews are not painted, the floor not paved or boarded and the whole has an unfinished appearance and is in bad repair. It was erected in the year 1822 and cost 113 pounds. The present house occupies the same site as a former house which was built in 1740 at the first establishment of a Seceding congregation in this parish. It will accommodate 182 persons, allowing 23 inches for each.

Gentlemen's Seats

Downhill, the residence of Sir James Bruce Bart, was built by Frederick Hervey, 4th Earl of Bristol and Bishop of Derry [insert footnote: see parish of Templemore], who bequeathed it to Sir Hervey Bruce, father to Sir James. The building was commenced in 1772. The picture gallery and library were added 3 years after, and the whole was cased with cut freestone about 1790. It is situated at the north extremity of the parish, on a commanding eminence near the edge of a perpendicular precipice overhanging the sea, and has a grand and imposing appearance from all parts of the surrounding country.

On the south side of the house at 340 yards distance is a mausoleum, 75 feet in height, erected by Lord Bristol about the year 1777 to the memory of his brother George, 2nd Earl of Bristol and Viceroy of Ireland. On the edge of the precipice on the north side of the house there is a temple, built in the year 1788 by Lord Bristol. The outside is a circle 40 feet in diameter with 16 Corinthian columns, and covered with a dome. The interior is of an octangular form, 31 and a half feet in diameter and is divided into 2 storeys. The upper storey is supported by arches springing from a column in the centre. The arches and dome are built of brick, but the other parts are freestone which, as well as that used in the house, was procured at Ballycastle and Dungiven. Lord Bristol, who was one of the greatest patrons of the fine arts in his time, has left Downhill richly endowed with paintings and statuary, which has always been most kindly shown to the public.

Bann Brook, near the shore of the River Bann, is at present occupied by a farmer and is in bad repair. It was built by William Ford Esquire in 1691, and an additional part was added by Lord Bristol in 1792. The house has been occupied by the following persons: William Ford Esquire, William Ford Esquire Jr, Doctor Barnett (Doctor of Divinity), Miss Robinson, James Boyle Esquire and Hugh Swan, the present occupier.

The Glebe House is situated in the townland of Blakes Lower, on the road from Coleraine to Downhill at 3 and a half miles from the former. It was built 1774, but on the arrival of Archdeacon Monsell in 1821 it was almost a ruin. He has made great improvements about it and rendered the house a good family residence.

There are some other good but small houses through the parish, and the farmers have generally comfortable dwellings.

Bleach Greens, Manufactories and Mills

There is no bleach green.

There are 2 corn mills and 5 flax mills in the parish. Of these, 4 are worked by the Articlave burn, from which the supply of water is constant except some parts of the summer.

Ardina flax mill is situated 1 mile above the junction of the stream with the Bann. It was built in 1827 and cost 90 pounds. It has a breast wheel 14 feet in diameter, 2 feet broad and a fall of water of 10 feet. There are 4 sets of skutches (or 4 men can work at the same time) and 4 rollers. All the works are wood and are in good repair.

The other 3 mills on this stream are situated higher up it, at the village of Articlave. One of them, a flax mill, is worked by a breast wheel 16 feet in diameter and 4 feet broad. It has 4 sets of skutches and 4 rollers. The cogs of the pit wheel are of metal screwed into a wooden rim and the rollers are cast iron.

Articlave corn mill is 350 yards above the flax mill. It has 2 water wheels, each 13 feet in diameter, on the same side of the mill and worked together by the same stream when there is a sufficient supply of water. One is 1 foot 2 inches and the other 1 foot 9 inches in breadth. The fall of water is 15 feet. The object of the 2 wheels is that one may shell and the other grind at the same time. The diameter of the pair of stones is 4 and a half feet. The kiln is 15 yards distant from the mill and is of sheet iron. The mill and kiln are both slated and all is in good repair, except the water wheels.

On the same stream, about 50 yards from the corn mill, there is a flax mill worked by a breast wheel 12 feet in diameter, 1 foot 8 inches broad and with 6 feet fall of water. There are 2 sets of skutches.

Ballywoodock flax mill is supplied, except sometimes in summer, from 2 small streams which rise in the mountains of the parish. It has a breast wheel 11 feet 8 inches in diameter, 4 and a half feet broad and a fall of water of 8 feet. There are 2 sets of skutches.

Ballywoodock corn mill is worked by the same stream. It has a breast wheel 13 and a half feet in diameter, 2 feet broad with 23 feet fall of water. The pair of stones are 4 and a half feet in diameter. The mill is thatched and is in bad repair. It is idle in summer from want of corn to grind, as most of it is now sold in the market. The kiln has a sheet-iron head and is attached to the mill.

Ballywildrick flax mill is situated in the townland of Ballywildrick Lower, and is worked by a connection of several small streams, except in summer when it is left idle. It has a breast wheel 12 feet in diameter, 1 and a half feet broad and a fall of 3 feet of water. The house is very small and is, as well as the water wheel, in bad repair.

Communications

No direct communication between 2 towns passes through the parish. The principal road is one from Coleraine to Downhill and the sea shore, through the village of Articlave. Its direction is from south east to north west. The length within the parish is 5 miles and breadth 21 feet clear of drains and fences. It was for the first time gravelled and made wider by the county about 60 years ago, and has been kept in repair by the same means since. There are several steep hills along the line, but it is kept in very excellent repair. Its direction might be improved. A road branches from it at the village of Articlave and pursues a south west direction for 3 miles, till it joins the old Coleraine and Newtownlimavady line of road. It was made and is kept in good repair by the county. Its breadth is 21 feet clear of drains and fences. Plan

and section of a proposed improvement on the road between Coleraine and Articlave, scale 1 inch to 1 mile. The proposed line is coloured red and is quarter of a mile longer than the present road which is coloured brown, [signed] Charles W. Ligar, 25 September 1835.

2 lines of road were made by Lord Bristol from Downhill to Newtownlimavady, passing through the north east corner of the parish. One of them, called the Black Road, leaves the west entrance to Downhill in a south west direction for 2 and a half miles through the parish. The other, which is called the Bishop's Road, leaves the strand and passes to the summit of the mountain in a direction nearly west. One and a quarter miles of it is within the parish. That part of the Black Road on the summit of the mountain was never finished by Lord Bristol and the other, the Bishop's Road, has been allowed since his death to go out of repair. Both roads are, however, about to be made passable by the county. See the parishes of Magilligan and Aghanloo respecting these roads.

There are 3 and a half miles of the old line of road between Coleraine and Newtownlimavady contained within the south extremity of the parish. It is kept in good repair but is very hilly and is not used as a direct communication.

The communication between Downhill and Newtownlimavady and between the parish and the barony of Innishowen is carried on by means of the strand, where the sand is hard and safe except in high tides in the winter.

There is a sufficient number of by-roads through all parts of the parish and are all in good repair.

There are a great many very good bridges on the several roads through the parish. The largest is one near Downhill on the Black Road. It consists of a single arch 24 feet in span and 16 and a half feet broad on the roadway, and is strong and well built.

The communication for foot passengers between the parish and Portstewart is by means of a ferry, 500 yards leading across the Bann near its mouth. No persons claim the exclusive right to the ferry. There are 3 men who, on the Dunboe side of the river, have boats. They charge 1d for each passenger. The ferry is at all times passable, and no difficulty occurs in procuring a boat.

ANCIENT TOPOGRAPHY

Ecclesiastical Buildings

The old church of Dunboe is situated on the west side of the road from Coleraine to Downhill, in the townland of Downhill and within half a mile of

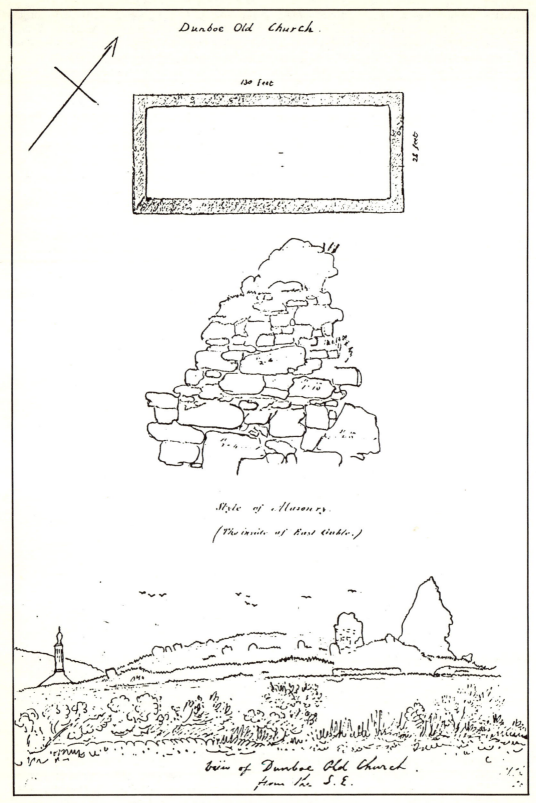

Dunboe old church

the sea shore. It is of a rectangular form, 63 and a half feet by 27 and a half feet, and lies in a direction from north west to south east. A small part of the north west gable and of the side walls is all that remains of it. The graveyard is much used, but there are no very old or curious tombstones or inscriptions. The most remarkable is a handsome vault surmounted by an ornamented shaft of freestone, on the top of which is an urn. It was built in 1810, as is shown by the following inscription on a stone tablet over the door, which is cast iron. The old church is said not to have been used for the last 200 years and tradition says it was founded by St Patrick [representation of inscription with words]: "The family burial place of Sir H.H.A. Bruce Bart, built 1810."

Near the old church to the north there is a well of excellent water. It is said that stations were formerly held at it, and was esteemed for its healing effects. During Lord Bristol's residence at Downhill, he enclosed the well with a wall and arched it over. The well was formerly called Tobar Jacob and is now known as Jacob's Well.

[Dunboe old church, ground plan, main dimensions 130 feet by 28 feet, walls 3 feet thick, scale 20 feet to an inch; style of masonry (inside of east gable); view of Dunboe old church from south east, showing monument in graveyard [neoclassical funerary urn]. [Signed] Charles W. Ligar, 26th September 1835.

Military Antiquities

There are no remains which can be classed under this head.

Pagan Antiquities: Standing Stones

There is no cromlech in the parish. There are standing stones in each of the following townlands: Ballywildrake Lower, Dunallis Upper and Quilly Upper, but they are not in a line or otherwise symmetrically arranged.

Giants' Sconce

The Giants' Sconce, which has a striking resemblance to the Grianan of Aileach (see parish of Templemore), is the most remarkable object of antiquity in the parish. [Insert footnote: The word giant is a modern addition to sconce. The name of the townland on which it is situated was formerly Lena Garran, or "horse meadow." It now takes the name of Sconce]. This stronghold is situated on a rocky eminence crowning the summit of a mountain 797 feet above the level of the sea. The

approach to it is very difficult on all sides except the east, where there is a well-formed entrance 5 feet broad, built on both sides with stone. The interior of the building partakes of an oblong shape and has been formerly surrounded by a very strong wall constructed with large stones without cement. This wall has, however, been destroyed except on the east side. Near the entrance it is 18 feet thick but decreases to 9 feet on the north extremity. Within the body of the wall there is a small passage 2 feet broad and 2 and a half feet high and 25 feet long, similar to the passage in the cashel of the Grianan. About 7 years ago a gentleman removed 4 or 5 feet of the wall which was above this passage, for the purpose of exploring it.

Adjoining the east side of the principal building a ledge of rock of inferior elevation has also been enclosed and strongly defended by a wall, which has, however, been destroyed.

Without the building at a short distance to the south there is a natural formation of rock resembling an armchair and is called the Giants' Chair; and on the west side of the building there is an enclosed space, the walls of which are fallen down. It appears to have been formed at the same time as the other parts of the building, and was probably intended to put cattle into at night. See drawing forwarded to Dublin previous to the writing of this Memoir.

Forts

There are 15 forts or raths in this parish, which are to be found in the following townlands: 1 in the Big Glebe, 1 in Ballyhacket Lisawilling, 2 in Dunalis Upper, 1 in Downhill, 1 in Killyveety, 1 in Ballymoney, 1 in Gorticavan, 1 in Altikeeragh, 1 in Ballyhacket Glenahorry, 2 in Ballyhacket Magilligan, 1 in Bannbrook, 2 in Ballyhacket Toberclaw. All of them are of the common character and form but the following are the most remarkable.

Fort in Big Glebe

Fort in the Big Glebe is situated in an open part of the country, and from its rising very abruptly to the height of 30 feet above a smooth and well-cultivated field, is a conspicuous object. It appears at first sight to be formed entirely of earth, but on a nearer examination the stones of which it is faced show themselves through the green sward which partly covers them. It is of an oval form and surrounded by a moat 30 feet wide, the greater part of which has been lately filled up. The most striking peculiarity about the fort is a ramp which leads in a circuitous ascent to the summit, the entrance to which has been carefully guarded, as may be seen from 2 stone gate pillars which still remain undisturbed. The interior has been surrounded by a stone parapet or wall, which has, however, been destroyed. In digging a hole at the top it appears that about 6 feet of its height is formed of small stones laid together without any regularity. In levelling and filling up the moat a kind of iron arrow was found, pointed at one extremity and terminating at the other with a flat knob. It has been lost, but from the description given it was of this shape: [drawing with measurement, 1 and half feet long].

A coin about half the thickness of a 6d was also found on the moat. The following is a copy: [reverse side with a crown, 4 leeks, 1675 and letters "Fran et Navarrae Rex"; obverse side with king's head and letters "Ludovicus XIII DGRA"].

[Plan and section drawings of Big Glebe Fort showing ramp and remains of stone gate posts, scale 3 inches to 132 feet, with dimensions]: distance from (A) to (B) 218 feet [diameter of outer rampart beyond moat]; from (C) to (D) 148 feet [diameter of outer bank of fort]; from (E) to (F) 79 feet [diameter of centre]; breadth of moat 21 feet; height above the bottom of the moat 30 feet. There appears to be no particular name by which this fort is now known; it is merely called the fort of the Big Glebe. [Signed] Charles W. Ligar, Drumagally, 12 November 1833.

Fort in Ballyhacket Lisawilling

Fort in Ballyhacket Lisawilling is situated on a rocky hill 30 feet high in a deep and retired glen on the side of the mountain. The hill has been made smooth and is surrounded by a moat. The fort is of an oval form, 84 feet by 44 feet, and in the inside there is a small, circular enclosure 24 feet in diameter. As the fort is surrounded on 3 sides by ground which commands it at about 90 yards distant, the parapet opposite those parts has been raised higher in order to protect the interior. The parapet, where it is high, has been furnished with a banquette or step of earth in order to allow persons from the inside to fire over it. There is no ramp or road up to the interior of the fort, but the entrance is on the north east side where the hill naturally is more easy of ascent. To the south of the fort and outside the moat is a small piece of level ground which, from its green appearance while the surrounding parts are covered with heath, would seem to indicate its having been once cultivated or the site of some place of defence. A supposition of the kind is strengthened by the existence of the foundations of a wall on one side and the remains of a bank of earth on 2 other sides, the remaining side being enclosed by the natural formation of the ground, which is steep and rocky. No other fort can be seen from the interior of this one, but from the top of the parapet at the south side of the fort the fort in the Big Glebe is visible. In the immediate neighbourhood there are, however, several forts.

[Plan and section of an old fort in the townland of Ballyhacket Lisawilling, scale 44 feet to an inch, with dimensions and orientation]: distance from (G) to (H) 204 feet [outer rampart beyond the moat]; from (E) to (F) 94 feet [outer bank of fort]; (C) to (D) [distance between outer and middle wall on top of fort not given]; from (E) to (F) 84 feet [between middle and outer wall]; height of the inside of the fort above the moat 30 feet; breadth of the parapet 5 and a half feet; height of the parapet (above the inside of fort) varies from 3 to 6 feet; breadth of moat from 12 to 29 feet]. There appears to be no particular name for this fort, [signed] Charles W. Ligar, Drumagally, 16 November 1833.

Dunalis Fort

Dunalis Fort is situated on a small hill, to the natural formation of which it owes all its strength. It has no moat round it, neither is there a parapet remaining at present. The fort is of an oval form, 57 feet by 33 feet, and on the south side of it there is a kind of seat in the rock 1 foot broad called the Chiefs' Chair.

Fort in the townland of Dunalis Upper [plan, dimensions 53 feet wide and 57 feet long, scale 40 feet to an inch] 10th September 1835.

[Chiefs' Chair in the townland of Dunallis Upper, height of chair 3 feet 8 inches].

Coves or Caves

There are 15 coves or caves in the parish, all of which partake of a similarity in their architectural construction. In the number of apartments and the manner they are disposed, [they] differ, however, in almost every one. They are to be found in the following townlands: 1 in Bankish hill, townland of Ballyhacket Glenahorry, 1 in Artidillon, 2 in Exorna, 1 in Ballyhacket Glenahorry, 2 in Dunalis, 1 in Ballyhacket Magilligan, 1 in Formullen, 2 in Ballywildrick, 1 in Farranlester, 1 in Bellany, 1 in Ballymadigan, 1 in Killyveety.

Bankish Hill Cove

Bankish Hill Cove, in the townland of Ballyhacket Glenahorry, is one of the most perfect in the parish. It is situated on the summit of a small hill, from which it takes its name. The entrance is very small and will scarcely admit a man, being only 1 foot high and 2 feet broad. From the entrance to the middle of the first chamber and from that point there is a gradual slope to the end of the third chamber, which terminates in a small passage resembling a sewer and which serves as such at present to drain off the rain water which makes its way through the roof. This passage at first sight appears to lead to another chamber but is too small to admit a man. A small boy might, however, make his way in. The number of chambers and the manner in which they are disposed will be best seen by reference to the annexed drawing. From the curved line which this small passage takes to the west, but a very short distance is all that can be seen of it. From the shape of the top of the hill, which is thrown into a ridge, it appears probable that there are similar chambers on the west side of these shown in the drawing, but this must remain doubtful as no opening can be found to them.

[Ground plan and section drawn through horizontally showing 3 chambers, entrance and end called sewer or air hole; top chamber (C) to (D) 22 feet 4 inches long by 4 feet wide; total length of cove (A) to (B) 48 feet 2 inches; widths at (E) to (F) 4 feet and at (G) to (H) 5 feet; depths (E) to (F) 4 feet, and (G) to (H) 5 feet; [profiles or vertical section drawings at 3 different intervals]: (C) to (D) [showing entrance] 4 feet deep; (E) to (F) 4 feet 10 inches deep by 3 feet across [with 4 feet of surface soil above]; (G) to (H) 5 feet 4 inches deep 3 and half feet wide [with 5 feet surface soil above]; scale 8 feet to an inch. [Signed] Charles W. Ligar, Drumagully, 25 November 1833.

Cove or Cave at Dunalis

The following is a plan and section of one of the caves in the townland of Dunalis: [plans and section drawings of 2 passages within the cave, scale 16 feet to an inch and dimensions: A to B 19 feet 6 inches plus 15 feet, C to D 25 feet 6 inches]. [Signed] Charles W. Ligar, 19 August 1835.

Nothing has been found in the coves of this parish which throws any light upon their original intention and use. Some few bones have been discovered in one and human teeth in another. The following remarks are applicable to all: 1st, that they are built at the top of rising ground and generally on small hills to ensure as it would appear a dry situation; 2nd, that they throw the surface of the ground into ridges and are easily traced from above, and in some cases pierce through the surface and expose the roofs and parts of the side walls; 3rd, that there are in some instances the foundations of ancient buildings over or very near them. In one instance, in the townland of Ballywoodock, the mouth of a cave opens from the inside of an ancient building, and in another the mouth is in the centre of a fort.

MODERN TOPOGRAPHY

General Appearance

The general appearance of the parish is rich and fertile. The farmers' houses are in most cases comfortable, and Downhill House, with its mausoleum and temple, are the most striking objects. The expanse of the northern ocean combines pleasingly towards the east with the headlands at the Giant's Causeway, the coast from Portstewart to Portrush and with the highly cultivated country on the opposite side of the broad and placid waters of the Bann.

Immediately at the shore near Downhill the dark basaltic cliffs, rising perpendicularly to the height of 200 feet, contrasted with the broad, white beach, form a bold foreground to the mountains of Inishowen <Ennishowen>. The roaring of the surf as it rolls on the strand produces a dull, monotonous sound not displeasing to the ear, and well suited to the surrounding objects. On a summer evening, as the sun sets behind the Inishowen mountains and leaves the rocks and all around in softened light, with his last rays reflected by the wet sand, a scene presents itself, the solitary grandeur of which is only occasionally broken by groups of figures moving along the beach or emerging from the lengthened shadows of the cliffs. Many of these possess much individual beauty, especially the overhanging mass under the temple at Downhill. There a natural arch has been formed through a projecting part, and from the interior of it the scene above described appears with the best effect.

SOCIAL AND PRODUCTIVE ECONOMY

Early Improvements

There appears to be no definite period at which the improvement of the parish may be said to have commenced. There is no doubt that many Scotch settlers came to the parish at the time of the Plantations of Ulster, but it is not thought that they brought with them a better system of farming than was at the time in the country. Lord Bristol, after he took up his residence in the parish about 1772, gave away a great number of wheel cars both to his tenantry and others. It is stated that at that time there were only 2 wheel cars in the parish. He also made several roads and rebuilt most of the houses of the poor. At the time Downhill House was in progress, the tenantry were employed in drawing stones and materials for building, for which each man received for himself, horse and car 1s 6d per day. This sum they were glad to earn as they could earn nothing with their horse before that time.

The linen weaving which exists extensively in the parish was a benefit to it during the time it flourished, but now only one-half of what was formerly to be made by it can be earned. The North West Farming Society has been of great service. Within the last 12 years Scotch ploughs made of iron have superseded the old Irish wooden plough, and other new implements are now made use of which were unknown before in the parish. Systems of farming such as drilling, green cropping and a regular rotation of crops have also been introduced through the example shown by the society. The excellent market of Coleraine has been likewise one great cause of the improvement of the parish, offering a ready sale for the rural produce.

Obstructions to Improvement

About one-half of the parish belongs to the Clothworkers' Company and is rented by the farmers from the lessee of the manor under a tenure depending on the life of an aged lady. This for the present obstructs improvement in a degree, as there are portions of ground which might be reclaimed and cultivated, and which is not done as the tenants think that their rent would be raised when the present tenure expires. In the other portion of the parish there is no obstruction to improvement. In the mountainous part of the parish, which fortunately does not constitute more than the twentieth part, the practice of dividing the farms among the children exists, and the people in that district have brought themselves to poverty by it, some of them being so very poor as to be unable, from want of good clothes, to attend their place of worship, having a great and unsurmountable objection to go when ill-dressed.

SOCIAL ECONOMY

Local Government: Justice and Crime

Sir James Bruce Bart, the only magistrate in the parish, is very highly respected. He does not act alone but refers the cases to Coleraine, where petty sessions are held every alternate Thursday and attended by 3 or 4 magistrates. In the village of Articlave are 3 constabulary police consisting of 2 privates and a sergeant, and at the mouth of the Bann 2 coastguard men in connection with the Portrush station, but there are no revenue police nearer than Coleraine. A manor court was held for one year in Articlave but was given up about 18 months ago. It would have been much frequented but for the bad attendance of the agent for the lessee of the manor of the Clothworkers' Company, who acted as seneschal.

Until the last 8 years petty robberies were very frequent. At that time a gang consisting of 10 men, natives of the parish, was broken up by means of a few firm prosecutions and consequent convictions. The number of these petty robberies are on the decrease. They amount to about 5 or 6 in the year and are all of a trifling nature, such as opening barns and stealing fowls and turf.

Illicit distilling exists in the parish. Lately a few seizures have been made by the police which has checked it for a time. The Presbyterian minister has also checked it by having refused to admit persons engaged in it to the Lord's supper or their children to baptism, as he considers they must necessarily break the Sabbath day in malting and other processes required.

Smuggling tobacco and rum was carried on extensively about 20 years since, but has been entirely put down by the coastguards.

Insurances could be easily effected on moderate terms in Coleraine, but the uncommon occurrence of fires have induced the inhabitants not to insure. The Glebe House is insured but no others.

Dispensaries

There is no dispensary within the parish: it is under the Coleraine dispensary; but as part of the parish is beyond the liberties of Coleraine, the surgeon is not obliged to visit the part so situated without the subscriber recommending the case pays him 5s, although medicines can be procured on the recommendation of a subscriber. It cannot be said that the dispensary has improved the health of the people, but it is considered to be very beneficial and a great source of comfort to them. The poorer classes avail themselves readily of it and of that part of it which supplies vaccination. A dispensary is required in the parish and might easily be procured if the land proprietors would unite in effecting it.

Schools

The schools have done much good and the people are anxious for instruction and knowledge. Previous to the introduction of the school in Articlave and over the parish in general, the children were left untaught. A decided improvement has been perceived in the morals of the inhabitants of the parish within the last 8 years. See table of schools.

Poor

There is no regular provision for the poor, aged or infirm. The following means are, however, used for their relief. The contributions collected every Sunday in the church are distributed among the poor of all denominations. The sum has been from 22 pounds to 26 pounds annually for the last 7 years. It is distributed half yearly at the discretion of the archdeacon, curate and churchwardens. The money collected at the Presbyterian meeting house is distributed to the poor every Sunday at the discretion of the minister and session. It amounts to about 20 pounds per annum. The collections at the Seceding meeting house amounts to about 10 pounds per annum, which is expended in relieving distressed persons, if the funds afford it, after defraying the repairs of the house, paying the travelling expenses of elders attending synods and paying young clergymen who sometimes officiate during the absence of the stationed minister.

The Clothworkers' Company give 15 pounds per annum to the poor of the parish, which sum is laid out in purchasing blankets for them. The poor receive great assistance in every way from the archdeacon's family. Mrs Monsell has a quantity of wool and flax made into linsey woolsey for the poor every year. It is spun by old women who are unfit for any other occupation and are employed by Mrs Monsell. In each of the years 1833 to 1834, 200 yards were made. The cost for weaving, spinning and dying 200 yards amounts from 12 pounds to 16 pounds. The cloth will last the wearer 1 year.

Religion

The parish is divided into the following religious persuasions according to the latest census: Protestants 529, Presbyterians 3,045, Seceders 633, Covenanters 66, Baptists 17, Roman Catholics 728, total 5,018.

Income of Clergy

The income of the archdeacon, the Rev. Thomas Bewly Monsell, including the Glebe House is 708 pounds, viz. tithe under the composition act 408 pounds, house and 30 acres of land attached 100 pounds, rent of glebe land received by the archdeacon 200 pounds, total 708 pounds. No objection whatever has been made by the parishioners to the payment of tithe. The archdeacon allows the persons who live near the mountains and whose tithe is 10s and under to supply turf instead of money at the same price as is given in Coleraine.

The Presbyterian minister receives 75 pounds regium donum and 60 pounds stipend, total 135 pounds.

The Seceding minister, the Rev. William Wilson, receives 50 pounds regium donum and 25 pounds stipend, total 75 pounds.

The Roman Catholic clergymen, the Rev. Daniel O'Doherty P.P. and the Rev. Bernard Magill, curate, who are connected with this parish, reside in the parish of Killowen. They receive 13 pounds 6d from stipends and 3 pounds 5s 6d from marriages and baptisms. One of them officiates every alternate Sunday at the temple at Downhill. Soon after the erection of the temple in 1788, Lord Bristol allowed his servants, many of whom were Roman Catholics, the use of the lower part of the temple for divine service and also gave 1 guinea per month to the officiating clergyman, which was paid till his death. Service was performed in it formerly once a month and now every alternate Sunday. During the prevalence of cholera morbus in the neighbourhood, Sir James Bruce Bart did not permit the people to resort to it, at which time mass was celebrated in the open air in the townland of Masteragwee.

Habits of the People

All the houses in the parish, except 5 which are built of mud, are built of stone and lime and glazed, but the windows are in general except in the wealthier farmers too small. There are about 30 slated houses which are 2-storeys high; the others are thatched and are in all cases 1-storey high. The poorer classes have generally 1 room and a kitchen, each room about 16 feet square. The floors are of earth. The farmers' houses are of a better description and are improving very much. They have generally 2 rooms and a kitchen. The people feel comfortable and contented in their manner of living, although they have too often a great scarcity of the necessary household utensils such as plates, cups and basins.

Food and Fuel

The diet of the wealthier class of farmers is good.

The farmers in general kill a cow at November and a pig in the course of the winter, which they salt and consume during the year. They also get a few fish taken on the coast. Their breakfast is stirabout and milk and the luxury of tea is creeping in among them: all classes take it on Sunday morning. The farmers' dinner consists of beef, pork or fish and potatoes. Their supper is flummery or potatoes and milk. The poorer classes fare something worse. Potatoes form the chief [dish], with fresh fish occasionally or salted herring. The latter is much used. They use also a considerable quantity of oatmeal.

The fuel used in the parish is turf procured from the mountains.

Dress

The dress of the inhabitants has nothing peculiar except what is generally worn throughout the country. It is good except in that part of the parish mentioned before and in some cases rather too extravagant. The men wear short body coats, the long greatcoat never used. Trousers are beginning to supersede short knee breeches. The cloth used by them is purchased in the shops and a finer quality is commencing to be used. The men always wear shoes and worsted stockings, but some of the females, when in the house and working in the fields, go without, but never make their appearance so in Coleraine or any other town. The children all go barefooted, but like the females it is often from choice than from want. The married females all wear good, white caps and the unmarried go bareheaded in the house with their hair tastefully arranged but never curled, and large combs are beginning to be esteemed by them. Bonnets are commencing to be used, generally when going to market and out of doors. Coloured cotton gowns are most frequently used, but white is the favourite colour for full dress at parties and other meetings.

Longevity, Family Size and Age of Marriage

No instance is there of longevity, but a great number live to the age of 80 and 90. The average number in a family is calculated to be 4 and a half; many families, however, consist of 10 and some of 12. The usual time of marriage is from 18 to 25. Many females, however, marry at 15 or 16 and many of the men at 18 or 19.

Amusements

There are a few dances throughout the year, 2 or 3 horses' [races] and Christmas Day and New Year's Day are entirely devoted to it and to "common" playing, but these amusements are carried on only during that part of the year. The horse races are got up by some publican offering a saddle and bridle to be run for as a speculation to collect persons to his house. The remainder of the day after the races are over is spent in social parties. Old Holyeve night is devoted to merrymaking and all kinds of amusement. The inhabitants have no legendary tales or poems, neither is the superstition respecting fairies general. See history of Articlave Reading Society.

Emigration

The following table shows the emigration for the years 1833 to 1834, the ages of the persons and to what part of America they have gone.

1833: males 24, females 17; males under 5 years old 3; males above 4 and under 10 years 1; males above 14 and under 20 years 2, females 2; males above 19 and under 30 years 13, females 10; males above 29 and under 40 years 3, females 4; males above 39 years 2, females 1; total 41, Protestants 5, Presbyterians 34, Roman Catholics 2; to Quebec 19, to St John's 12, to Philadelphia 10, total 41.

1834: males 13, females 7; females under 5 years old 2; females above 4 and under 10 years 1; males above 14 and under 20 years 4; males above 19 and under 30 years 8, females 4; males above 29 and under 40 years 1; total 20, Presbyterians 19, Roman Catholics 1; to Quebec 3, to St John's 3, to New York 3, to Philadelphia 11, total 20.

Remarkable Events

The most remarkable circumstance in the parish was the erection of Downhill House by Lord Bristol.

Articlave Reading and Debating Society

[J. Stokes] The Articlave Reading Society was established in the beginning of the year 1825. It consisted at first of 7 members, who subscribed each 10d, Irish currency. With this and a pound advanced by one member they purchased their first stock of books and agreed to meet on the first Friday of every month, and to subscribe 5d each at every meeting. At the end of the first year the currency having been changed, the subscription was reduced to 3d per month.

In a short time the members increased to 40 in number. Religious and political subjects were excluded from the debates and to this the permanence of the society is ascribed, as several others of the same kind have sprung up in the parish and without observing this exclusion have failed. They are kindly patronized by the Venerable the Archdeacon of Derry and family, who give an annual donation of 1 pound or books to that amount with an occasional new publication. 2 pounds were also received from the Honourable Mrs Knox. The stock consists at present (July 1835) of 450 books, viz. theology 127, civil history 23, ecclesiastical history 19, biography 15, commentaries 14, periodicals 12, Jewish antiquities 10, controversy 8, medicine and veterinary works 7, gardening and farming 6, arts and sciences 6, novels 6, natural history 6, voyages and travels 5, poetry 4, miscellaneous 179.

The following are the rules of this society:

1, The members meet on the first Friday of every month in Articlave schoolhouse, at 6 p.m. in the winter and 7 o'clock in the summer.

2, Those who are not present to answer their name when the roll is called are each fined 1d.

3, Each member has his first choice of books according as his name stands on the list.

4, Each is allowed to borrow 2 books at a time. On returning them he is fined according as they may have been abused. If he does not return them in 1 month he is fined 3d, and 3d for every month following. If the book be lost, the price is forfeited by the borrower.

5, No member is permitted to lend a book under the penalty of one ha'penny.

6, To refuse to pay fines is to forfeit all claim to the fellowship of the society.

7, Any member wishing to withdraw must signify his intention at least one night previously and his successor must come in by ballot.

8, Each member on withdrawing receives the full amount of his subscription.

The present number of members is 40.

PRODUCTIVE ECONOMY

Trades and Occupations in Articlave

[C.W. Ligar] Weavers of linen 21 (12 of them also hold small farms), carpenters 6, wheelwright 1, cooper 1, sawyers <sawers> 2, blacksmiths 2, masons 2, nailors 1, reed maker 1, basket maker 1, flax dresser 1, miller 1, tailors 3, shoemakers 4, publicans 4 (2 of them also hold small farms), grocer, cotton and woollen draper, ironmonger, delph, general dealer and postmaster 1, fishermen, who are occasional labourers also, 6.

SOCIAL ECONOMY

Table of Schools by J. Bleakly

[Table contains the following headings: name, situation and description, when established, income and expenditure, physical, intellectual and moral education, number of pupils subdivided by age, sex and religion, name and religious persuasion of master or mistress. No physical education].

The Dunboe parish school, situated in the village of Articlave, a good house built of stone and lime, slated, established in 1824; income: London Hibernian Society 3 pounds, from pupils 10 pounds; intellectual education: books published by the London Hibernian Society; moral education: visited by the clergy of the Established Church, catechisms and Authorised Version; number of pupils: 40 under 10 years of age, 56 from 10 to 15, 2 above 15; 98 total number of pupils, all male, 16 Protestants, 76 Presbyterians, 6 Roman Catholics; master William Donnally of the Established Church.

The Dunboe parish female school, held in the same schoolhouse, established in 1821; income: from Mrs Monsell 5 pounds per annum, from pupils 5 pounds; intellectual education: books published by the London Hibernian Society; moral education: visited by Mrs and Miss Monsell; number of pupils: 70 under 10 years of age, 19 from 10 to 15; 89 total number of pupils, all female, 15 Protestants, 64 Presbyterians, 10 Roman Catholics; mistress Eliza Creevy of the Established Church.

Downhill school, near the entrance to Downhill House and built of stone and lime, slated, established in 1824; income: Sir James Bruce 5 pounds, from pupils 8 pounds; intellectual education: books published by the Kildare Society and extracts from the Authorised Version of the Scriptures; moral education: visited by the clergy of the Established Church; number of pupils: 14 under 10 years of age, 22 from 10 to 15, 4 above 15; 40 total number of pupils, all male, 4 Protestants, 33 Presbyterians, 3 Roman Catholics; master William Anderson of the Established Church.

Downhill female school, held in the same house, established in 1824; income: from Sir James Bruce 3 pounds, from pupils 3 pounds; intellectual education: books published by the Kildare Society and extracts from the Authorised Version of the Scriptures; moral education: visited by the clergy of the Established Church; number of pupils: 18 under 10 years of age, 4 from 10 to 15; 22 total number of pupils, 8 Protestants, 12 Presbyterians, 2 Roman Catholics; mistress Lettitia Dallas of the Established Church.

Glebe school, on the new road from Garvagh to the sea, a small house of stone, thatched, established in 1828; income: London Hibernian Society 6 pounds, from pupils 6 pounds; intellectual education: books published by the London Hibernian Society; moral education: by the clergy of the Established Church, Authorised Version; number of pupils: males, 15 under 10 years of age, 10 from 10 to 15, 5 above 15, 30 total; females, 20 under 10 years of age, 10 from 10 to 15, 30 total; 60 total number of pupils, 16 Protestants, 7 Roman Catholics; master John Ross of the Established Church.

Knockmult school, on the road from Coleraine to Newtownlimavady, a good house of stone, thatched, established in 1832; income from pupils 14 pounds; expenditure: 1 child is taught free for house rent, 6s; intellectual education: books published by the London Hibernian Society, Authorised Version; moral education: by the Presbyterian clergy, catechism is taught by master; number of pupils: males, 26 under 10 years of age, 26 total; females, 24 under 10 years of age, 24 total; 50 total number of pupils, 2 Protestants, 26 Presbyterians, 1 Roman Catholic, 21 Seceders; master Samuel McIntyre, a Seceder.

Ballinrees school, above the Seceding meeting house, a good house of stone, thatched, established 1828; income: London Hibernian Society 6 pounds, from pupils 11 pounds; intellectual education: books by London Hibernian Society and Authorised Version of Scriptures; moral education: by clergy of the Established and Presbyterian Churches; number of pupils: males, 30 under 10 years of age, 6 from 10 to 15, 36 total; females, 40 under 10 years of age, 4 from 10 to 15, 44 total; 80 total number of pupils, 12 Presbyterians, 3 Roman Catholics, 65 Seceders; master Robert A. Lennox, a Methodist.

Ballystrone school, in townland of Ballystrone, a tolerable house of stone, thatched, established in 1834; income from pupils 10 pounds; intellectual education: *Manson's Spelling book* and Authorised Version of Scriptures; moral education: Seceding minister, catechism is taught by master; number of pupils: males, 20 under 10 years of age, 7 from 10 to 15, 27 total; females, 10 under 10 years of age, 3 from 10 to 15, 13 total; 40 total number of pupils, 2 Protestants, 4 Presbyterians, 4 Roman Catholics, 30 Seceders; master John Allen, a Seceder.

Quilly school, in townland of Quilly on road from Coleraine to Articlave, small house, thatched,

established 1830; income: London Hibernian Society 4 pounds per annum, from pupils 12 pounds; intellectual education: books by London Hibernian Society and Authorised Version of Scriptures; moral education: clergy of Established and Presbyterian Churches, catechism taught; number of pupils: males, 14 under 10 years of age, 26 from 10 to 15, 40 total; females, 23 under 10 years of age, 1 from 10 to 15, 24 total; 64 total number of pupils, 4 Protestants, 60 Presbyterians; master John Doherty, a Presbyterian.

Cranagh hill national school, on lower road from Coleraine to Downhill, a bad house, established 1834 with National Board and 50 years altogether; income: from National Board 8 pounds per annum, from pupils 6 pounds; intellectual education: books published by the National Board; moral education: by Presbyterian clergy, Authorised Version is taught; number of pupils: males, 16 under 10 years of age, 10 from 10 to 15, 4 above 15, 30 total; females, 3 under 10 years of age, 23 from 10 to 15, 26 total; 56 total number of pupils, 49 [5 ?] Protestants, 41 Presbyterians, 10 Roman Catholics; master John Lyons, a Presbyterian.

Altikeeragh school, on the mountain road from Downhill to Newtownlimavady, established 1830; income from pupils 4 pounds; intellectual education: books published by the London Hibernian Society; moral education: visited by the Presbyterian clergy, catechism taught by master; number of pupils: males, 28 under 10 years of age, 2 from 10 to 15, 30 total; females, 24 under 10 years of age, 6 from 10 to 15, 30 total; 60 total number of pupils, 1 Protestant, 41 Presbyterians, 12 Roman Catholics, 6 other denominations; master David Lindsay, a Presbyterian.

Killyveety school, on the road from Coleraine to Newtownlimavady by Articlave, established 1835; income from pupils 4 pounds 4s per quarter; intellectual education: books published by the London Hibernian Society; moral education: visited by the Presbyterian clergy, catechisms taught by master; number of pupils: males, 20 under 10 years of age, 10 from 10 to 15, 30 total; females, 25 under 10 years of age, 1 from 10 to 15, 26 total; 56 total number of pupils, 2 Protestants, 48 Presbyterians, 6 Roman Catholics; master William Clarke, a Presbyterian. 23 and 24 September 1835.

Table of Sunday Schools by J. Bleakly

[Table contains the following headings: name, situation, when established, superintendent, teachers, number of scholars subdivided by religion and sex, hours of attendance, societies with which connected, observations].

The Articlave church Sunday school, held in the church, established in 1821, superintendent Archdeacon Monsell; teachers 4 males, 4 females, total 8; scholars: 12 Established Church, 61 Presbyterians, 2 Roman Catholics, 27 males, 48 females, 75 total; hours of attendance: from 2 till 3 o'clock p.m.; Sunday School Society give books; concludes by prayer.

Quilly, held in the day schoolhouse, established 1835, superintendent John Doherty; teachers 1 male, 1 female, total 2; scholars: 31 Presbyterians, 17 males, 14 females, 31 total, 23 exclusively Sunday school scholars; hours of attendance: from 4 to 6 p.m.; societies with which connected: none; no singing or prayer.

Ballinrees, held in the day schoolhouse, established 1829, superintendent Robert A. Lennox; teachers 14 males, 14 total; scholars: 33 Presbyterians, 7 Roman Catholics, 60 Seceders, 40 males, 60 females, 100 total, 20 exclusively Sunday school scholars; hours of attendance: from half past 7 to 10 o'clock a.m.; London Hibernian Society give books; commences by singing and prayer and concludes with the same.

Knockmult, held in the day schoolhouse, established 1830, superintendent Thomas Moore; teachers 7 males, 2 females, 9 total; scholars: 4 Established Church, 34 Presbyterians, 2 Roman Catholics, 34 Seceders, 41 males, 89 females, 120 total, 68 exclusively Sunday school scholars; hours of attendance: from 7 to 10 a.m.; London Hibernian Society give books; commences by singing and prayer and concludes with the same.

Downhill, held in the day schoolhouse, established 1824, superintendent Miss Bruce; teachers 3 males, 4 females, 7 total; scholars: 21 Established Church, 62 Presbyterians, 1 Roman Catholic, 42 males, 42 females, 84 total, 48 exclusively Sunday school scholars; hours of attendance: from 9 to 11 a.m.; Sunday School Society give books; concludes with prayer.

Glebe, held in the day schoolhouse, established 1828, superintendent John Ross; teachers 1 male, 1 female, total 2; scholars: 16 Established Church, 33 Presbyterians, 4 Roman Catholics, 23 males, 30 females, 53 total, 26 exclusively Sunday school scholars; hours of attendance: from 9 to 11 a.m.; Sunday School Society give books.

Ballystrone, held in the day schoolhouse, established 1832, superintendent John Allen; teachers 5 males, 3 females, 8 total; scholars: 2 Established Church, 12 Presbyterians, 86 Seceders, 48 males, 52 females, total 100, 56 exclusively Sun-day school scholars; hours of attendance: from 7 to 10 a.m.; Sunday School Society give books at a reduced price; commences with singing and prayer and concludes with the same.

Altikeeraght, held in the day schoolhouse, established 1830, superintendent Mr Samuel Greer; teachers 6 males, 2 females, 8 total; scholars: 1 Established Church, 88 Presbyterians, 10 Roman Catholics, 12 other denominations, 61 males, 50 females, 111 total; hours of attendance: from 7 to 10 o'clock a.m.; Sunday School Society give books; concludes by singing and prayer.

Articlave meeting house Sunday school, held in the Presbyterian meeting house, established in 1823, superintendent Rev. William Lyle; teachers 6 males, 3 females, total 9; scholars: 1 Established Church, 74 Presbyterians, 2 Roman Catholics, 25 males, 52 females, 77 total, 35 exclusively Sunday school scholars; hours of attendance: from 9 till 12 a.m.; Sunday School Society give books at a reduced price; commences with singing and prayer and concludes with prayer.

Killyveety, held in the day schoolhouse, established 1835, superintendent William Clarke; teachers 11 males, 11 total; scholars: 6 Established Church, 61 Presbyterians, 3 Roman Catholics, 30 males, 40 females, 70 total; hours of attendance: from 8 to 10 o'clock a.m.; just established, commences with singing and prayer and concludes with the same. [Signed] John Bleakly, 26 September 1835.

Notes on Place-Names by J. O'Donovan

Memoir Writing: Natural State

Place-Names

Ballanrus, Ballinrus: Ballan, Ballin *baile-an, baile-in,* "town of the." Custom favours the latter spelling. When the article "an" falls into the middle of a compound word it should be written "in" in English, as Ballin, Tullin. Custom favours this remark in almost every instance, and the article "an" is commonly written "in" in old manuscripts and pronounced ion by those who speak Irish. What I principally insist upon is that Ballin should not be changed to Ballan upon the mere grounds that the article is at present written "an."

Burrian, B[oundary] Surveyor; Barnis Sampson; Burren, Down Survey. I would be inclined to think Burren, the name on Down Survey, the best spelling, to agree with Burren in the county of Clare.

Downhill is called Dunbo on Down Survey map, and this townland as being that on which the parish church had stood has given name to the parish. There is generally in every parish a townland of the same name with the parish. Its present name is from the house built there by Lord Bristol, Bishop of Derry, in [blank].

Drumagully is on Down Survey map Drumneguille alias Drumnegully i.e. "dorsum sylvae."

Gortigran is on Down Survey map called Gortnegrane i.e. "the field of trees."

Masteraguie is on Down Survey map called Massregee alias Magherebwee, the latter of which signifies "yellow plain." Mass, the first part of the first, appears to be a corruption of *mais* "a heap." Copy of Officer's Report

NATURAL FEATURES

Hills

The west side of this parish from the Atlantic Ocean towards Dungiven consists of a bold ridge of mountains, being a part of the chain in which Binevenagh <Benevenagh> mountain stands. Those mountains do not fall precipitously on this eastern side, though the descent is in some places very rapid. This range ascends gradually to the southward and from the southern part of it in this parish there is a general ascent eastward to a very remarkably shaped hill called the Giant's Sconce, which is 797 feet high above the level of the sea. From this there is a considerable descent to the east and north, and the remainder of the parish consists of generally undulating features.

Lakes and Rivers

Lakes [blank].

Besides the River Bann, which at its mouth is the boundary of a small portion [at the ?] north east of the parish, there is none of any consideration. The principal stream is the Articlave river, which runs through the centre of the parish emptying itself into the River Bann at Pottagh, close to the sea. There are a great number of small streams taking their rise from the mountains on the south west of the parish and which generally fall either into the Articlave river or at another small stream which falls into the sea at Downhill.

Bogs

There is not much bog in any part of this parish, with the exception of the mountains where there is a considerable quantity.

Woods

With the exception of a few trees at the Glebe House and at the picturesque planted valley surrounding from sea to sea on each side the abrupt-sided hill on which Downhill House stands, there is scarcely a tree to be met with in the whole parish. As far as I have been able to see, there is not much indication of the former existence of forests to any extent.

MODERN TOPOGRAPHY

Towns

The little village of Articlave is the only one in the parish of any note. It is a very small and rather an insignificant one consisting of very few houses, and these not remarkable for size.

Public Buildings

There are in the village of Articlave an Established church and a Presbyterian meeting house standing nearly together.

Gentlemen's Seats

Downhill, the residence of Sir James Bruce Baronet, who is a constant resident landlord: the mansion at Downhill is a magnificent building covering a large portion of ground. It is erected on the middle of a nearly flat hill which is surrounded east, west and south, particularly to the latter, by a beautiful and an extensive valley, the descent to which is very abrupt and in some parts precipitous, and on the north by the perpendicular cliff down to the sea. North of the house and close to the edge of the cliff stands the temple, the use of which is given by Sir James Bruce to those of the Roman Catholic persuasion as a place of worship, there being no chapel in the parish. South of the house and near the edge of the hill stands the monument which was erected by the late Sir Hervey Bruce to the memory of the Earl of Bristol, who was Bishop of Derry, from whom the property descended and who built the mansion. The western side of the mansion consists almost exclusively of a library and a picture gallery, which contains a splendid collection of paintings, many of them originally by the old masters.

Bleach Greens and Manufactories

There is an extensive flax mill in this parish.

Communications

The eastern part of this parish is well intersected

by roads, but not so the western side. The principal one is that leading from Coleraine to Magilligan through the parish from south east to north west, passing the demesne of Downhill till it reaches the strand of Magilligan. This strand, which is perfectly flat and, at low tide, in excellent, hard order for travelling, is situated directly under the high, perpendicular cliffs which are the northern boundary of the parish, and forms the continuation of the road for some distance west of this parish, when it again strikes inland southward towards Newtownlimavady <Newtownlimavaddy>. This is the best communication between the western part of this parish and the towns of Newtownlimavady and Londonderry.

As before remarked, this strand is in good, hard travelling order at low water. It becomes more difficult and heavy as the tide advances and at high spring tides is impassable and dangerous. This road is very hilly, particularly at Downhill where there is a long and steep descent to the strand, but is kept in very good repair and has lately undergone much improvement of a very expensive nature, particularly where it passes through the south of Downhill demesne. From this another road branches off near Coleraine, and entering the parish at Cranagh hill, proceeds by Bannbrook and Pottagh along the low ground of the parish near the sea till it joins the former about half a mile west of Articlave. This road is tolerably good and not quite so hilly as the former. From these two on the eastern side of the parish another runs south through Quilly to Macosquin. This is in tolerable order. The old road from Coleraine to Newtownlimavady passes through the southern part of this parish east and west under the Giant's Sconce hill. From this last another communicates from the south west with Articlave north east. These two last are very bad, hilly roads and not much used, as well as one or two roads over the mountain on the west which are all in the parish.

Fair Sheets by J. Bleakly, June to August 1835

MODERN TOPOGRAPHY AND PRODUCTIVE ECONOMY

Mills in Articlave

The corn mill in the townland of Articlave has 2 water wheels which are abreast, and both placed on the same side of the mill and turned by the same stream, and at the same time, if the water is plenty.

Each wheel is 13 feet in diameter, 1 wheel is 1 foot 2 inches broad at the buckets and the other is 1 foot 9 inches broad. Both wheels are in bad repair. The fall of water on each wheel is 15 feet. The water proceeds from springs called the Clear Holes on Altikeragh <Artikeragh> mountain and forms a stream called Articlave burn. There is a hopper, a pair of stones and a pit wheel to each water wheel. One part of the machinery can be shelling while the other is grinding. The pit wheels are each 7 feet in diameter. The stones are each 4 and a half feet in diameter and can grind 3 barrels per hour and can work a little in summer by collecting the water in the mill-pond. The corn kiln is about 10 yards from the mill and was built of stone and lime, slated, in 1817; the head of the kiln is of sheet iron. John Alexander Esquire of Newtownlimavady, head proprietor; occupying tenant of the mill is James Clarke, occupying tenant of the kiln is William Cochran.

The flax mill is on the same stream with the corn mill and about 50 yards distant from the corn mill. The water wheel is a breast and 12 feet in diameter and 1 foot 8 inches broad. The fall of water on the wheel is 6 feet. The pit wheel is 7 feet in diameter with metal segments screwed on a wooden rim. There are 2 scutches with 2 men to attend, and can scutch 6 score per day. James Clarke is the proprietor. Information obtained from Robert Porter and James Clarke.

Articlave Flax Mill

Articlave flax mill (no.2) is wrought by a pressure of water from a cistern on the water wheel, which is 16 feet in diameter and 4 feet broad across the rim. The cog wheel is 8 feet in diameter, with metal segments screwed on a wooden rim. This mill has 4 scutchers and can scutch 12 score per day with 4 men and can work a little at all seasons of the year by a stream proceeding from springs called the Clear Holes on Altikeeragh mountain. There are 4 rollers of cast iron attached to this mill. James Clarke is the proprietor, Lesly Alexander Esquire, a minor, is the head proprietor. A premium was granted to the proprietor, William Cochran, in 1831 for being the best mill in the parish. This mill was built and insured in 1829, cost of insurance 20 pounds, premium granted by Linen Board 20 pounds.

Mills in Ballywoodock

The flax mill in the townland of Ballywoodock is on the estate of Sir James Bruce Bart. William Graham is the proprietor of this mill, which is on a small stream and takes its source from springs in Ballyhacket mountain and falls into the sea at the Back Strand near Aull's Hotel. The water wheel is a breast and 11 feet 8 inches in diameter and 4 and a half feet broad. The fall of water is 8 feet. The pit wheel is 7 feet in diameter. There are 2 berths <births> i.e. 2 scutchers, one person to each stock and one person to attend. The mill is idle part of the summer from want of water.

The corn mill is also in Ballywoodock. The head proprietor is Sir James Bruce. The water wheel is a breast, 13 and a half feet in diameter and 2 feet broad at the buckets. The fall of water is 23 feet. The pit wheel is 6 feet 8 inches in diameter. The stones are each 4 and a half feet in diameter and can grind 2 barrels per hour. This mill is on the same stream with the flax mill. The occupying tenant William Graham pays 15 pounds per annum to Sir James Bruce Bart. The tenants of Sir James Bruce are bound to make their oatmeal at this mill. The mill is built of stone and lime, thatched and in bad repair, idle also in summer from want of water and work, as the greater part of the corn is sold in the markets. The corn kiln is attached to the mill and has a sheet-iron head. From William Graham, proprietor and James Graham, his son. 23 June 1835.

Pound in Ballywoodock

The pound in Ballywoodock is on William Allen's farm and is 68 feet by 48 feet. The walls are 5 feet high and 2 feet thick. A good spring is in the pound with a stream which passes east and west. The pound is situated 100 yards east of the corn mill. This is the only pound in the parish and is for the use of the tenant[s] of Sir James Bruce Bart. The poundage for 1 cow is 4d and if 10, 20 or 30 is put in together, no more is charged. From Joseph McMichael, poundkeeper.

Flax Mill at Ballywildrake

Ballywildrake flax mill is on the estate of Lesly Alexander Esquire; James Blair is the proprietor. Breast wheel and 12 feet in diameter and 1 and a half feet broad, fall of water 3 feet, water wheel in bad repair; the house, a mere cabin, in bad repair. The cog wheel is 6 feet 3 inches in diameter. 2 berths or scutchers in this mill, can scutch 1 cwt per day, idle part of the summer from want of water. Information obtained from William Blair.

Flax Mill in the Townland of Ardina

John Smith is the proprietor of this flax mill which is situated in the townland of Ardina, on the estate of Lesly Alexander Esquire. This mill was built in 1827 of stone and lime, thatched and cost 90 pounds. The water wheel is a breast, 14 feet in diameter and 2 feet broad and is placed inside the walls of the mill. The cog wheel is 7 feet in diameter, the fall of water is 10 feet. There are 4 berths or stands at which 4 men with one to attend are employed, and can scutch 1 cwt per day, but idle part of the summer from want of water. The stream to this mill has its source from springs called the Clear Holes in Altikeeragh mountain. The works of the mill are of wood and in good repair. There are also 4 rollers of wood attached to this mill. Information obtained from John Smith, farmer and proprietor of the mill.

Downhill House

Downhill House is situated on a beautiful eminence 5 miles west of Coleraine and [blank] feet above the level of the sea, which bounds it on the north and north west. The house was built of black stone procured on the ground by Bishop Hervey in 1770. The plan was first laid by Mr James Wyatt of London and built under the superintendence of Michael Shanahan, architect, and agent to the bishop at that time, and was afterwards cased with freestone in 1787 under the superintendence of David McBlain, architect.

Temple

The temple was also built by Lord Bristol in 1788; from the foundation to the cornice under the superintendence of Michael Shanahan, and from the cornice to the top of the dome by David McBlain. The stones for the temple was brought from Ballycastle in the county Antrim and from Dungiven. The temple is circular outside and 31 feet in diameter and an octagon inside. From the base or cut stone to the top of the cornice is 24 feet high and from the springing of the arch or centre of the dome to the top is 15 feet high. The door is on the south side and is 8 feet by 4. From the foundation or surface to the cut stone where the door commences is 6 and a half feet high, of basalt rock and is north east of Downhill House. The floor of the upper part of the temple is of Portland flags. The door on the lower part of the temple is 5 and a half feet by 3 feet 3 inches. The pier in the centre which supports the temple is 5 feet 8 inches high. The roof of the lower part of the temple is of bricks, not plastered; 2 small windows, a semicircle on the lower part. The floor is of earth and very rough. There are 3 large windows oblong and are each 5 feet by 11 on the upper part of the temple.

About 48 years since, the bishop gave the lower part of the temple to the Roman Catholics for a chapel, as many of the servants at Downhill at that time were Roman Catholics and also gave 1 guinea per month to the priest, which sum ceased at the death of the bishop. This is the only Roman Catholic chapel in the parish of Dunboe. Formerly mass was held only once a month, now every second Sunday. The year in which cholera prevailed in this part the people were prohibited by Sir James Bruce to come to the temple, during which time mass was celebrated in the open air, in the townland of Masteragwee, on John Doherty's farm.

A splendid library of good books was also deposited in the upper part of the temple by the bishop but are all long since removed, some to Downhill House and some to Derry. A number of plaster of paris images of the heathen deities with a number of marble busts are still to be seen in the temple. Many of the images are the workmanship of "Joseph Torrenti for 1789", but are much out of repair. The skeleton of a crocodile 7 feet 2 inches long, 1 and a half feet broad on the back in the widest part; the head is 1 foot 4 inches long, the 2 forelegs are each 1 foot 3 inches long, the 2 hind legs are the same length; from the hind legs to the top of the tail is 2 feet 10 inches long. The animal is 3 feet 2 inches round the body, which is stuffed with shavings of wood. There is also a petrifaction which has the appearance of a sponge <spunge>.

St Columkill's <Columkiln's> Iron Chest

Tradition says an iron chest was also in the temple in which was deposited a number of old books and ancient manuscripts of St Columkill. It was said that this chest could not be opened but by a man who had never been born, and who was to ride on a white horse without a black hair, and which had never been foaled. The bishop, thinking himself possessed of the above necessary qualifications, procured a white horse on which was not a black hair and which had never been foaled but was taken out of the mare's side, as he (the bishop) had by skilful surgeons been taken out of his mother's side and proceeded to open the chest. The consequence was that the bishop could not sleep 2 nights in one house and from the disquiet state of his mind fled to Rome where it is said he died a papist and in a miserable state. The above chest was afterwards removed to Derry. Information obtained from John Wisely, weaver and David McBlain, architect.

Monument at Downhill

The monument at Downhill was erected about 50 years ago by Bishop Hervey, under the superintendence of David McBlain and Michael Shanahan, architects, and is 75 feet high and 250 yards south of Downhill House. The statue is of white marble executed by an Italian in Naples and cost 1,000 pounds [insert query by C.W. Ligar: figure or monument?]. Information obtained from David McBlain, architect.

Old Church at Downhill

The old church at Downhill, i.e. the ruins, is 63 by 21 and a half feet. The walls are 3 feet thick. The churchyard and burial <burrial> ground contains 2 roods. [Crossed out: The annual value of the ground is 1s]. Tradition says this church was founded by St Patrick.

Fish Ponds at Freehall near Downhill

There are 2 artificial fish ponds in the townland of Freehall, the property of Sir James Bruce Bart. These ponds were made by Bishop Hervey, in which was deposited a few trout and eel. The ponds are both together except a small parapet with an aperture to let the water from one to the other. These ponds both together are 125 yards long by 35 yards broad and 36 yards from the precipice over the sea and 150 feet above the level of the sea and on a rock.

Banbrook House

Banbrook House was built by Squire Ford in 1691, the sexangular part by Bishop Hervey. The Boyle family were the late inhabitants of Banbrook House after the Barnetts. Information obtained from David McBlain, architect. 1 August 1835.

Ancient Geography Book

Ancient <antient> geography left at Bannbrook House by Bishop Barnett was republished 1st January 1836 at Amsterdam in Holland by Henry Hondius, John Johnston and Henry Hexam. This ancient book was originaly published under Gerard <Gerrard> Mercator, Duke of Gulick, and in the confines of Flanders.

Glebe House

The Glebe House is situated in the townland of Blakes near the road between Articlave and Coleraine. This is the residence of Archdeacon Monsell and was built in 1774 by Michael

Shanahan, architect. The supposed cost is 700 pounds. From David McBlain.

Residence of the Clergy

Isaac Hazlett's house in the townland of Liffock was formerly the residence of a curate of the name of Golden, and was the only residence for the clergyman of the parish at that time as there was no Glebe House. From Isaac Hazlett, farmer. 1 August 1835.

Isaac Hazlett's House

Isaac Hazlett's house in Liffock was built by Rector Golden in 1691.

Village of Articlave

The village of Articlave is situated 3 and seven-eighth English miles west of Coleraine and on the road leading from Coleraine to Downhill. In this village there are 57 houses. The following is a list of the trades and occupations: 5 publicans, one of which is a publican [crossed out: grocer and hatter, 2 grocers], 1 cloth shop and grocer and general dealer, 2 blacksmiths, 1 nailor, 3 tailors, 1 hackler, 1 miller, 2 stonemasons, 6 carpenters, 1 wheelwright, 1 cooper, 2 sawyers, 4 shoemakers [crossed out: 1 gravedigger], 21 weavers of linen, 1 reed maker, 1 basket maker, 6 fishers who labour occasionally. There is also a post office, established 11th May 1832, a general penny post on foot from Articlave to Coleraine, a distance of 3 and seven-eighth miles; time allowed 1 hour and 10 minutes, daily dispatch at 15 minutes past 8 o'clock a.m. and arrives at Articlave 50 minutes past 4 o'clock p.m., James Dugan, postmaster. There are 12 persons in Articlave who have 2 occupations each. The curate, the Rev. Joseph Knox, resides in Articlave.

A small river passes at the east end of the village in which the salmon come up in great quantities at a time of fresh or flood [water]. Many are seen leaping against the rocks in the river and are taken by poachers with torch and gaff. Information obtained from James Dugan, postmaster.

Linen Weavers in Articlave

There are 21 linen weavers in Articlave, 6 of which hold small farms. The other 15 chiefly depend on weaving for their living.

SOCIAL ECONOMY

Local Government

There are 3 police in the parish of Dunboe, stationed in Articlave.

There are 2 coastguards stationed at the bar mouth.

The only resident magistrate is Sir James Bruce Bart, who resides at Downhill. Sir James Bruce, Archdeacon Monsell and the curate of the parish are the only resident gentry in the parish.

Occupations

There are 7 blacksmiths, 7 tailors and 13 shoemakers in the parish of Dunboe.

MODERN TOPOGRAPHY

Samuel Dunn's House

The 2-storey house in Articlave opposite the meeting house was built by Fredrick Lafferty, a slater in Coleraine, and purchased by Joseph Orr, publican, of Coleraine.

Bridge at Articlave

The bridge on the road from Downhill to Coleraine which divides the village of Articlave from Dartress has 3 arches, 2 of which are each 16 feet in the span, the other a small arch 7 feet in the span. The bridge is 17 feet broad on the top on the road leading from Downhill to Coleraine. The wall of the bridge is 170 feet long, 2 and a half feet high and 18 inches thick and in good repair. There is also 3 arches to this bridge, each 11 feet 10 inches in the span and 14 feet broad on top, the wall 3 feet high and 90 feet long, on the road leading from Newtownlimavady to [blank], in good repair at the expense of the county. 26 June 1835.

Bridge at Glebe

The bridge at Glebe has 1 small arch 4 and a half feet in the span and 4 feet high. The top of the bridge is 12 and a half feet broad, walls 39 feet long, 3 feet high and 18 inches thick. This bridge is on a road leading to Newtownlimavady and is in good repair at the expense of the county.

Small Bridge at Killyveety Schoolhouse

The small bridge at Killyveety schoolhouse has 1 arch which is 5 and a half feet in the span and 5 and a half feet high and 18 feet broad on top. The wall is 40 feet long, 1 and a half feet high and 14 inches thick. The wall of this bridge is in bad repair, made at the expense of the county.

Bridge at Ardina

This bridge divides Ardina from Ballywildrake

and has 2 arches each 18 feet in the span and of good architecture. The wall is 280 feet long, 3 feet high and 18 inches thick. The bridge on the top is 17 and a half feet broad, 10 feet of the wall is in bad repair. This bridge is on the leading road from the Downhill road to Coleraine through Banbrook and near Ardina flax mill. The road leading to this bridge is 17 feet wide, of stones and gravel, all made and kept in repair at the expense of the county.

Bridge at Aull's Hotel

The bridge at Aull's Hotel near Downhill entrance has 1 arch which is 20 feet in the span. The wall is 24 yards long, 3 feet high and 18 inches thick, but in bad repair. The bridge on the top is 18 feet broad. The road leading to Coleraine near this bridge is 21 feet broad, of stones and gravel, made and kept in repair at the expense of the county. This bridge is about 53 years built.

Glen Bridge

The Glen bridge near Downhill has 1 arch 24 feet in the span. The wall is 54 feet long, 2 and a half feet high and 1 and a half feet thick. This bridge is 16 and a half feet broad on the top. This bridge is of excellent architecture and made at the expense of Bishop Hervey <Harvey>. The road leading to this bridge, which is the mountain road to Newtownlimavady from the road at the entrance to Downhill House, is 24 feet broad in the clear, in good repair at the expense of Bishop Hervey, now kept in repair at the expense of the county. The architect of this bridge was Michael Shanahan <Shanaghan>.

Bridge and Roads at Isaac Hazlett's

This is a small bridge in the townland of Drumliffe. It has 1 small arch 4 feet wide and 3 feet high. The wall is 24 and a half feet long on one side and 35 and a half feet on the other side and 3 and a half feet high and 14 inches thick. This bridge on the top is 24 and a half feet broad.

Also the road leading to Articlave and Coleraine across this bridge is 21 feet broad of stones and gravel. Another road leading from the road at this bridge to the mountain and to Newtownlimavady is 21 feet, of stone and gravel. The above bridge and roads made and kept in repair at the expense of the county.

Bridge at Ballywoodock

This bridge has one arch which is 10 feet in the span and 5 feet high. The wall is 120 feet long, 2 feet 10 inches high and 1 and a half foot thick and 20 and a half feet broad on the top. The stream which passes through the arch of this bridge divides the townland of Ballywoodock from the townland of Ballymadigan and is on the road near the corn mill leading from the Coleraine road to Newtownlimavady. The bridge is 50 years built and in good repair. The road leading to the bridge is 17 feet of stones and gravel and in good repair at the expense of the county.

Bridge in the Townland of Dartress

This small bridge has 1 arch 6 and a half feet wide in the span and 6 and a half feet high and 18 feet wide on the top. The wall is 22 feet long, 2 feet high and 18 inches thick, lately built at the expense of the country. The stream which passes thro' the arch of this bridge divides Ballywildrake from Dartress.

Roads and Roadmaking

The Rock Road, commonly called Allen's Glen, is 21 feet in the clear and is about 36 years made at the expense of Bishop Hervey, but now kept in repair at the expense of the county. Part of this road near Aull's Hotel was made through a rock, at the blasting of which a man named William Peebless was killed.

In 1815 a man named Isaac Wark was killed at the blasting of a limestone rock on the strand beyond Aull's Hotel.

The road leading from Garvagh to the sea near the schoolhouse is 22 feet in the clear of banks, drains and fences, and 16 feet of stones and gravel but not finished, at the expense of the county.

The road leading from Quilly to the bar mouth is 27 feet in the clear, in good repair at the expense of the county.

The road leading from the Coleraine road to the Banbrook road is 21 feet in the clear.

Road from the bar mouth to the leading road from Downhill to Coleraine: this is an accommodation road leading from the bar mouth through the townland of Exorna to the leading road from Downhill to Coleraine, and is 16 feet, of stones and gravel, in good repair at the expense of the county. Information obtained from the Rev. William Lyle and James Dugan, shopkeeper in Articlave.

The road leading from Quilly to the old leading road to Londonderry is 16 feet, of stones and gravel and 21 feet in the clear from ditch to ditch, made and kept in repair at the expense of the county and in good repair. From Thomas Ray, farmer. 29 June 1835.

Bar Mouth

Originally this part of the River Bann emptied itself by 2 mouths into the sea.

Old Road

The old road which formerly led from the lower road at Ardina near the bridge and flax mill at Ardina and to the bar mouth is now closed up.

SOCIAL ECONOMY AND MODERN TOPOGRAPHY

Population

Population of the parish of Dunboe taken in 1831: Established Church there are 529, Presbyterians 3,045, Seceders 633, Covenanters 66, Baptists 17, Roman Catholics 728, total 5,018. Copied from enumerator's book. Information obtained from James Dugan, shopkeeper in Articlave.

Church at Articlave

The church at Articlave is situated 3 English miles west of Coleraine and on the leading road from Coleraine to Magilligan Point, and 2 miles east of Downhill; was built in 1691 by consent of Bishop Hopkins who also consecrated it the same year. The outside of the church is 63 feet 7 inches by 25 feet 4 inches. The tower is 14 feet 2 inches by 11 and a half feet, with 4 pinnacles on the top with a weathercock on each. Inside the church is 51 and a half feet by 20 feet 9 inches. The vestry room is at the west end of the church and is 7 feet 4 inches by 4 feet 10 inches inside. The floor of the aisle is of freestone flags and 6 feet 2 inches broad. There are 3 oblong windows on the front or south side, and 1 window of an arch form which is at the east end; no window on the north side. There are 9 seats each 7 feet 4 inches by 4 feet 10 inches, and 1 single seat 7 feet 4 inches by 3 feet. There are 4 double pews [crossed out: 2 of which have a canopy overhead]. One of these pews is occupied by Sir James Bruce and family; the other pew was formerly occupied by the Barnett family who resided at Banbrook. Each of these double pews measure 10 feet 9 inches by 7 feet 2 inches. The 2 pews at the east end of the church are of this shape: [small drawing] and 12 feet 8 inches by 7 feet 4 inches in the widest part. One of these pews is occupied by the archdeacon and family, with any strange lady or gentleman who may come to worship in the church. The other pew was built for

Alick Alexander Esquire, the proprietor of the ground on which the church is built.

The pulpit and reading desk is at the centre of the south wall. There are 2 stoves in the centre of the church and a globe with 5 branches to light the church for evening service during the winter season. Suspended from the east wall at each side of the communion table are 2 tablets of wood, one containing the Lord's Prayer and the Apostles' Creed, the other contains the Ten Commandments. Over the vestry room door is a tablet containing a text of Scripture taken from Nehemiah VIII chapter and 8th verse. Over the inside porch door is a tablet on which is written a text from Genesis 28th chapter and 17th verse. Over the arch door at the inside entrance at the aisle is a tablet on which is written a text from Ecclesiastes, 5th chapter and 1st verse. A poor box of copper on which is written the following inscription: "The gift of Mr William Ford in 1771." The outside door is 6 and a half feet by 4 feet, the inside or porch door is the same, the vestry room door the same. The archway is 5 feet 10 inches wide. The walk leading from the church door to the street is 6 and a half feet broad and 120 feet long. The wall in front of the churchyard is 5 feet 9 inches high and 18 inches thick. The door at this wall is 5 feet 2 inches wide. The tablets and stoves have been put up at the expense of Sir James Bruce and the archdeacon, the light and fuel at the expense of the archdeacon.

The church and churchyard contains 2 roods. The annual value of the land is 4 pounds; the annual value of the house, deducting one-third, 6 pounds 6s, total value 6 pounds 10s. The church is about to be repaired at the expense of the Board of First Fruits. The repairs required is thorough: lights, with new windows and to alter the pulpit and reading desk. A gallery is also required but will not be erected until a future period. The church is in good repair except the above alterations which is really necessary.

There is not at present a pew standing in the church, but are all broken up and about to be repaired at the expense of the Ecclesiastical Commissioners. Sir James Bruce paid for one stove and the archdeacon paid for the other. 16 September 1835.

Note on Epitaph

Epitaph on a tombstone in Articlave churchyard to the memory of Robert Castles, master, and John Jameson, supercargo, and 6 sailors who perished in the brig Trader of Greenock near the

Castle rock under Freehall (half a mile west of the bar mouth), on the night of the 24th November 1826. Information obtained from John Watson, farmer, Freehall and James Dugan, postmaster, Articlave, and the tombstone.

Annual Income of the Clergy

The annual income of Archdeacon Monsell, including Glebe House and land, is 708 pounds viz. tithe composition 408 pounds, house and 30 acres of land attached 100 pounds, rent of glebe land received by the archdeacon from the tenants 200 pounds, total 708 pounds. The annual income of the curate, the Rev. Joseph Knox, is 75 pounds, paid by the archdeacon. Information obtained from the archdeacon and James Dugan, church-warden.

Bequest of Sir Hervey Bruce in 1818

In 1818 Sir Hervey Bruce Bart left 5 pounds in the hands of the Rev. George Huston, curate of the parish at that time, to be distributed among the poor of the parish of Dunboe.

Poor Money

The following sums have been collected in the parish church of Dunboe (from the year 1828 to the year 1835) and distributed half-yearly at the discretion of the archdeacon, curate and church-wardens of the parish indiscriminately among the poor of the different religious denominations: viz. 23 Protestants, 56 Presbyterians and 19 Roman Catholics, making a total of 98 poor persons who receive help from the parish church of Dunboe.

Poor money collected half-yearly in 1828 13 pounds 1s 1d, 12 pounds 7s 5d, total for 1828 25 pounds 8s 6d.

In 1829 11 pounds 5s 7d ha'penny, 13 pounds 5s, total for 1829 24 pounds 10s 7d ha'penny.

In 1830 12 pounds 3s 9d ha'penny, 12 pounds 2s 9d, total for 1830 24 pounds 6s 6d ha'penny.

In 1831 12 pounds 5s 5d ha'penny, 14 pounds 7s 10d, total for 1831 26 pounds 13s 3d ha'penny.

In 1832 13 pounds 3s 1d ha'penny, 11 pounds 2s 6d ha'penny, total for 1832 24 pounds 5s 8d.

In 1833 14 pounds 4s ha'penny, 11 pounds 1s 6d, total for 1833 25 pounds 5s 6d ha'penny.

In 1834 11 pounds 14s, 11 pounds 4s 8d ha'penny, total for 1835 [sic] 22 pounds 18s 8d ha'penny.

Total from 1828 to 1835 173 pounds 8s 10d ha'penny. In addition to the sums collected for the poor in the church, there are 4 poor persons who receive each 6d per week i.e. poor housekeepers.

In 1832 a charity sermon was preached in the parish church of Dunboe by the Rev. Joseph Knox (curate), at which 9 pounds 1s 6d was collected for the purpose of cleansing the houses of the poor and purchasing fresh straw for their beds during the time of cholera. From James Dugan, church-warden, and from the preacher's book.

Provision for the Poor

During the last 6 or 7 years the dead were interred by act of vestry (i.e.) funds raised by act of vestry for that purpose, and 5 of a committee appointed for that purpose, a coffin to be provided with a certificate signed by 3 of the committee and the amount specified. Now the poor are interred by the benevolence of the inhabitants of the neighbourhood in which poor reside. From James Dugan, post office.

Presbyterian Meeting House

The Presbyterian meeting house is situated at the [blank] end of the village of Articlave, and was built by subscription of the congregation in 1785 and cost 350 pounds. The house was enlarged in 1830 by raising it a storey higher, the cost of which amounted to 250 pounds, including the gallery. Lord Bristol gave 50 pounds towards the erection of the old part. Sir James Bruce Bart gave 20 pounds towards the latter. The total cost of the meeting house has been 600 pounds.

The house is 78 feet by 32 feet outside, with 12 windows on each side and 1 window in each end, a door on each end and 1 door on the back part outside, with stone steps leading up to it and the gallery. Each window on the lower part of the house is 5 feet 8 inches by 3 feet. There are 2 of the windows on the front, circular at top. The aisle <ile> is 6 feet wide and flagged. There are 4 double pews, one at each corner of the meeting house, each 11 and a half feet by 6 feet. There are 40 single pews each 11 and a half by 3 feet. The pews on the ground floor are in bad repair. There are 20 single pews on the gallery each 7 feet 8 inches by 3 feet, and 6 double pews each 7 feet 8 inches by 5 feet 8 inches. Forms occupy part of the gallery which from the want of funds the congregation is unable to finish. The pulpit is at the centre of the front wall of the meeting house. The house is built of stone and lime, slated, the walls, aisle and roof in good repair, the pews and pulpit in bad repair. The doors are each 3 feet 8 inches by 6 feet.

The names of those who contributed towards the erection of this meeting house are as follows:

the Earl of Bristol 50 pounds, Sir James Bruce Bart 20 pounds, Lesly Alexander Esquire of London 10 pounds, the Clothworkers' Company 50 pounds, the Rev. William Lyle, minister of the congregation, 10 pounds, [total] 140 pounds, the remainder by the congregation which amounted to 460 pounds, making the total cost of the meeting house 600 pounds. The congregation pay for their seats. The meeting house is on the estate of Lesly Alexander Esquire, a minor. The following inscription is cut on a stone on the front wall of the meeting house: "This house was built AD 1785 under the care of our late worthy pastor the Rev. William Knox, who after 37 years ministerial labour resigned his breath to God who gave it. 20th August 1801."

The congregation is composed of Presbyterians, many of whom come from the following parishes viz. Macosquin, Magilligan and Killowen. The meeting house is too small to contain the present congregation. An aisle is about to be erected, the cost of which will amount to 350 pounds. The congregation consists of 800 families, the average number of each family is about 4 and a half. The late repair of the meeting house was built under the superintendence of Mr Hugh Swan, a respectable farmer of this parish. The congregation is increasing and *appear* respectable. 27th June 1835.

Additional Notes on Meeting House

The Clothworkers' Company gave 25 pounds towards the original ceiling and flooring of the Presbyterian meeting house and 25 pounds towards the late repairs, i.e. raising the house a storey higher. Information obtained from the Rev. William Lyle, minister of the congregation. 19 September 1835.

The meeting house and graveyard contains 1 acre and 20 perches. Annual value of the land is 19s, annual value of the house, deducting one-third, 9 pounds, total 9 pounds 19s [insert additional note: taken from the valuation of the county]. The stones for the late repairs of the meeting house have been procured on the Rev. William Lyle's farm in the townland of Upper Articlave. There are 15 graves in the meeting house yard and only 1 tombstone, to the memory of Margret Anne Louden.

Income of the Presbyterian Clergyman

The annual income of the Presbyterian clergyman of this parish, the Rev. William Lyle, is 135 pounds viz. 75 pounds regium donum and 60 pounds stipend. Has a comfortable residence in the townland of Upper Articlave about quarter of a mile south west of the meeting house and on the estate of Lesly Alexander Esquire, minor. The house is built of stone and lime, slated, to which is attached a good farm of land. Service commences in this meeting house every Sunday at 12 o'clock a.m. and continues till 5 o'clock p.m., with the intermission of 1 hour. The new system of singing has been lately introduced into this meeting house. The money collected for the poor in the meeting house is distributed every Sunday after the service at the discretion of the minister and session of the congregation. The gallery was put up at the same time the house was built.

Poor Money

The average sum collected in the Presyterian meeting house of Dunboe for the poor amounts to 20 pounds, which is distributed among the poor indiscriminately at the discretion of the session. A day is appointed before the sacrament and the money collected from the congregation. Information obtained from Samuel Glenn, session clerk.

Seceders' Meeting House in Ballinrees

The meeting house in the townland of Ballinrees is called the Whin meeting house and was built of stone and lime, thatched and by subscription of the congregation in 1740. This was the first time of establishing a Seceding congregation in the parish of Dunboe. This house was rebuilt in 1820 of stone and lime, slated and cost 113 pounds, by the congregation. The Rev. Alexander Stewart was the first minister who preached in this meeting house, the Rev. Charles Campbell was the second, the Rev. Samuel Weir was the third, the Rev. Joseph Thomas was the fourth. The congregation is composed of people from Macosquin, Killowen and Dunboe. The Rev. William Wilson is the present clergyman, whose annual income is 75 pounds viz. 50 pounds regium donum and 25 pounds from the congregation.

The meeting house is 69 by 26 feet and 10 feet high, a door on each end of the house; each door is 6 feet high and 3 feet 3 inches wide. There are 37 pews; one of these is a double pew opposite the pulpit and would contain 14 sitters. There are 4 pews, 2 at each end of the house, with a canopy over each; these 4 pews would contain each 8 sitters. According to the above calculation the house would contain 270 (i.e. 7 sitters to each pew of 32). The house when crowded <crowed> would contain in the pews 300 who could sit. The pews have a door to each and are in pretty good repair, but not painted. The pulpit is in the centre of the east side of the house. No floor better than earth and sods in the pews or aisles. There are 6 windows on each side of the house which are oblong; 4 of those are larger than the others and in the centre of the house. There are 2 pews opposite the pulpit which are railed, and 2 pews at each end of the house which are railed also and are higher than the other pews of the meeting house. Some of the pews have straw mats on the floor. The house is 100 yards west of the road leading from Coleraine to Newtownlimavady and on a bank called the Whinny hill on Mr Richardson's land. The meeting house and yard contain 1 acre 1 rood and 36 perches. Annual value of this land is 5s, annual value of the house, deducting one-third, 3 pounds 4s, total 3 pounds 9s. 13 July 1835.

Poor Money

The poor money collected at the meeting house in belonging to the Seceding congregation amounts to 5s per Sunday during the summer half year and in the winter to 3s per Sunday; total for each year 10 pounds 8s. Information obtained from the Rev. William Wilson, minister of the above congregation.

SOCIAL ECONOMY

Articlave Reading Society

[Letter addressed to John Bleakly, Royal Engineers Department, Liffock, from James Dugan, Articlave, 10 July 1835].

Sir,

The Articlave Reading Society was established in the beginning of the year 1825 by a few young men anxious not only for their own improvement but that of others less favourably circumstanced than some of them were for readable matter. At first I think it consisted of but 7 members who subscribed each 10d (it was then Irish currency), and with this sum and a pound or two advanced by me we purchased our first stock of books. We agreed to meet on the first Friday of every month and to subcribe 5d each at every meeting. At the end of the first year (the currency having been then changed) we reduced our subscription to 3d per month, which sum we continue to pay till this day.

The good effects of it now began to be seen and *felt*, and some who perhaps had never read a single volume in their life began to talk of such works as Hervy [? Henry], Erskin, Paly [Paley],

Hull etc., thus exhibiting proofs that they were evidently growing wiser and I trust better than when they first joined the society. Numbers now began to seek admission and some who, perhaps from a mistaken idea of their own dear selves, we thought the society scarcely *respectable* enough for *them* to join it, and from ignorance of the *value of such an institution*, were found most anxious to have their names enrolled on our list, till our numbers in a very few months amounted to 40.

From the manner in which our rules are drawn up and the strictness with which they are enforced, I am happy to say the utmost harmony prevails. We have also occasionally a debate on some moral or scientific subject, but *religious or political* subjects are never once touch[ed] at; and to this I mainly attribute the permanency and prosperity of our society, for several societies have from time to time sprung up in our parish on nearly similar principles but have invariably failed from the above cause.

We are kindly patronised by the Venerable the Archdeacon of Derry and family. We receive an annual donation of 1 pound or books to that amount and an occasional new publication. This, with the exception of 40s received from the Honourable Mrs Knox, is the only help we have received from any quarter.

Our stock of books consist[s] at present of 450 volumes viz. natural history 6, civil history 23, ecclesiastical history 19, theology 127, controversy 8, poetry 4, Jewish antiquities 10, commentaries 14, biography 15, medicine and veterinary works 7, gardening and farming 6, voyages and travels <travails> 5, arts and sciences 6, periodicals 12, fiction 6, miscellaneous 179, [total] 459. Thus, you see, the diligent and attentive reader has had an opportunity of perusing no less than 450 volumes on almost every subject.

There has been an objection raised against our society and societies in general as being calculated to lead the mind from the study of the Bible, but the very contrary is the fact, as many of our books require to be read being held in the *one hand* and the Bible in the *other*. But with greater propriety might it be said that the time spent reading our books would be spent in the *alehouse*, the *country dance* or perhaps at the *card table*. For we know that the mind of man is an active principle, and when not employed in a laudable pursuit is not, nor cannot be idle, but must find out something or other wherein to engage. When the shades of evening (a winter's evening in particular) draws in upon the toil-worn son or servant or the care-worn parent or master, with what avidity will he draw to his favourite volume, and forgetting the labours of the day at once get absorbed in the contemplation and study of the works of those whom he well knows to have been wiser and perhaps better than himself.

If he is a farmer, with what pleasure will he draw to and with what eagerness will he pore over the last number of the farmer's calendar <callender> or magazine. How will he stand amazed when he is told that the very limestone that lies imbedded in one corner of his field obstructing the progress of his plough share, that the bed of deep rich shell marl <marrel> (the deposit of ages long since bygone) that rendered another portion of his farm in a manner useless, that a third piece of quagmire which at present answers no good purpose but is a continual source of trouble and loss by tempting the unsuspecting ox to hurl his unwieldy form to the false and unstable sward, that these, together with the [river ?] that at present roams idly by, except perhaps at an improper season when it is sometimes permitted to overrun his low, lush meadow ground leaving the seeds of devastation, famine or death to the cattle; how, I say, will it startle him when he is told that these *very things are* in themselves, through a judicious course of management, the very springs of wealth and of comfort and induce him to exclaim "I have found the philosopher's stone."

Or is he a mechanic? Give him one of the many useful publications of the society for diffusing useful knowledge and there will he not only find the wheel within the wheel, but himself becoming the centre of the revolving circle. He will contemplate with growing wonder the mighty power of mechanism, and from admiration of the finite works of art be led not only to improve his own particular calling but with growing wonder and expanded mind to look up from art to nature and to nature's God.

Or may he rather wish to take a survey of the heavens, when in a frosty night the stars are shining in all their effulgent <efulgent> glory? Why not take Sir Isaac Newton by the hand, who will gently lead him from orb to orb and from world to world and till each of them by name and as system upon system are brought revolving upon his astonished sight, how will he be induced to exclaim "in wisdom hast thou made them all."

Or should he rather be disposed to explore the hidden treasures of the earth, let him descend the narrow dark and precipitous "shaft" in company with (I had almost said Mr Hacket) this geologist, who will teach him the various strata of which our

earth's crust is composed, pointing out the primary, secondary and calcareous rocks; and passing on through beds of limestone, sandstone, quartz and calp, at length reaches the resting place of the source of Britain's wealth and power: coal. Here he will point out the various fossil remains of animal, vegetable, serpent and shell that must have been deposited at a period long antecedent to any historical record.

Or should he chance to diverge from his *downward path*, here he may trace the several springs through all their serpentine, gravelly <gravly> paths now labouring to ascend the highest hill, now bumping rapidly down the deepest vale till at length reaching the highest range of mountains where, by its attraction of damp and vapours, he finds to his astonishment that the Grey lough and the Clear Holes, that before he considered as perfectly useless, are the very basins <basons> or reservoirs to supply the wants of thousands. Or should he take an opposite direction and "sail with the tide", how will he be surprised when his pathway (to use a technical <technicl> phrase) having "crossed out", he finds a delightful, pure, sparkling stream start from the foot of the barren rock and that, perhaps at his own garden side, to accommodate him with one of the greater comforts and blessings with which providence has been pleased to bless one country.

Now I would ask, can it be possible that amid such a pleasing and delightful study he can be prevailed on by any power on earth to quit such a mental feast and join the *heart-sickening, soul-destroying* revel <revul> of a country alehouse carouse. I would not, at least, be the person [who] would ask him to do so. As each individual takes 2 books, it is invariably the practice of each member to take a religious volume to supply him with Sunday <Sundy> reading, and here is no less than 40 families entertained and instructed in the several callings and avocations throughout the week and edified and comforted with the practical teachings of such men as Rutherford, Brown, Henry, Scott or Burke throughout the solemn sabbath. You will perceive by our rules that the subscriber *loses nothing* by joining our society, as he gets his full amount of his subscription whenever he pleases to withdraw. Thus he becomes possessed of a little library of his own, a thing he never could nor would have had otherwise.

Our number, as I said before, is 40. Were we able to get through the business, we could have 4 times that number. It is a pleasing reflection that not a single unpleasant word has ever passed in the society since its first commencement, nor has there been a death of one of its members while in connection with us. I have endeavoured to give you an outline of the workings of our society with a sketch of the rules. Should I have omitted anything you would wish to know, I will most gladly furnish you with it, and am your obliged servant, James Dugan, Articlave, 10 July 1835.

Reading Society

The Reading Society at Articlave is held in the schoolhouse. The following is an abstract of one of the rules: any subscriber taking a book out of the library may keep it 1 month.

Dispensary

There is no dispensary in this parish: the people go to Coleraine dispensary. The subscribers to the Coleraine dispensary from the parish of Dunboe is Sir James Bruce, Archdeacon Monsell and John Alexander Esquire of Newtownlimavady. Visiting tickets are given, signed by some of the subscribers, which tickets compel the physician Doctor Neil to visit the patients. If out of the liberties of Coleraine, the subscriber pays the doctor 5s, inside nothing.

Schools in Downhill

Downhill male and female school was established in 1824 upon the estate of Sir James Bruce Bart. The schoolhouse is built of stone and lime, slated and is 40 feet 11 inches by 15 feet 7 inches. The side walls are 11 feet high. The house was built by the Kildare Society and cost 119 pounds 12s 2d ha'penny. The schoolhouse is situated 5 miles north west of Coleraine <Colerane>, on the road leading from Coleraine to Magilligan. The floor of the schoolroom is of earth. The teacher's dwelling house is a short distance from the schoolhouse, to which is attached 1 rood of ground with turf bog. The house and ground and bog was granted by Sir James Bruce and valued at 6 pounds per annum. This is a pay school: the annual income of the master is 13 pounds in cash viz. 5 pounds from Sir James Bruce and 8 pounds from the children, making a total (including the house and ground) of 19 pounds. The children pay as follows: reading, writing and arithmetic 1d ha'penny per week, spelling 1d per week. There are 5 windows on the front of the schoolhouse and 2 windows on the back with 2 doors, one on each end of the house, with a wall between the male and female apartments. There are 2 Protestants, 47 Presbyterians and 2 Roman Catholics, males 39,

females in the male apartment 12, total 51. There is 1 fireplace in the schoolhouse and is placed in one end of the partition wall which has 2 open doorways. Information obtained from William Anderson (a Protestant), teacher. 19 June 1835.

Downhill female school, Letitia Dallas (a Protestant), teacher: this is also a pay school. The income of the mistress is 8 pounds per annum, viz. 5 pounds from Sir James Bruce and 3 pounds from the children. The average attendance for the last 3 months was 23 girls: of the Established Church there are 8, Presbyterians 13, Roman Catholics 2, total 23. This is under the same roof with the male school. The Kildare system is taught in both schools. Sir James Bruce, Lady Bruce with the younger branches of the family, Archdeacon Monsell and the Rev. Joseph Knox are visitors of the school. A Sunday school is also held in this schoolhouse from 9 to 11 o'clock a.m. on Sundays. After the school is dismissed, the children repair to their respective places of worship. Information obtained from Letitia Dallas, teacher.

Dunboe Parish School for Boys

This school is held in the townland of Articlave and is situated 27 yards south of the church, William Donnelly, a Protestant, teacher. This is a pay school. The master receives 6 pounds per annum from the patron of the school Archdeacon Monsell, with 1 acre of land, a dwelling house or apartments which are attached to the schoolhouse and valued at 5 pounds per annum, and 12 pounds per annum from the children, making a total of 23 pounds per annum. The schoolhouse including the master's apartments is 60 feet 10 inches by 21 feet. The walls are 8 and a half feet high and built of stone and lime, slated, with 2 windows on the front and 3 windows on the back. The schoolhouse was built by a grant from the Kildare Society and a grant from Archdeacon Monsell. There are 12 children of the Established Church, 3 Roman Catholics and 45 Presbyterians, total 60 boys. 20 June 1835.

Dunboe Parish Female School

Articlave female school is under the same roof with the male school, with a partition wall between them. In the wall there is 2 open-arch doorways; the fire is placed in one doorway and the master's desk in the other. The mistress, Eliza Creevey, is of the Established Church. Her annual income is 13 pounds viz. 5 pounds from Mrs Monsell and 8 pounds from the children. Each girl pays the mistress 1s 6d per quarter. There are 16 children of the Established Church, 64 Presbyterians and 10 Roman Catholics, total 90 girls. There are 18 of those girls educated and clothed at the expense of Mrs Monsell, who also provides each girl in the school, whose parents will allow them to accept of it, with a working slip. Those slips are not to be taken out of the school. 30 of the girls in this school attend Miss Monsell 3 days in each week i.e. Tuesday, Thursday and Saturday, in order to receive religious instruction. Saturday is exclusively devoted to singing sacred music. The school is visited each week by some of Mrs Monsell's family. From Eliza Creevey, teacher.

Glebe School

The Glebe school was established in 1828, is built of stone and lime, thatched and cost 23 pounds. The schoolroom is 15 and a half feet by 16, was originally a farmhouse and was purchased in 1828 by Archdeacon Monsell, with a small garden which is attached to the schoolhouse. Both free and pay school: the master receives 6 pounds per annum from the Hibernian Society and 2 pounds from the archdeacon, with the house and garden which is valued at 1 pound 10s per annum and 6 pounds from the children, making the master's income 15 pounds 10s per annum. There are 14 children of the Established Church, 27 Presbyterians and 7 Roman Catholics, males 20, females 28, total 48. The schoolhouse is situated on the road leading from Garvagh to the sea and is connected with the London Hibernian Society, who also supply the school with books. The school is inspected 3 times a year by an inspector from the society. There are 12 poor children taught free, for which the master receives 12 pounds per annum with the house and garden. Each child in the school, except the above 12, pay the master 1s per quarter. Information obtained from John Ross, a Protestant, teacher. 22 June 1835.

School at Ballyhacket Toberclare

This school commenced the 1st of June 1835, Charles Newell, a Seceder, teacher. A pay school, held in a barn 13 and a half by 14 and a half feet, for which the master pays the sum of 1 guinea per annum. There are 26 Presbyterians, 1 Seceder and 8 Roman Catholics, 23 males and 12 females, total 35. The children sit on round sticks and stones, and blocks of wood. The school is connected with no society, supported by the children who pay the master 1d per week each. The house

is in bad repair and on the estate of Lesly Alexander, a minor. From Charles Newell, teacher and Edward McLaughlin, proprietor.

School in Killyveety

The schoolhouse in Killyveety is of stone and thatched and is 14 by 15 feet, is a small room attached to the master's dwelling house. The master purchased the house with a garden containing half a rood for 11 pounds in May 1835 from Mr Isaac Hazlett. There is no furniture in the school: the children sit on planks and stones. There are 52 Presbyterians, 3 Roman Catholics, 2 Seceders and 0 Protestants, 1 Covenanter, 35 girls and 23 boys; each child pays the master 1s 6d per quarter. The school is connected with no society. The house is situated about half a mile north east of Articlave and on the road leading to Newtownlimavady. Information obtained from William Clarke, a Presbyterian, teacher.

School in the Townland of Quilly

The school in Quilly is on the estate of Sir James Bruce Bart and was established in 1830. John Doherty, a Presbyterian, is the teacher, who receives 20 pounds per annum viz. 2 pounds 3s 6d from the London Hibernian Society for the last quarter. The grant from this society is paid according to the number and proficiency of the children. Thomas Ray, the proprietor of the schoolhouse, pays the master 12 pounds per annum, which he collects from the children afterwards. Each child must pay Thomas Ray 2s per quarter. The schoolhouse is attached to Thomas Ray's dwelling house and is built of stone and lime, thatched and in very bad repair. The children sit on round sticks and blocks of wood. The house is 16 feet by 16 feet. The house is on the leading road to Coleraine and 2 miles south west of Coleraine. There are 4 children of the Established Church, 66 Presbyterians, 4 Seceders, 2 Covenanters and 1 Roman Catholic, males 38, females 39, total 77. The school is visited by Archdeacon Monsell and the Presbyterian minister. Information obtained from the teacher.

School at Altikeeragh

David Lindsay, a Presbyterian, is the teacher of this school, whose annual income is 13 pounds paid by the parents of the children. There are 67 children in the school viz. 53 Presbyterians, 13 Roman Catholics and only 1 Protestant, 33 males and 34 females. The house is built of stone and lime, thatched and is 17 by 14 feet 4 inches, the walls 7 feet high and cost 15 pounds. The house was built by subscription of the inhabitants who subscribed among themselves 6 pounds; the remainder was done in work by those who gave no money. The school was established in 1828. The house has 2 small windows on the back or west side. The floor is of earth and very uneven with the fire in the centre, an empty barrel being the only chimney on the house. There are no forms in the school: the children sit on sticks and blocks of wood. The master has no stated place of residence but goes with the childen to the houses of their parents. Each child pays the master 1s 1d per quarter for their education. The present master is only 1 and a half year teaching in this school. The children are in great want of books. This school is connected with no society at present but was about to be established under the National Board; but from influence of the clergy of the Established Church and the opposition met with by the people, they did not succeed. From the teacher and James Dugan, shopkeeper. 4th July 1835.

Sunday School in Articlave Church

The Sunday school is held in the church at Articlave from 2 to 3 o'clock p.m., superintended by the archdeacon. His lady and daughter are teachers. This school was established in 1821 in connection with the Sunday School Society for Ireland, who supply the childen with books. The average attendance for the last year was 75 viz. 12 of the Established Church, 61 Presbyterians and 2 Roman Catholics, 27 male and 48 female, total 75. There are 8 gratuitous teachers viz. 4 males and 4 females in this school, concluded by prayer. Information obtained from the archdeacon.

Sunday School at Quilly

The Sunday school at Quilly was established in May 1835. The average attendance is 31. There are 17 boys and 14 girls, all Presbyterians. There are 23 of those who do not attend day schools viz. 12 are boys and 11 are girls. There are 3 gratuitous teachers, 1 male and 2 females. The children have received no books yet from any society. Held in the day schoolhouse, held from 4 to 6 o'clock p.m.

Day School in the Townland of Ballinrees

Ballinrees day school was established in connection with the London Hibernian Society in 1829 and held in a small thatched cabin near the gate of the meeting house yard. The present schoolhouse is situated about 300 yards east of the meeting house and on the road leading from Coleraine to Newtownlimavady. The house was built in 1827 of stone and lime, thatched, with 2 small windows on each side of the schoolhouse, and the door on the north side. The house is 22 by 17 feet, built and furnished by the inhabitants. The greater part gave work instead of money. This is a pay school: the annual income of the teacher is 20 pounds viz. 8 pounds from the London Hibernian Society and 12 pounds from the parents of the children, which sum comes through the hands of a committee who are appointed to superintend the school. Each child pays to the committee, for the master, 1s 6d per quarter. There are 20 of the children Presbyterians and 50 Seceders, 40 are boys and 30 are girls, total 70. The school is in connection with the London Hibernian Society, 12 perches of free land attached to the schoolhouse. Information obtained from Robert Arthur Lennox, a Protestant, teacher. 14 July 1835.

Sunday School at Ballinrees

The Sunday school at Ballinrees is held in the day schoolhouse and was established at the same time, in 1829, in connection with the Sunday School Society for Ireland. There are 100 in attendance at this school viz. 40 males and 60 females, 20 of those are exclusively day school scholars. There are 14 gratuitous teachers, all male. The school is open from half past 7 to 10 o'clock a.m. and from half past 5 to 7 o'clock p.m. The Sunday School Society supply the school with books.

Day School in the Townland of Ballystrone

John Allen, a Seceder, is the teacher of this school which was established in January 1834. This is a pay school. The annual income of the master is 10 pounds, paid by the parents of the children. The house is 22 by 18 feet outside, the walls are 7 feet high, built of stone and lime, thatched, but not finished. The present cost is 7 pounds 15s and 5 pounds more will finish it. Built by subscription of the inhabitants but not yet furnished. The children sit on temporary seats, no desks or forms. There are 4 windows on the house viz. 2 in front and 2 in rear. This is the first time of a school being in this townland, and connected with no society. There are 42 Presbyterians and 3 Roman Catholics, no Protestants, 22 males and 23 females, total 45. From John Allen, teacher.

Sunday School at Ballystrone

Ballystrone Sunday school was established at the same time of the day school. There are 96 scholars in attendance at this school and 7 gratuitous teachers viz. 4 males and 3 females. 17 July 1835.

Day School in the Townland of Knockmult

Knockmult day school was established in 1833 and built of stone and lime, thatched, by subscription of the inhabitants and cost 20 pounds. The house is 18 by 15 feet 3 inches. There are only 2 children of the Established Church, 5 Roman Catholics, 21 Presbyterians and 27 Seceders, 27 males and 28 females, total 55. This is a pay school. The annual income of the teacher is 16 pounds 10s, paid by the parents of the children. 6 of a committee superintend the school and meet once a month to see into the necessary repairs of the house. The house is situated 4 miles south west of Coleraine and on the road leading from Coleraine to Newtownlimavady, on the estate of Lesly Alexander Esquire and on Benjamin Rath and William Caskey's farm. The house is well furnished with double desks and forms at the expense of the inhabitants. The house would contain 60 children with a fireplace at each end of the house. Each child pay the master 1s 6d per quarter. The floor is of earth. There are 3 windows on the house, 2 on one side and 1 window on the other. This is the first quarter for the present master. This school has not been connected with any society since its commencement. Information obtained from Samuel McIntyre, a Seceder, teacher. 21 July 1835.

Sunday School at Knockmult

Knockmult Sunday school is 5 years established. 90 is the average attendance, many of whom are adults; 55 of the above number are day school scholars and 35 are exclusively Sunday school scholars and there are 9 gratuitous teachers. The Sunday school is held in the day schoolhouse. Information obtained from the teacher of the day school, Samuel McIntyre.

Reading Society held in the Schoolhouse of Knockmult

This society was established in 1834 for the purpose of reading the Scriptures and conversing on religious subjects. The members of the society are Seceders and meet in the schoolhouse once a month. From the Rev. William Wilson, Seceding minister.

Day School in the Townland of Farranlester

This is called the Cranagh school and was established in 1780; was 6 years at first in connection with the London Hibernian Society and 7 years afterwards with the Kildare Society, the remainder of the time up to the year 1834, a private school, that is connected with no society. In 1834 it became connected with the National Board and still continues. The master, John Lyons, is a Presbyterian. This is a pay school. The annual income of the master is 16 pounds viz. 8 pounds from the National Board and 8 pounds from the parents of the children. The schoolhouse, which is very old and a mere cabin built of stone and mortar, thatched, is 15 and a half by 12 and a half feet. The walls are 5 and a half feet high and cost 10 pounds. In 1832 the Kildare Society gave 1 pound 16s towards the furniture, desks and forms. There are 5 small desks. There are 8 children of the Established Church, 36 Presbyterians and 15 Roman Catholics, 24 males and 35 females, total 59. The house is situated 1 and a quarter miles north west of Coleraine, on the road leading from Coleraine [to] the shore by Banbrook and on the parish boundary of Killowen and Dunboe. Two-thirds of the house is in the parish of Dunboe. The National Board supply the children with books. Information obtained from John Lyons, teacher. 29 July 1835.

Sunday School at Downhill

The Downhill Sunday school is held in the day schoolhouse and was established in 1824 in connection with the Sunday School Society for Ireland, who supply the children with books. The school is superintended by Miss Bruce and held from 9 to 11 a.m. in winter and from 8 to 11 in summer. There are 7 gratuitous teachers viz. 3 males and 4 females. There are 8 males and 13 females of the Established Church; there are 34 males and 28 females, Presbyterians; there is only 1 Roman Catholic. Total of the Established Church 21, Presbyterians 62, Roman Catholics 1, 42 males and 42 females, total 84. There are 48 who are exclusively Sunday school scholars. Hours of attendance from 9 till 11 a.m. Information obtained from William Anderson, teacher, a Protestant.

Glebe Sunday School

The Glebe Sunday school was established the same time [as] of the day school and is held in the same house. There are 16 Protestants, 4 Roman

Catholics and 33 Presbyterians, males 23, females 30, total 53. There are 26 of those who do not attend day schools. Connected with the Sunday School Society for Ireland. Information obtained from the teacher of the day school and Sunday school, John Ross, a Protestant.

ANCIENT TOPOGRAPHY AND NATURAL FEATURES

Cave on Baccus Hill

Baccus Hill Cave is in the townland of Ballyhacket, is 21 feet long east and west, the mouth of which is 2 feet wide and 1 foot high. Inside this cave is 4 and a half feet in the widest part and 5 feet high. Another wing, the mouth of which is inside, is 2 feet 5 inches wide and 1 foot high. This part extends to the north, is artificial and on Samuel Cooper's farm. Information obtained from Edward McLaughlin, farmer.

Fort in the Townland of Downhill

This is called the Dungannon Fort, the centre of which is of stones covered with blackthorn, is circular and 50 feet in diameter. The fort itself is of earth and is 150 by 108 feet and 20 feet high. The entrance is 8 feet wide. The trench is 9 feet wide. This fort is situated in the centre of a planting near the old church at Downhill and on Sir James Bruce's estate.

Fort of Earth in the Townland of Killyveety

Killyveety Fort is of earth and of this shape: [drawing with dimensions of parapet wall], shape all destroyed except 15 feet of the parapet which is 3 feet high. The fort before it was destroyed was 6 feet high; is now planted with potatoes. This fort is supposed to have been circular.

Cave in Killyveety

There is an artificial cave on Andrew Hutchison's farm and about 100 yards from his house. The cave inside is 10 and a half feet long, 4 feet high and 4 and a half feet wide. Another apartment inside, the mouth of which is 2 feet wide and 8 inches high; the outside mouth is 3 feet wide by 2 and a half feet high.

Bogs

Bog in Carn and Ballybright also, nearly all cut away.

Ballymoney flow bog is on the estate of Lesly Alexander Esquire and was originally a slane turf bog, but now cut away. Hand or baked turf is now made of the refuse or cutaway bog. This bog is 4 feet deep. The imbedded timber consists of oak stumps which are useless except for fuel. The bog is covered with rushes which are used to tie or bind flax and to make manure or thatch cabins. In Magilligan they are used as a substitute for candles by taking off the rind or bark and dipping in fish oil. From Mr Isaac Hazlett, farmer. 25 June 1835.

Fort in the Townland of Ballymoney

This is called the Carn Fort, is of earth and 105 feet in diameter, and is circular with a hollow or low in the centre where water remains during the winter. The parapet is 4 feet high and undisturbed. The entrance is 12 feet wide and 40 feet long, on Samuel Dunn's farm and on the estate of Lesly Alexander Esquire. The trench of this fort is 17 feet wide.

Cave in Artidillon

An artificial cave in the townland of Artidillon at Thomas Hunter's door and extends upwards of 50 feet north: inside this cave is 4 feet high and 3 and a half feet wide. The mouth is 3 feet wide and 2 feet high, on the estate of Lesly Alexander Esquire.

Discoveries

About 15 years ago in the townland of Ballywoodock, on William Graham's farm near the corn mill, a quantity of bones (supposed to have been human) was discovered 6 feet below a hard subsoil, resembling iron in a gravel pit. Information obtained from James Gage, farmer, who procured some of the bones but are now all lost.

Fort in Townland of Glebe

The fort in the townland of Glebe is circular, of stones and is 70 feet in diameter. The wall is 6 feet broad. The entrance <enterance> is 6 feet wide, with 2 stones on the north side. The largest stone is 2 feet 9 inches long, 2 feet high and 1 foot thick. The smallest stone is 2 feet long, 1 foot high and 1 foot thick. The fort is 20 feet high tapering to the top. A trench is round the fort which is 21 feet broad in the broadest part. 24 June 1835.

Fort of Earth in the Townland of Gortycavan

The fort in the townland of Gortycavan is on a hill called the Bullock Park, on James Blair's farm.

This fort is of earth and planted with potatoes, is circular and 76 feet in diameter. The entrance is 15 feet wide. The fort is 30 feet high, with a trench around it which is 20 feet wide. The outside parapet is 5 feet high and 4 feet wide. The trench is covered with long, coarse grass and filled with water during the winter.

Standing Stone in the Townland of Quilly

This stone serves as a guide or object for seamen coming to the bar mouth. It stands upon an hill on David Kennedy's farm and on the estate of Sir James Bruce Bart. This stone is supposed to be 8 feet under the surface. The part which remains above the surface is on the east face, 9 and a half feet high, 8 and a half feet broad. On the north and south side it is 6 feet 9 inches high and 5 and a half feet high at the north side. From John Kennedy, farmer. 30th June 1835.

Flow Bog in the Townland of Quilly

The flow bog in the townland of Quilly was originally slane turf, but all cut away. The cut away part is now made into hand or baked turf and some of the moss is drawn to the farmyards for manure. This bog is 4 feet deep. The imbedded timber chiefly consists of oak stumps, some of which present the appearance of pinnacles from 1 to 3 feet above the surface. Some of the roots of the oak stumps extend 15 feet along the surface of the cutaway bog. These stumps are raised for fuel. Sir James Bruce Bart, proprietor. Information obtained from John Kennedy.

Standing Stone

This standing stone is on William Finley's farm in Ballywildrake and is 5 feet 8 inches high and 3 feet 3 inches broad on the face of the north side. The face of the south side is 3 feet wide. The face of the west side is 2 feet 5 inches wide. This stone stands in the centre of a stone ditch 2 feet high, on the estate of Lesly Alexander Esquire. Information obtained from William Finley, farmer. 1st July 1835.

Deer's Horn

[Marginal drawing of deer's antler] This deer's horn was discovered about 40 years ago by Isaac Hazlett deceased <diseased>, grandfather to the present Isaac Hazlett of Liffock. It is affirmed by the people that the deer from which this horn was taken made its escape from the deerpark at Downhill, and passing through Liffock the horn was broken off by a throw of a stone. The animal was hunted to Altikeeragh mountain where it was killed by a gunshot. This horn is flat and of a dark brown colour and measures 2 feet in length; was much longer, which is evident from the forked part at the top, the branches of which have been broken off. A cord passes through the hole at the top, from which the horn is suspended and is used as a substitute for pegs on which hanks of yarn is suspended by Mrs Samuel Hazlett in the townland of Liffock. Information obtained from Isaac Hazlett, farmer.

Artificial Caves in Exorner

The artificial cave is at the west end of James Horner's dwelling house; the south end of the barn is built over part of the cave. The cave is 22 feet long east and west and 5 feet deep, with 2 feet deep of water and is 6 feet wide. The east end of the cave is like an arch, on the estate of Lesly Alexander.

Another cave is in the townland of Exorner on Mrs Gutrie's farm, in a clover field near the road from Downhill to Coleraine. This cave was discovered about 33 years ago and is said to have been 5 feet high and 5 feet broad. Burnt flax seed, bones and human teeth were found in this cave, but is now closed up at the mouth. From James Gutrie, farmer.

Fort of Earth and Stones in the Townland of Altikeeraght

Altikeeraght Fort is 88 feet by 120 feet and in its original form very uneven, with large stones interspersed through the centre which is grown in parts with heather. The entrance, which is at the east side, is 7 feet wide. The parapet is nearly all of stones, 3 feet broad and 6 feet high at the east side. The fort is 30 feet high in the highest part. Lesley Alexander Esquire is the head proprietor. 3 July 1835.

Remarkable Cave in Artidillan

The following is the plan and elevation of this remarkable cave, which is in the townland of Artidillan at Thomas Hunter's house and on the estate of Lesley Alexander [plan of cave and passages with key positions lettered]: (A) is the east end of the first apartment and which is 8 feet long, 3 feet wide and 3 and a half feet high; (B) is the entrance to the east end; (C) is a stone which is placed across the mouth of the cave and forms it into 2 small entrances; (D) is the entrance to the west end of the cave; the mouth of the cave from small (a) to (b) (including the stone across the mouth) is 3 and a half feet long by 2 and a half feet wide; (E) is the west end of the first large apartment and is from the entrance (D) to (E) 27 feet 10 inches long, 3 and a half feet wide near the entrance and 4 and a half feet high; (F) is the entrance into the north and south apartments. This mouth is 2 feet wide and 2 and a half feet high; (G) is the south end of this apartment and measures from this to the entrance 10 feet 2 inches long and 4 feet wide and 4 feet 10 inches high. From the entrance (F) to the entrance (H) is 14 and a half feet long, 4 feet 10 inches high and 4 feet in the widest part. (H) is the entrance to the smaller east and west apartment and is 1 foot 7 inches wide by 1 foot 10 inches high. From (I) to (J) is 21 feet 10 inches long, 5 feet 2 inches wide in the widest part and 4 feet 10 inches high. From (K) to (L) is 3 feet long. 4 July 1835.

Cave and Fort in the Townland of Ballyhacket Glenahorry

This artificial cave is on Samuel Hindman's farm and is 20 feet long, 5 feet 9 inches high and 4 feet 10 inches wide. The entrance is 18 by 18 inches, with a frame of wood to keep the earth from falling in. Malt is frequently deposited in this cave for illicit distillation. 4 other caves are attached to this, but are now all closed up except the above. The above cave is situated in the centre of a fort of earth. This fort is circular and 112 feet in diameter, but was destroyed about 36 years ago except part of the parapet on the east and north west side of the fort. This fort is all sown with corn and appears to be 9 feet high in the highest part. This fort in which is the above caves is on the estate of John Alexander Esquire and on Samuel Hindman's farm.

Discoveries

An ancient plough iron, a water can and a quern stone was discovered in a small, brittle bog by John Nowry, deceased, in the townland of Ballyhacket Glenahorry.

Fort of Earth

In the Townland of Ballyhacket Magilligan on Jacob Finley's farm: this fort is 280 yards south west of the fort in Ballyhacket Glenahorry and was of the same dimensions, that is 112 feet in diameter, but now all destroyed and planted with potatoes except a few yards on the south west

side. The parapet, of which a few yards remain undisturbed, is 3 feet high and 3 feet broad and is of stone. A fairy bush was originally in the centre of this fort but is now cut down. Information obtained from James Gage and Samuel Hindman, farmers. 6 July 1835.

Caves in the Townland of Dunalis

There are 2 artificial caves in a field now sown with flax on Alexander McCracken's farm. These caves are 175 yards asunder but so difficult of access that a man must creep on hands and feet to enter them, that is, the inside apartments. James Gage and Daniel McAlees states that a man could stand upright with extended arms and in some parts so high as to admit of the arms being extended above the head. One of these caves has 4 apartments extending east, west, north and south. Stones have been put in and obstructed the pass so as to render it too difficult of access. The entrance to one of these caves was from the roof like a trapdoor, inside of which bones were found. These caves cannot be explored until the flax is pulled off the field where the caves are.

Fort of Earth and Stones in the Townland of Ballyhacket Magilligan

This fort retains its original shape which is nearly circular and well fortified on the east side by a waterfall. The parapet around this fort is of stones, 7 feet broad and 6 feet high at the west side which is the highest. This fort is 52 by 58 feet and low in the centre, with large stones interspersed through it. From the base of the fort to the bottom of the river is 15 feet of a solid rock. No regular entrance to this fort. Information obtained from James Gage, farmer.

Cataract in the Townland of Ballyhacket Magilligan

The fall of water from this cataract is 10 feet from a solid rock, the face of which is 22 feet wide. The water falls into a pond which is 22 feet in diameter and from whence small trout are often taken. From James Gage, farmer.

Fort of Stones in the Townland of Ballyhacket Lisawilling

This fort is on the estate of Lesly Alexander Esquire and on the farm of Robert Doherty and is situated about 700 yards south west of the waterfall and fort in the townland of Ballyhacket Magilligan. This fort is of an oval shape, 82 feet long and 50 feet in the widest part and 40 feet wide near the entrance, which is at the east side. The parapet is 4 feet high and 7 feet broad. At the north end of this fort is a smaller fort like a platform or quarter-deck of a ship and is 25 feet in diameter and 1 and a half foot higher than the large fort, which is 34 feet high. The trench around this fort is 14 feet wide, with small parapets of stone which form small apartments at the south east side. The hill on which this fort is situated has the appearance of a sugar loaf wanting the top, and in a natural state quite undisturbed.

Discoveries in the Townland of Ballyhacket Lisawilling

About 50 yards north of this fort and in the same townland on Robert Doherty's farm a quern stone and a spur of brass of unusual size with a quantity of Danes' <Deans'> pipes were found at this place. Robert Doherty says the spur was as thick as a man's wrist, with rollers as thick as a man's finger. From Robert Doherty, farmer. 8 July 1835.

Discoveries

In 1830 an ancient pot was discovered 3 feet below the surface on the mearing between Ballyhackett Tuberclare and Ballyhacket Lisawilling by Patrick McGunigle and Alexander Tosh, farmers.

Caves

There is a cave, artificial, in a narrow lane on the march between Ballyhacket Magilligan and Ballyhacket Tuberclare, on the farm of John McAlees and Alexander Tosh.

Standing Stone in Dunalis

This standing stone is in a reclined position or rather flat, and forms part of a ditch of earth and stones on a lane or narrow pass leading to James Morrison's house. About 35 years since, James McLaughlin dreamed 3 times of money being deposited under this stone, in search of which his thigh-bone was broken by this stone falling on him while in the act of searching for the money by night. Information obtained from Thomas Hunter, farmer.

Fort of Earth and Stones in Dunalis

This fort is situated on a rocky hill covered with stones and whins on Samuel Reed's farm and on the estate of Lesly Alexander Esquire, and is of an

oval shape, 58 feet long by 32 feet in the widest part and 27 feet in a narrower part and 9 feet at the narrowest part. At the east and round to the west side is a solid rock, the face of which is 14 feet in the highest part. At the south side on the face of the rock is a chair called the Chief's Chair, the seat of which is 1 foot 2 inches wide in the front or face and 1 foot 2 inches on the surface of the seat and 1 and a half foot high and 10 inches high on the side where the arms rest. The back of the chair is 2 feet wide. The first step at the ground appears to be artificial and is 6 inches high; the second step is 2 feet 8 inches high and 3 feet broad; the third step is 1 foot high; the fourth step is where the feet rest, is 1 and a half feet high and 2 feet 5 inches broad. 9 July 1835.

Large Fort of Earth and Stones in Dunalis

This fort is situated 800 yards north of the smaller fort and 50 yards south of Alexander McCracken's house, on the estate of Lesly Alexander, and is nearly oval and 73 by 90 feet, with whins growing in several parts of the fort in the centre, which is the lowest part. Part of the centre have been taken off for manure and has small stones interspersed through it. The entrance is east and west. The wall or parapet is 4 feet high outside, which is the highest part of the fort. The parapet inside is 2 feet high. Brackens or ferns are growing through the fort.

Cave on Alexander McCracken's Farm

There is also a cave in a flax field on Alexander McCracken's farm in the townland of Dunalis, but now closed up at the mouth and cannot conveniently be opened until the flax is pulled. This is also an artificial cave and is on the estate of Lesly Alexander Esquire. Information obtained from Alexander McCracken, farmer. 10 July 1835.

Murder Hole

The Murder Hole is in the townland of Altibrian and on the old road leading from Coleraine to Newtownlimavady. It is said that Cushey Glenn with a gang of robbers lodged at this hole. It was at this Murder Hole where Cushey Glenn was shot by James Hopkins of Bolea.

Cave in the Townland of Fermullen

[Marginal drawing of cave entrance] This cave extends 61 feet nearly north and south. The mouth is 1 foot 7 inches by 1 foot 3 inches. From the mouth to the second entrance is 16 feet long, 5 feet high and 3 and a half feet wide. The second door is 1 foot 10 inches wide and 1 foot 9 inches high. From this door to the next apartment or entrance is 30 feet long, 4 and a half feet high and 3 and a half feet wide. From this to the end of the cave is 15 feet long, 2 feet wide at the end, 3 feet 9 inches in the widest part or middle, 5 feet 4 inches high in the highest part. The roof or top stone is 2 feet wide, the cave throughout. This cave is in a potato field on Joseph Caskey's farm and on the estate of Lesly Alexander Esquire.

Caves in Ballywildrake

A cave in James Lighton's farm in Ballywildrake in a corn field, but now closed up. Another on James Love's farm in the same townland, in a corn field and closed up also. 20 July 1835.

Sconce Hill

This remarkable hill is of an oval shape and 160 by 94 feet in the widest part. At the north side is the trigonometrical station, convenient to which is a spring well. An artificial cave is also on this hill which extends north and south and is 40 feet long and 2 feet wide, but now nearly all filled up with stones. The parapet at the south east side is 3 feet high and 11 feet 8 inches wide inside, and 6 feet high at the east side. The entrance is at the south east side and is 17 feet long by 5 feet wide, regularly formed like the foundation stones of a house.

Fort and Giant's Grave adjoining Sconce Hill

The fort adjoining the Sconce hill is of a semi-oval shape and 126 feet by 78 inside the parapet, which is 6 feet wide. Inside this fort is a giant's grave with a hole in the centre, from whence it is said bones were taken. The Sconce is 16 feet above the level of this fort. The fort is 30 feet above the grazing field below.

Giant's Chair

The Giant's Chair is 20 paces east of the entrance to the Sconce hill. The front of the seat is 1 foot 10 inches high and 2 and a half feet wide; from front to back is 1 foot 7 inches broad. The back is 3 feet high by 2 and a half feet wide, from front to back of the south arm is 2 feet and from back to front of the other arm is 1 foot 4 inches high. The Sconce hill is in the townland of Sconce, the fort and grave is in Bellgarrow, the Giant's Chair is in Knockmult. From John Walker, farmer. 22 July 1835.

Cave in the Townland of Farnlester

[Marginal drawing of cave and passages with key positions lettered] This is an artificial cave in the townland of Farnlester, in a field of barley on a farm the property of John Watson of Freehall. The following is the dimensions: from (A) which is the first entrance to (B) which is the second is 13 feet 3 inches long, 3 feet 9 inches high and 2 feet 4 inches wide at the bottom. The entrance (A) is 2 feet wide by 1 foot 9 inches high; (B) is the second entrance and is 2 feet 10 inches wide and 1 foot 8 inches high. From (B) to (C) is 18 feet 8 inches long, 3 and a half feet wide, 3 feet 3 inches high and 3 feet wide at the top or cap stone. (E) is the third entrance and is square, 1 foot 8 inches by 1 foot 8 inches. From (E) to (D) is 16 feet 9 inches long, 4 feet high, 3 feet wide at bottom and 2 feet wide at the top. The entrance to this cave is in a gravel hole. The cave appears to have extended many feet longer at the east end, but the stones have been taken away at the clearing of the gravel pit. A large stone has fallen into the entrance (B) which almost obstructs the passage. Information obtained from John Lesly. 23 July 1835.

Cave in Bellany

This cave is in a corn field in Bellany is called Steen's Cave, now closed up.

Fort of Earth in the Townland of Banbrook

A fort of earth was originally in the townland of Banbrook on the farm of Hugh Swan, but now all destroyed. A horse, the property of Hugh Swan, fell dead in harrowing over this fort. Information obtained from Henry Swan.

Natural Cave on the Strand

[Plan of cave with key positions lettered] This cave is 10 paces east of the parish boundary of Magilligan and Dunboe, in a rock on the strand. The following is the dimensions: from (A) to (B) is the end and is 10 feet wide and 5 feet high; from (C) to (D) is 7 feet wide and 4 feet high; from (E) to (F) is 5 and a half feet wide and 3 feet high; from (G) to (H) is 4 feet 9 inches wide; from (I) to (K) is 6 feet 10 inches wide and 8 feet high; from (L) to (M) is the mouth and is 7 feet 9 inches wide; from (N) to (O) is 11 feet long; from (O) to mouth is 18 feet long; total length of the cave is 29 feet. 30 July 1835.

Tory Cave

White cave called the Tory Cave, natural: this

cave is also on the strand and 150 paces west of the other cave and is 24 feet long, 14 feet 3 inches wide in the widest part and very high. The entrance is a narrow cliff between 2 high rocks and is 28 feet long and 2 and a half feet wide. The narrowest part of the entrance is 1 and a half feet wide and 3 feet at the widest. This is called the Tory Cave from Cushy Glenn, a noted robber with a gang of others, resided in it. This is a natural cave.

Large Natural Cave

[Plan of cave with key positions lettered] A large natural cave 100 paces east of the white cave in the face of the rock; the following is the dimensions: from (A) to (B) is the end and is 8 and a half feet wide and 12 feet high; from (C) to (D) is 19 feet wide; from (E) to (F) is 5 and a half feet wide; from (G) to (H) is 24 feet wide; from (I) to (J) is 8 feet wide; from (K) to (L) is 15 feet wide; from (M) to N is 4 feet 10 inches wide and 2 and a half feet high; from (O) to (P) is 17 feet wide; the mouth is 5 feet wide and 13 feet high; from (R) to (S) is 54 feet long; from (S) to (T) is 15 feet long; from (T) to mouth is 101 feet long; total length of the cave is 170 feet and 12 feet high in the highest part.

Small Natural Cave

[Plan of cave with key positions lettered] This is the smallest natural cave and is 7 yards east of the larger or white cave; the following is the dimensions: from (A) to (B) is 5 and a half feet wide; from (C) to (D) is 3 feet wide; from (E) to (F) is 4 and a half feet wide; mouth is 3 feet wide and 3 feet 4 inches high; from (K) to (L) is 16 feet long; from (M) to (N) is a small apartment attached to the larger and is 3 feet wide and 3 feet 4 inches high.

Natural Caves: Gull Cove

[Plan of cave with key positions lettered] The Gull Cave is a large natural cave in the face of the rock above the sea near Freehall; the following is the dimensions: from (A) to (B) is 11 feet 9 inches wide; from (C) to (D) is 7 feet 8 inches wide; from (E) to (F) is 23 feet wide; from (G) to (H) is 57 feet long; from (I) to mouth is of water and 64 feet long and 10 feet wide at the mouth; total length of the cave is 121 feet and very high.

Temple Cave

[Plan of cave with key positions lettered] The Temple Cave is in the face of a rock under the temple; the following is like the shape and dimensions: from (A) to (B) is 10 feet wide and 20 feet high; from (C) to (D) is 9 and a half feet wide; from (E) to (F) is 16 feet wide; the mouth is 15 feet wide; from (G) to (H) is 20 feet long; from (H) to mouth is 38 feet long; total length of the cave is 58 feet, inside interspersed with large stones. The mouth extends wider into the sea and is about 12 feet above the level of the sea.

Permir Cave

[Plan of cave with key positions lettered] Permir Cave: from (A) to (B) is 7 feet wide; from (C) to (D) is 18 feet wide; from (E) to (F) is 22 feet wide; from (G) to (H) is 29 feet wide; from (I) to mouth is 108 feet long. The mouth is 30 feet wide and 40 foot high. This is called the Permir Cove, from a great number of those small birds of the web-footed kind building in it. 4 August 1835.

Pigeon Cove

[Plan of cave with key positions lettered] The Pigeon Cave is also natural and in the face of the rock above the sea; the following is the dimensions: (A) is the end of the cave and is 2 feet wide and 1 foot high; from (B) to (C) is 9 feet wide; from (D) to (E) is 12 feet wide; from (F) to (G) is 7 feet wide; (H) is 2 and a half feet wide; (O), (P) and (Q) are 3 stones in the centre; (K) is a large rock in the centre of the cave which almost obstructs the pass; from the end of the cave to this rock at (S) is 93 feet long; from (S) to the mouth is 37 feet long, total length of the cave is 130 feet. The mouth is 8 feet wide, the floor is of sand.

Natural Cave

[Plan of cave with key positions lettered] This [is] another natural cave and is like a cleft <cliff> in the rock; the following is the dimensions: (A) is near the end of the cave and is 2 feet wide; (B) is 3 feet wide and 3 feet high; (C) is 2 feet 8 inches wide; from (D) to (E) is 19 and a half feet wide. This cave is 75 feet long and 18 and a half feet wide at the mouth and 24 feet high and narrow at the top, with stones scattered throughout. The above caves could not be explored without a boat.

Springs

The following is a list of the springs in the parish of Dunboe: in the townland of Articlave there are 5 springs viz. 1 on James Clarke's farm, 1 on James Dunn's farm, 1 on William Cochran's farm and 2 on William Lowry's farm; 1 on Samuel McCurdy Greer's farm in Bogtown, 1 on James Horner's farm in Exorner, 1 mineral spring on Isaac Dugan's garden in Ballywillan, 1 on John Hunter's farm in the townland of Artidillan, 2 springs in Freehall, 1 in Blakes, 1 in Liffock, 1 in Downhill glen, 1 in Dartress, 1 on the Sconce hill and the Clear Holes in the townland of Altikeeragh.

Fort of Earth and Stones

The fort in the townland of Ballyhackett Tubberclare on a rundale <run deal> farm and on the estate of Lesly Alexander Esquire: this fort is of an oval shape, 70 by 52 feet. The entrance is east and west, the parapet is 3 feet high, chiefly of stones and from 9 to 11 feet wide. The entrance is 4 feet 9 inches wide. A small fort is inside, near the south east end, and is circular, 16 feet in diameter. The parapet is 1 and a half foot high and 3 feet wide, nearly all of stones. The entrance of this small fort is east and 3 and a half feet wide. The large fort is on the brink of a precipice about 30 feet high.

Artificial Cave in Ballymaddigan

The artificial cave in the townland of Ballymaddigan, in a potato field near Downhill House, was discovered in 1833 by a labourer of Sir James Bruce Bart. This cave is now closed up at the mouth and cannot be explored till the potatoes are dug. A large pipe, small at the mouth and wide at the bottom, was found in this cave and would contain an ounce of tobacco. From James Morrisson, farmer. 5 August 1835.

Cave in Dunalis

This artificial cave is in a flax field on Alexander McCracken's farm and runs east and west, 16 feet long, 5 and a half feet high, 3 feet wide at the bottom and 1 and a half feet wide at the top. The mouth is like a trapdoor and is 2 feet by 1 foot 3 inches wide. 18 August 1835.

PRODUCTIVE ECONOMY

Fishery at Freehall

The number of fish taken at Freehall strand for this season up to this date, 20 August 1835, amounts to 120 salmon fish; each fish on an average weighs 6 lbs. The fishery at this shore is not yet ended and it is supposed will not be a profitable fishery next season, as there is always a rough sea at this point and the nets generally

broken. The right of fishery at this strand belong to the owners of the land adjacent to the shore. The right of the Bann fishery, together with 500 fathoms from low water mark on either sides, belong to the Honourable the Irish Society. The sea being a free common, it is only necessary to obtain the liberty of trespass upon the owner of the land.

Fisheries

The fishery at Freehall strand was established for salmon fishery in 1833 by a few Scotchmen, by permission of Sir James Bruce and on his estate, and continued during the months of May, June, July and August during the years 1833 and 1834 by nets, and re-established this year 1835 by Sir James Bruce and John Watson, by whom 4 men are daily employed with one boat. The fish are sold in the parish and in Coleraine at from 4d to 5d per lb.

The following is a list of the names of the fish taken occasionally on the coast and river in the parish of Dunboe: salmon, codfish, a few, fluke or flounder, gurnets <gornets>, hardheads or creenans, sole, haddock, murlagh, brazerfish, dogfish, gallashans, eels and skatefish. Only the fins of the latter is used.

The shellfish are as follows: mussels <muscles>, limpets, periwinkles, crabfish, crubans, shrimps and giggans. Shrimps are sometimes used as baits for fluke. Giggans are only found after a north storm and are driven or come against the wind. Information obtained from John Watson and Isaac Hazlett, farmers.

SOCIAL ECONOMY

Water Guards

The water guards came to the Back Strand in this parish in 1831 where they remained for 7 years, and in 1828 came to the bar mouth where they still remain. From John Watson, James Dugan and Samuel Foreman.

Prevailing Names

The most prevailing names in this parish is Clarke, Cannings and Lees: Christian names John, James, William and Robert, the Clarkes indiscriminately, the Cannings along the mountain foot, the Lees indiscriminately.

Temperance Society

The temperance society at Articlave was established in 1831 through the instrumentality of

Archdeacon Monsell and held in the schoolhouse at Articlave.

Ferry Boats

There are 2 ferry boats at the bar mouth. The right of ferry belongs to the owner of the boat: charge for each passenger crossing the river 1d, paid to the owner of the boat, i.e. any person who may wish to put a boat on the river. Information obtained from James Dugan and Isaac Hazlett. 20 August 1835.

Faction Fight

About 35 years ago a fight took place on the Back Strand between the inhabitants of Magilligan and the inhabitants of Dunboe, the latter seeming to become the victors. The Magilligans got a reinforcement and beat those of Dunboe, no lives lost. The fight ended with a retaliation of the Dunboes upon the Magilligans by beating them coming from the markets of Coleraine. 31 July 1835.

Superstition

The Roman Catholics believe that while they have a St John's book suspended about their neck they can neither be drowned nor burned to death. From Isaac Hazlett.

Fair Sheets by Thomas Fagan, 22 October 1835

MEMOIR WRITING

Answers by Thomas Fagan to Queries

Queries relating to the parish of Dunboe, answered.

1. There are 6 2-storey houses in Articlave.

2. The ancient church of Dunboe is 65 feet 6 inches in length from out to out and 27 feet 9 inches in breadth from out to out.

3. There is no other house than the Glebe House known to be insured in the above parish.

4. The money collected at the Seceding meeting house of Dunboe is collected to defray expenses incurred by repairing and making improvements on the meeting house from time to time; also to pay up any debt <dept> due to a minister at the time of being changed. From that charge also to pay young clergymen giving weekly attendance in the absence of a stationed minister; also to defray the travelling expenses of the clergy

and elders of the congregation incurred by attending presbyteries and also to relieve poor distress[ed] persons, where the funds afford it. Informant William Watson, elder.

5. The Christian name and surname of the Archdeacon of Derry is Thomas Bewly Monsell.

6. Rules of the Articlave Reading Society is that any member of the society will get, on the first Friday of each month, any work or book he may choose, which work or book is to be returned to the library on the first Friday of the ensuing month. If not returned, in accordance with the rules of the society, there is a fine of 3d struck against the person so trespassing on the rules of the society, and for every such trespass he is fined 3d per month till the work or book is returned. If not returned at all, he forfeits the full value of the work or book. Information obtained from James Dugan, postmaster. [Signed] Thomas Fagan, 22 October 1835.

SOCIAL ECONOMY

Emigration in 1833

[J. Bleakly] List of persons who have emigrated from the parish of Dunboe during the year 1833. [List gives name, age, year in which emigrated, townland of residence, religion and port emigrated to].

Nancy Donahy, age 25, Presbyterian, from Articlave to St John's.

Frances McGauney, age 30, Established Church, from Articlave to St John's.

James McGauney, age 22, Established Church, from Articlave to St John's.

Mary Smith, age 22, Presbyterian, from Articlave to Quebec.

Robert Smith, age 4 months, Presbyterian, from Articlave to Quebec.

Cochran Coleman, age 18, Established Church, from Articlave to St John's.

Mary Coleman, age 30, Established Church, from Articlave to St John's.

Stephen Thorpe, age 18, Established Church, from Articlave to St John's.

William Paul, age 50, Presbyterian, from Articlave to St John's.

Sarah Paul, age 16, Presbyterian, from Articlave to St John's.

Elizabeth Paul, age 45, Presbyterian, from Articlave to St John's.

Alexander Broster, age 40, Presbyterian, from Knocktogher to Philadelphia.

Cochran Sterling, age 28, Presbyterian, from Knockmult to St John's.

Gilbert Smith, age 22, Presbyterian, from Bennarees to Quebec.

Elizabeth Smith, age 22, Presbyterian, from Bennarees to Quebec.

Robert Fulgrave, age 24, Presbyterian, from Fermoyle to St John's.

Ellen Black, age 22, Presbyterian, from Fermoyle to Quebec.

George Lestly, age 30, Presbyterian, from Bratwell to Philadelphia.

John Clarke, age 21, Presbyterian, from Bratwell to Quebec.

Nancy Clarke, age 30, Presbyterian, from Bratwell to Quebec.

Jane Clarke, age 2, Presbyterian, from Bratwell to Quebec.

Mary Ross, age 22, Presbyterian, from Sconce to Quebec.

Margret Ross, age 22, Presbyterian, from Sconce to Quebec.

Thomas Ross, age 36, Presbyterian, from Sconce to Quebec.

Jane Ross, age 24, Presbyterian, from Sconce to Quebec.

Robert Ross Jr, age 6, Presbyterian, from Sconce to Quebec.

Thomas Ross, age 4, Presbyterian, from Sconce to Quebec.

George McLaughlin, age [?] 23, Roman Catholic, from Mullan Head to Quebec.

William Smith, age 22, Presbyterian, from Fermullen to St John's.

William Deveny, age 20, Roman Catholic, from Farnlester to Quebec, returned 1834.

John Smith, age 22, Presbyterian, from Ballyhacket Glenahoy to Quebec.

Ellen Smith, age 32, Presbyterian, from Ballyhacket Glenahoy to Quebec.

John McLaughlin, age 1, Presbyterian, from Ballyhacket Glenahoy to Quebec.

James Blair Sr, age 26, Presbyterian, from Ballywildrake to Philadelphia.

Mary Blair, age 20, Presbyterian, from Ballywildrake to Philadelphia.

John Clarke, age 20, Presbyterian, from Ballywoodock to Philadelphia.

Thomas Broster, age 20, Presbyterian, from Glebe to Philadelphia.

Mary Broster, age 18, Presbyterian, from Glebe to Philadelphia.

Jane Broster, age 20, Presbyterian, from Glebe to Philadelphia.

Isaac McMullen, age 20, Presbyterian, from Ardina to Philadelphia.

Charles Hazlett, age 35, Presbyterian, from Bogtown to Philadelphia.

Emigration in 1834

List of persons who have emigrated from the parish of Dunboe during the year 1834.

Hugh Evans, age 20, Presbyterian, from Articlave to St John's.

John Beaty, age 28, Presbyterian, from Articlave to New York.

Robert Ray, age 18, Presbyterian, from Knocknogher to Philadelphia.

Margret Hindman, age 22, Presbyterian, from Killyveety to Quebec.

Charles Wilson, age 25, Presbyterian, from Pottagh to Philadelphia.

John Bond, age 32, Presbyterian, from Bratwell to Philadelphia.

Anne Bond, age 27, Presbyterian, from Bratwell to Philadelphia.

Mary Bond, age 5, Presbyterian, from Bratwell to Philadelphia.

Margret Bond, age 2 and a half, Presbyterian, from Bratwell to Philadelphia.

Barbara Bond, age 2, Presbyterian, from Bratwell to Philadelphia.

John McLaughlin, age 25, Roman Catholic, from Bellany to Philadelphia.

Jane Dunlop, age 23 and a half, Presbyterian, from Drumagully to New York.

Thomas Johnston, age 26, Presbyterian, from Drumagully to St John's.

Robert McClement, age 19, Presbyterian, from Drumagully to St John's.

William McLaughlin, age 29, Presbyterian, from Ballyhacket Glenahoy to Quebec.

Mary McLaughlin, age 25, Presbyterian, from Ballyhacket Glenahoy to Quebec.

James Blair, age 22, Presbyterian, from Ballywildrake to Philadelphia.

Isaac Wark, age 20, Presbyterian, from Ballywoodock to Philadelphia.

John Alexander, age 18, Presbyterian, from Ballywoodock to Philadelphia.

James Williams, age 18, Presbyterian, from Altibrian to New York.

Parish of Magilligan (Tamlaghtard), County Londonderry

Memoir by C.W. Ligar, July 1835, with sections by J. Bleakly

MEMOIR WRITING

Memoir Writing

Read and forwarded to Lieutenant Larcom, 8 September 1835 [signed] R.K. Dawson, Lieutenant Royal Engineers.

NATURAL FEATURES

Hills

The following are the highest points of land in the parish: Binevenagh <Benyevenagh> [insert note: name, see Toland's *Druids*; T's opinion, however, is not the received one [initialled] George Downes], 1,260 feet, Long hill, 1,119 feet, Tircreven grey rocks, 912 feet and Eagle rock, 694 feet above the level of the sea. All these points form part of one large mountain known generally under the name of Binevenagh, and rather less than the half of the extent of the parish is comprised of the north west extremity of it.

Binevenagh is the last of the basaltic range that stretches through the county. It presents a steep face to the west and south west and slopes very gradually in the opposite direction. The steep face is crowned by a high precipice, at the base of which the ground falls in steps or ridges parallel to the direction of the precipice, and descends 1,200 feet at the highest part in a distance of 1 mile. These ridges are much broken by small, conical hills and pointed rocks which give great variety to them and present a profile of striking beauty, adding considerably to the picturesque scenery of the country to the south. The line of precipice is also much cut up by small streams passing over it, particularly by one that separates the townlands of Lower Ballyleighry and Tircreven. Here the precipice disappears for a distance of half a mile and admits of a road passing to the summit of the mountain.

The remainder of the parish consists of a triangular plain, the sides of which are nearly equal and are bounded by the ocean, Lough Foyle and the base of Binevenagh <Benyevena>. The side formed by the ocean lies in a direction from south east to north west and is 5 miles long. The side formed by Lough Foyle lies in a direction nearly north to south and is 6 miles long. The side formed by the base of Benyevena lies in a direction from

south west to north east and is 6 and a half miles in length. This plain, which is now said to be losing ground, was evidently covered by the ocean at a remote period, and, at the base of Binevenagh, the former margin of the water can be distinctly traced. The following map will show the difference of the present and former boundary. [Plan of the parish of Magilligan, showing the present and former boundary of the sea. Memo: to complete on this plan the line of ancient coast through the parishes of Finlagan, Faughanvale and Clondermot. Scale of 1 inch to a mile. 16th July 1835].

Lakes and Rivers

There is no lake in the parish.

Rivers: before falling into Lough Foyle, the Roe divides this parish from Tamlaght Finlagan and Aghanloo for one and a half miles. Its direction for this short distance is from east to west, breadth when first connected with the parish 200 feet and at its mouth 700 feet. It is within the tideway for the whole distance, which rises at the mouth from 5 to 6 feet but is only navigable at high water to the Wooden bridge at Bellarena, a distance of 1 and five-sixth miles from its mouth, owing to the piers of the bridge having collected a quantity of sand. At the mouth there is a long island, 1,686 feet in length and 300 feet broad, on the north side of which there is a channel from 6 to 7 feet deep at high water. [Insert note: There was formerly a channel on the south side of the island but it has been closed up for the purpose of allowing cattle to graze on the island]. Beyond this island the water spreads over the mud beach which is 2 miles broad opposite the river. Conolly Gage Esquire has 2 flat-bottomed boats, each of which will carry 14 tons for the purpose of bringing in shells and mud, the latter is locally called glar from Lough Foyle, for manure. These 2 flat-bottomed boats, a fishing and a pleasure boat of Mr Gage's are the only boats on the river. The following will show the state of the water at Bellarena bridge: distance between the bed of the river and the underneath part of the roadway of the bridge is 9 feet; depth of water at low water 6 inches; depth of water at high water 2 foot 6 inches. Floods in the river cause the depth to be much greater: in this case it is from 5 to 6 feet in depth. The Roe in its course through the parish does not overflow its banks.

There are several small streams in the parish. The most important is one which takes its rise on the summit of Binevenagh and at its base falls into the Big Drain between the townlands of Lower Ballyleighry and Tircreven. The high grounds in the parish are supplied with numerous and excellent springs which gush out from the mountain. The lowlands are also abundantly supplied with water from wells.

[Insert addition: the Roe was formerly remarkable for the quantity and size of the fish which were taken in it. Salmon were caught with the leister, weighing from 30 to 40 lbs each. The river was rented from the Right Honourable Sir Thomas Conolly for a number of years by Thomas Smith Esquire, provost of Newtownlimavady, secondly by Edward Ross of Mulkeeragh and lastly Doctor Gillespie. During their tenures there were regular water-keepers employed, and salmon were so abundant as to sell in Newtownlimavady for 1d ha'penny per lb and trout also at an equally moderate price. About the year 1793, the landed proprietors along the Roe discovered that Mr Phillips, when dividing the county, omitted inserting in any of the company's books the River Roe, consequently any tenures given of it by the Conolly family or any others was invalid. The landed proprietors entered a lawsuit, the result of which was that each landholder along the river is at liberty to fish opposite his own land and the public are only subject to the penalty of trespassing].

Bogs

There is a large extent of bog in the mountain part of the parish, which is from 1,100 to 700 feet above the level of the sea. In some parts it is 10 feet deep, but generally it varies from 2 to 5 feet in depth. The only imbedded timber found in it are the roots of fir. The substratum is clay and rock. The bog in the lowlands has been either cut away or reclaimed. It varied from 2 to 10 feet in depth. There have been yew and oak trees found in it which were lying generally with their tops pointing to the east. No fir has been found in the bogs of the low ground.

Woods

From the timber which has been found imbedded in the bogs and the small patches of a stunted growth in the townlands of Woodtown, Umbra,

Duncrum, Tamlaght and Milltown along the steep face of Benyevenagh, it is evident that this parish was formerly well clothed with wood.

The ornamental planting of Bellarena demesne and the planting on the face of Binevenagh are at present the only extensive planting in the parish. The latter is in the townlands of Tamlaght and Milltown where, under the enterprising exertions of Conolly Gage Esquire, this steep and otherwise useless land has been converted into a flourishing wood. It consists of 60 acres, Cunningham measure, and has been planted at 2 different periods. The first, consisting of 15 acres, was planted in 1818 and in the 17 years which have elapsed, some of the trees have attained a height of 40 feet. The other part which consists of the remaining 45 acres was commenced in 1831, at which time 200,000 trees were planted, and since that time 100,000 have been also planted to replace those that had died and to fill some parts which had before been left vacant. The planting consists of all kinds of forest trees, but the principal number are oak, ash and larch. The larch bears the greatest proportion and has been interspersed among the oak and ash so that it may be cut out to give the other sufficient space when about 10 years old, at which time each larch fir will sell for 1s. As the planting is on the side of the mountain facing the west, it is exposed to the north, south and west winds and protected only from the east. It extends from 200 to 480 feet above the level of the sea and although thus exposed, the trees are doing extremely well, contrary to the generally conceived opinions on this subject.

Coast

This parish is bounded on the north east by the ocean and on the north west by Lough Foyle. These 2 sides form a point called Magilligan Point, which is the east side of the entrance to Lough Foyle, and from it there is a ferry to the opposite coast of Inishowen <Ennishowen>. Both beaches are of sand, and carriages can with safety pass along them between the high and low water marks. The breadth of the beach between the high and low water mark on the side next the ocean averages 200 yards, but the Lough Foyle side has a beach averaging 2 miles in breadth between the high and low water.

Climate

The air of this parish is considered to be very healthy. The following are the different periods at which the various crops are generally sown and ripen. The time at which the various crops are generally put down and become ripe in the low ground of the parish of Magilligan: wheat put down from 1st October, ripe from 15th August; barley put down from 1st April, ripe from 12th August; oats put down from 1st March, ripe from 15th August; flax put down from 15th August, ripe from 1st August; potatoes put down from 15th April, ripe from 1st October; clover and hay seed put down from 1st April, ripe from 20th May, cut down for green feeding; turnips put down from 12th June, ripe from 1st November, given to cattle; field peas put down from 1st March, ripe from 15th August; vetches put down from 1st March, ripe from 1st July, cut for green feeding; rye put down from 1st February, ripe from 15th August.

In the mountain part of the parish, the crops are from 12 to 28 days later than in the low grounds.

Letter on Natural History

[Insert note: See the *Anthologia <Anterlogia> Hibernica* for a copy of this letter. This copy has been procured from the Rev. Samuel Butler, Presbyterian minister of the parish of Magilligan].

[J. Bleakly] Extract from the Statistical Report of the Rev. Robert Innes, curate of Magilligan, to the Lord Bishop of Derry (Nicholson), dated 2nd June 1725.

"To the Right Rev. Dr William Nicholson, Lord Bishop of Derry.

My Lord,

In obedience to your lordship's commands, I have made the best inquiry I could of anything singular hereabouts. Did I understand botany, I believe this parish could afford as good a collection of herbs as any one place in the three kingdoms. In a word it is the *physic garden for the Irish doctors both far and near*.

That this land was formerly sea there is sufficient reason to believe, for along at the foot of the mountain and all the coast is the old bank to be shown and [over] which the sea hath formerly flowed, at the foot of which everywhere is sea, sand and shells to be dug up; and the Giant's Grave, another curiosity in this place, proves it. It is a mile and a half long: one limb of him lies at Ball'spoint, at the mouth of the River Roe, passes by Mr Gage's house and under my house (the Glebe House) and along the highway a quarter of a mile farther. It is a ridge of stones, such as the sea throws upon beaches mixed with sand and sea-shells. Besides, near my house, a mile from the sea at the foot of the grave, is the quicksand raised

at the second spade, and at the digging seems to be a small skull but when some days in the air, turns to dust. The other limb of the giant the Irish fables make lost in the battle, but of late they have discovered some more of him inside Ballycastle orchard, 2 miles from the sea up the River Roe, and another bank of shells a mile further up at Strieve near the road from Newtown to Coleraine <Colerane>.

As to Magilligan, it is so far from gaining that it bears no proportion to the land that has been, and it is every year losing on Lough Foyle side. *There are men alive who know the land to have lost above 100 yards*, and if we can make anything of Irish fables, the flats of Lough Foyle which extend in some places a full league have been formerly a part of this land.

There is a rock on the side of the mountain called *The Poor Woman* (in Irish *Calliagh Veerbogth*) which tells us that when she was a maid, the place where she stands was corn ground and Lough Foyle so narrow that a lamb could skip from Magilligan Point to Greencastle, which is now near 2 sea miles distant, and the fairy that lived on the Ton <Tuns> banks which lie at the mouth of Lough Foyle (mostly formed, I believe, of what was borne away from the shore), having a carpet stolen from her by one of this parish, cursed it and threatened that every year the breadth of the carpet should be swept away." From Rev. Samuel Butler. 17th June 1835.

MODERN TOPOGRAPHY OR ARTIFICIAL STATE

Towns

[C.W. Ligar] There is no town or village in the parish.

Public Buildings

The parish church, the Presbyterian meeting house, the Roman Catholic chapel and the Martello tower are the public buildings in this parish.

Parish Church

The parish church is situated on the west side of the high road leading from Newtownlimavady to the shore and Downhill. It measures 72 feet by 30 on the outside, was built in 1787 at the supposed cost of 700 pounds, 150 pounds of which was raised off the parish and the remainder by subscription. It is furnished with 11 single and 3 double pews each 9 feet long, which will accommodate 100 persons, allowing 6 to each pew. It is supplied with a good bell and belfry and is strong and well built.

Presbyterian Meeting House

The Presbyterian meeting house is situated in the townland of Margymonaghan, on the west side of the lower road leading from Newtownlimavady to the shore and Downhill. It was erected in 1803 and cost 205 pounds. The principal contributors were Sir Hervey Bruce Bart and Marcus Gage Esquire. The latter also gave 1 rood of ground on which the building stands. [Insert note by J. Bleakly: William Allison Esquire, M.D. also gave 60 pounds towards the pews in the Presbyterian meeting house in the parish of Magilligan]. It measures on the outside 52 feet by 25, is lighted by 5 windows on one side and one in the end and is furnished with 34 pews and allowing 6 to each, it would accommodate 204 persons.

Roman Catholic Chapel

Situated in the townland of Tamlaght, in the immediate vicinity of the old parish church; was built by subscription in 1826; the sum at present expended is 575 pounds. Many persons of the Established Church and Presbyterians contributed towards its erection. It is of a rectangular form, 70 feet by 30 (measured on the inside) with a projection behind the altar of 10 feet 4 inches by 15 feet 8 inches (measured in the interior). The building lies in a direction from south west to north east, and the altar, which is of large dimensions, is in the centre of the south east side. From the want of funds, it has not yet been finished in the interior. There are no pews. Forms supply the deficiency and a beam has been left at each extremity for the purpose of erecting galleries at some future time. The inside is not painted or ceiled, but as far as the work has been carried, it is substantial and well finished. The walls are 2 feet thick and built of basalt. There are 5 Gothic windows in the south east and 2 doors on the opposite side. On the north east gable is a stone cross, underneath which, on a stone tablet, is the following inscription: "To the true and living God, AD 1826."

Martello Tower

At the point of Magilligan at the entrance to Lough Foyle, there is a Martello tower which was commenced in 1812 and finished in 1817. It is of a circular form, 166 feet 10 inches in circumference measured above the basement, which is sunk 16 feet deep. The walls are 11 feet thick above and 13 below the basement, of cut freestone from the quarries in Ballyharrigan in the parish of Bovevagh. It mounts one gun, which turns on a pivot and can be presented to any quarter. In the centre of the tower there is an excellent spring.

Gentlemen's Seats

Bellarena, the residence of Conolly Gage Esquire, is pleasantly situated on the side of the River Roe at one mile above its junction with Lough Foyle. The present dwelling house has been erected at 2 different periods: one part being built in 1797 and the other in 1822. The demense is kept in the most exact order and with great taste. The garden and orchard consists of 2 acres and is in the highest state of cultivation, and abounds with all kinds of fruits and flowers with extensive hothouses for grapes. The bold rock of Binevenagh in the immediate vicinity is seen with much effect through the vistas formed by the planting of the demesne.

Glebe House, the residence of the Rev. John Graham, rector: on the glebe is a substantial house and offices built about the year 1774 by the Rev. Alexander Skipton [insert marginal note: exact date not known]. There is no charge on it. It is unpleasantly situated between the High and Low Roads which traverse the parish and branch off near it, being only 150 yards asunder at the point where the house is built. Although commanding a beautiful view of Binevenagh mountain, does not itself add anything to the surrounding scenery from the want of ornamental planting. It is used as a landmark by vessels passing to and from Derry through Lough Foyle.

There are also several other good but small houses in the parish, the most important of which is Castle Lecky, the residence of Mrs Lecky. It is situated near the junction of the upper and lower roads on the east side of the former. Its situation at the base of Binevenagh is retired and commands a fine view of the flat grounds of the parish, the sea, Lough Foyle and the Inishowen mountains.

Cottages in Umbra Townland

At the Umbra, a townland at the foot of the precipice of Binevenagh, there are 3 small cottages built by the late Dr Tyler and the Messrs Moody and Cather of Newtownlimavady, whose families occasionally reside there in summer for the benefit of sea bathing.

Corn Mills

There are 3 corn and 1 flax mill in this parish.

Bellarena corn mill: the water wheel of this mill is 15 feet 4 inches in diameter and 4 and a half feet broad. It works 2 pair of stones, each 4 feet 10 inches in diameter and can grind and shell 5 cwt of oatmeal per hour. It can work all seasons of the year, the water being collected from 11 springs in the parish and reserved in a large pond 200 yards long and 50 broad. At 100 yards from the mill is a good kiln with a metal head. Conolly Gage Esquire is the proprietor of this mill and he holds it in his own hands. It was established in 1806.

Ballycarton corn mill: this mill is supplied from a spring on the mearing between this parish and Aghanloo called Tubberduell. It has one pair of stones and is worked by a breast wheel 13 and a half feet in diameter and 2 feet 4 inches broad. The cog wheel is 8 feet 10 inches in diameter with metal segments screwed into a wooden rim. The stones are 4 feet 9 inches in diameter and can grind 2 and a half cwt per hour. A kiln with a metal head is under the same roof and the grain is conveyed from the kiln to the mill by means of a trough. The greater part of the inhabitants of the parish of Aghanloo bring their corn to this mill. It can work at all seasons of the year. Mr Benjamin Lane is the proprietor.

Craig corn mill is situated in the townland of Craig, on the high road in the immediate vicinity of Castle Lecky. It is on the estate of Sir James Bruce Bart and is held by Edward McCoristin. But little corn is ground at this mill, as most of it is now sold at the markets. It is wrought by a breast wheel 14 feet in diameter and 2 feet broad, with a fall of water of 16 feet. It has one pair of stones which are 4 feet 10 inches in diameter. From the want of work and water, this mill is idle during part of the summer. With a sufficient supply of water it can grind 2 barrels per hour. The water which supplies this mill is procured from springs in the mountain, the principal one of which is in the townland of Craig.

Duncrun Flax Mill and Bleach Green

Duncrun flax mill is wrought by a breast wheel 15 feet in diameter and 2 feet 4 inches broad and is supplied by a small stream proceeding from 2 springs, one called Tubbernaleck in the townland of Ballyleighry and the other called the Big Well in the townland of Duncrun. The supply of water enables the mill to work at all seasons of the year. It was established in 1821. There are 4 stocks (that is, 4 men can work at the same time) with 6 handles or scutches to each stock. It can scutch 10 score of flax in a day, of 20 lbs to the score. The head proprietor of the farm in which the mill is situated is Conolly Gage.

Duncrun flax mill occupies the site of one of the houses which formerly belonged to a bleach green which has ceased to work for 69 years. Nothing now remains of it but the engine house, furnace house, the wash mill and the broughan or eating house.

Communications

From the secluded situation of this parish, it is not the medium of direct communication between any 2 towns. It is, however, well supplied with accommodation roads. The principal of these is a road called the Low Road, which extends through the parish from south west to north east to the sea shore. It carries on the 2 roads on either side of the River Roe after their junction, by means of the wooden bridge at Bellarena. It was made about 40 years ago and is kept in repair by the county for the accommodation of the parishioners. After it reaches the sea the communication is extended to the east to Downhill, the residence of Sir James Bruce Bart, distant 2 and a quarter miles, by means of a sandy beach which is firm and hard close to the edge of the water, where the sand is kept wet by the waves. This beach is safe and passable at all times except in high tides in winter, at which season the water comes too near the precipice which extends along it for the distance of one mile from Downhill. [Blank] miles of the Low Road from the Wooden bridge to sea shore is in this parish. It is 21 feet broad clear of fences and drains.

At one-eighth of a mile from the Wooden bridge at Bellarena, a road called the High Road branches from the Low Road and joins it again in the north part of the parish at one and one-eighth miles from the sea. This is the ancient road of the parish. It is very hilly and was impassable except for slide cars and horses until about 60 years ago, when it was for the first time gravelled and made broader at the expense of the county. It is not used except for foot passengers and persons residing along it.

The Bishop's Road

In the mountain part of the parish there are portions of 2 roads made at the expense of the late Lord Bristol, Bishop of Derry, intended as a communication between Downhill, at that time his residence, and Newtownlimavady. One of these roads is called the Bishop's Road and was made about 52 years ago. One mile and a quarter of it is within the boundary of the parish, but since his death it has been allowed to go out of repair. The other is more direct than the former and was made after it. That part on the summit of the mountain was never completed and is impassable. The county keep these roads in repair into the mountain only as far as is necessary to the procuring of turf. Half a mile of the Black Road is within this parish.

Bridges

At Bellarena there is a bridge over the River Roe (the only one between the Newtown bridge and the mouth of the river) called the Wooden bridge, which divides this parish from Tamlaght Finlagan. Its length across the river is 189 and a half feet and breadth 16 and a half feet. The roadway is of wood stretched across stone piers, forming 6 openings or arches. The money for building it was advanced by the late Marcus Gage Esquire and cost 500 guineas, 300 pounds of which was repaid by the county, who keep it in repair, and the remainder was given by him. It was commenced in May 1799, the former bridge having been carried away by a quantity of ice coming down the river in the previous winter. The bridge thus swept away was

Doorway of old church

built by Thomas Mitchell in 1798 and cost the county 300 pounds. It was formed by piles driven into river, over which were laid beams of wood, and the whole was covered by branches of trees and grass sods. Before this, there was no bridge at this part of the River Roe.

There are several good but small stone bridges over the streams and drains, made and kept in repair at the expense of the county. Amongst the most important of them is the bridge over the Big Drain on the Low Road and the bridge at Duncrun near the wall of the church, over a small stream. Both of these are of the same dimensions and consist of a single arch 12 feet in span and 19 feet broad across the roadway.

Ferry at Magilligan Point

There are 2 boats employed at this ferry, a large one for conveying cattle and a small one for passengers. Sir Arthur Chichester, the proprietor of Greencastle, to whom the boats belong receives part of the produce of the ferry: one half being received by him and the other going to the boatmen. Cattle, goods and passengers are boated over at all seasons of the year at the following prices: 6d for a person of respectable appearance, 3d for a poor person, 1s 8d for a cow or horse, 3d for a sheep or pig, 6d for a sack of potatoes containing 5 bushels.

ANCIENT TOPOGRAPHY

Ecclesiastical: Old Parish Church

Under this head the old church of the parish in the townland of Tamlaght, Screen old church and the abbey of Duncrun will have to be classed.

The old parish church is situated in the townland of Tamlaght. It measures 55 feet long (on the inside) and the breadth inside varies from 14 feet 8 inches to 15 feet 2 inches. The breadth of the wall of the west gable is 3 feet 6 inches and the other gable and 2 side walls are each 3 feet thick. It was erected by William Gage Esquire shortly after the Restoration in 1660. It is not known at whose expense, but as Mr Gage was at that time the bishop's agent and these lands being a part of the estate of the see, it is probable that it was defrayed by the bishop. It occupies the same site and was built out of the ruins of the former church which was burnt by Phelimy Roe O'Neill in 1642. After the new church was built in a more central part of the parish and divine service transferred to it, the Roman Catholics made use of this church up to the time of the erection of their new chapel.

The following is a plan showing the remains of the church which was burnt and the one which was built out of its ruins: [ground plan with annotations showing where there are indistinct traces of a foundation; foundation of the church burnt by Sir Phelimy Roe O'Neill in 1642, window and buttress; dimensions inside 55 feet long, widths 14 feet 8 inches, 14 feet 9 inches and 15 feet 2 inches wide, wall thickness 3 feet and 3 feet 6 inches, width of east end outside 22 feet 10 inches]. The parts shaded with crossed line are the remains of the church which was burnt by Sir Phelim Roe O'Neill in 1642. The part shaded with single lines is the church built by William Gage Esquire.

Antiquities connected with Old Church

AD 635, Aidan, an Irishman educated at Iona, went from that island to Northumberland at the request of King Oswald. He died in 651 from grief at the murder of King Oswald by his subjects. His 4 immediate successors in the see of Lindisfarne <Landisfarne> were Irishmen, educated in Iona. Their names were Cellach, Finton, Dima and Colman. 13 years after the death of Aiden in 664, St Colman, the last of these four, resigned his see and returned to Ireland, bringing with him the bones of his predecessor Aiden. The cause of leaving his see was a controversy with the son of the late King Oswald as to the proper time of observing the feast of Easter. This quarrel and also the act of transferring the bones is recorded in Bede's <Bead's> *Ecclesiastical History*, but does not mention where the bones were deposited. There is in this parish a tradition that they were deposited outside the eastern window of the old church in the townland of Tamlaght. The grave is covered with hewn stones.

There is near the grave a well called Tubber Aspug Aidan which means "the well of Bishop Aidan"; and also a natural formation of rock on a hill above the church called Aidan's Pulpit, from which a person might preach to a great multitude of persons.

[Drawing of grave and windows of church, with dimensions of individual stones in wall: 1 foot 6 inches, 1 foot 4 inches. Inscription on separate tombstone: "Here lies the body of Patrick Canning of Aughtymore, who departed this life March the fifth 1812, aged 57 years"].

View showing the grave of Bishop Aidan on the outside of east window of the old church of Magilligan in the townland of Tamlaght, and also the character of the architecture of the building.

Height of the window 10 feet (from A to A), breadth of window 1 foot 6 inches, length of Bishop Aidan's grave 9 feet, height of grave 2 feet 4 inches. [Signed] Charles W. Ligar, 19th June 1835.

[Drawing of door of the old church, showing part of interior with benches, height 6 feet 3 inches, breadth 3 feet].

[Drawing of Magilligan or Tamlaght old church, showing the east gable and Bishop Aidan's pulpit in the distance].

List of Rectors

List of rectors of the parish of Magilligan since the Reformation: 1630 John Mayor M.A.; 1635 [blank] Holland M.A.; 1666 Jonathan Edwards D.D.; 1672, May 21, Richard Griffith; 1675, December 30, James Webster; 1694 James Graffan; 1703 John Leather M.A.; 1750 Benjamin Bacon A.M.; 1770, April 2nd, Alexander Skipton; 1782, April 2nd, Robert Graham; 1784, April 1, Harrison Balfour; 1797, June 5, John Torrens; 1803, May 28th, David Christie; 1817, October 9th, William Knox; 1821, September 22nd, Arthur William Pomeroy; 1824, April 27th, John Graham.

Plantation History

1615, November 9th: precepts were issued by the Irish Society to the 12 companies, for certificates of their works and operations in regard to their plantations, the several proportions of which they had engaged to secure by a stipulated number of Protestant settlers upon each of them, in order that the society might be able to give an account thereof to government when they should be ordered to do so, which they hourly expected. The companies made the required returns. The Irish Society at this time ordered each of the London companies to send 1 or 2 artisans with their families into Ulster to settle there, and directions also were given that the city of Londonderry should not for the future be inhabited by Irish (meaning members of the Church of Rome); that 12 of Christ's Hospital and other poor children should be sent there as apprentices and servants; and that the inhabitants should be prohibited from taking Irish (Popish) apprentices. Directions also were given to the companies to repair the churches on each of their proportions and to furnish each of the ministers with a Bible, Common Prayer Book and a communion cup. The following represents a communion cup which is supposed to have been given to this parish. Communion cup: the following is the inscription round the cup: "A communion cup for ye parish of Tamlaght and alias Ard Magilligan [drawing of cup and lid, with dimensions: 4 and a quarter inches diameter of lid, 8 and a half inches high].

Skreen Old Church

This old church is situated in the townland of Craig, on the east side of the road leading from Newtownlimavady to the shore and to Downhill. It measures inside the walls 48 feet by 21 feet. The walls are nearly level with the ground and the whole is grown over with blackthorn and briars. It was formerly used used as a chapel of ease to this part of the parish, as will be seen from the following extract from the visitation book of the Diocese of Derry for the year 1718.

"Tamlaght Ard: Johannes Leathes [Leather] M.A., rector, Robert Innes, curatus, Michael Haynes, clericus paroch. Hugo McLauglin, ludimagister, Johannus Cust and Jacob D[remainder blank], churchwardens, John Caen and William Granaghan, sidesmen. This parish is divided by a great bog, so that some of the inhabitants cannot come to church in winter without travelling 6 miles. Hereupon Bishop King with the rector and parishioners repaired an old chapel farther distant from the church, where the incumbent is obliged sometimes to officiate, the benefice being too small to support him and a curate."

The century which has elapsed since this record was made, has made a material alteration and improvement. The great bog has been intersected with roads and converted into arable lands. The church has been built in a central part of the parish and a glebe and house have been provided for the incumbent.

Duncrun Abbey

The ruins of the abbey of Duncrun is situated on the west side of the high road through this parish, on a small hill on the west side of which is a steep bank that was evidently the former boundary of Lough Foyle, whose waters have retired to a distance of 1 and three-quarter miles. All that now remains of the abbey are the foundations of what is said to be the chapel, and the traces of the burial ground. The former give the dimensions of the chapel to have been 35 feet long and 19 broad and the thickness of the wall 4 feet. The burial ground is immediately adjoining it on the south side. There is at present lying in the interior of the building a stone on which there is a well defined cross, and also a separate drawing of the stone

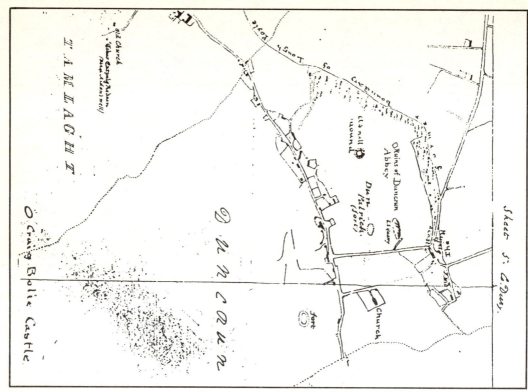

Duncrun and neighbourhood

with the cross on it. The founder of this abbey was O'Cahan (as is recorded by Archdall in his *Monasticon Hibernicum*). He also endowed it with the whole of the lands of the surrounding tract of country called Ard Magilleogan, opposite the barony of Inishowen, then called Kinfleogan. This abbey was called the throne of St Columba and in time became one of the richest in Ulster. [Insert marginal note: In the year 1203 it was plundered by Diarmitt Hua Lochluinn who, at the head of a party of foreigners, attempted to plunder Inishowen, but the lords of the country perceiving them, Diarmitt was killed with many of his party. Archdall's Monasticon].

About 100 yards south of the ruins of the abbey is a small mound apparently artificial, of a conical form with a base of 70 feet and an elevation of 30 feet. See plan and section.

[Plan of ruins of Duncrun abbey and remains of burying ground showing modern fence, remains of the wall of the graveyard with section drawing, scale 40 feet to an inch].

[Drawing of grave stone engraved with a double cross]. The stone which is at present lying inside the ruins of Duncrun abbey. It stood formerly in the fence outside of the ruins. 18th June 1835.

[Plan and section drawing of a small artificial mound about 100 yards south of Duncrun abbey, 30 feet high, scale 40 feet to an inch].

Holy Well: Tubberdonagh Spring

In the townland of Gortmore there is a well called Tubberdonagh, "Sunday Well", from the people resorting to it on Sunday to perform stations. It is said that the primitive form of baptism was also performed at this well.

Military Topography: Castle in Duncrun

The remains of an old building said to be a castle exists in the townland of Duncrun. The cellar with the steps leading down to it was destroyed and obliterated about 20 years ago. Some barley hulls were found which appeared to have been discoloured by fire, and some water-worn stones which had been used as weight and had been lettered indicating their weight. See drawing of one of these, weighing 14 lbs. A small part of the walls of this castle is all that can at present [be] seen. See accompanying plan taken from the Ordnance maps showing the position of the castle with respect to the surrounding country. [Plan of

Duncrun and area showing buildings, mounds and other antiquities].

[Drawing of] a stone weight found in the remains of a castle in the townland of Duncrun in the holding of John McLaughlin, weighing 14 lbs, length 11 inches, breadth 4 inches, thickness 4 inches.

Witch Hill

In the townland of Gortmore, at the foot of the precipice, is a small, oval-shaped hill of natural formation rising to the height of 25 feet, with a base 160 feet long and 40 feet broad. This hill is termed by the local inhabitants the Witch hill. On its summit is a large stone which it is said was formerly supported by 4 others in the manner of a table. This cromlech <cromleach>, for such it appears from this to have been, was destroyed by persons digging underneath it for supposed treasures. The cavity thus made is at present existing and in it the large stone is now lying.

[The Witch hill, townland of Gortmore [ground plan showing area and stones scattered for which dimensions are supplied in a key, and section drawing showing hole made by treasure seekers 5 feet high; scale of 40 feet to an inch; key to stones: A, length 5 feet 6 inches breadth 2 feet depth 4 feet; B, 3 feet by 2 feet 6 inches by 1 foot 6 inches; C, 4 feet 6 inches by 3 feet by 2 feet; D, 2 feet 9 inches by 1 foot 6 inches by 1 foot 6 inches; E, 4 feet by 3 feet by 2 feet 6 inches; F, 2 feet 6 inches by 2 feet 6 inches by 1 foot 6 inches; G, 1 foot 6 inches by 6 inches by 9 inches; H, 3 feet 6 inches by 1 foot 6 inches; I, 4 feet by 2 feet by 2 feet 6 inches. This stone is said to have been thrown up the hill by an earthquake].

Forts: Craigbolie Castle

The following are forts or raths which are to be found in this parish: Craigbolie Castle, Tamlaght Fort, 2 forts in the townland of Duncrun and Ballycarton Fort.

The first and most important is Craigbolie Castle, which has been described and drawings made of it and forwarded to Dublin in December 1833.

[Insert addition: Craigbolie Castle, or Dun Crutheni, situated in the townland of Tamlaght: this fort is admirably situated for defence and ranks among the strongest in the county. It is situated about 200 yards from the bottom of the precipice of Binevenagh <Bennyevena>, which would have saved it from attack in that direction before the invention of gunpowder. It occupies

the top of a steep and rocky eminence, the slope of which to the country opposite the precipice is exceeding steep but smooth and regular. There is also a slope back towards the precipice but which though steep is not more than 30 feet. It will be seen therefore that it is well defended by nature both in front and rear, and as the 2 sides are protected by additional parapets the approach in both those directions being along the top of the narrow tops of small hills, that on which the fort stands itself forming one of the same chain. The other particulars will be shown by the drawing. The breadth of the parapets is about 7 feet at base, decreasing towards the top to almost a point. They are built of stones intermixed with earth, but the facing of them is completed with stones. After a minute examination of the different and especially of the lower parts, I can find no traces whatever of the action of fire on them.

This fort is not only in itself strong, but there are 2 others which from their style of architecture and materials would lead to the supposition that they were built about the same time and were outposts to it. One is situated immediately below and about 200 yards from it. The other is situated to the north west and is distant [blank] yards, both enjoying a much less commanding position. The former is scarcely elevated above the slope on which it is and is only defended by a single parapet which is, as I said before, of the same materials as the large one. Its figure is also the same, being of an oval form. Like the larger, it has also in the centre a circle of a single row of stones, but as these are not very connected, it is hard to say whether they are or are not the foundation of a superstructure, but I should scarcely think they were. The other, though not exactly the same shape, is built of the same materials. It is called Duncrun Fort and is situated immediately above the parish church of Magilligan. I send a sketch of both these forts with some few particulars respecting them and shall confine myself in this paper more to the principal fort.

The circle in the centre, <of> which [is] called by Lieutenant Larcom the keep, is composed only of a single row of stones the whole way round, and from it, I should scarcely think possible to raise the wall to any height. Besides, they are not good square stones which would in such a case have been used but are of various sizes and very irregular. A reason also to support the opinion of their not serving as a foundation for a wall of any height is that the present stones are not above half buried by the sod and earth, and there are none others beneath them. A medium size for all the stones is

13 inches by 16 inches by 12 inches. In the centre of this circle there is a oblong space 3 feet 2 inches long and 2 feet broad, and has the appearance of having served as hearths for a fire, the stones which now remain serving to keep the ashes and fuel together. In removing digging down below the fireplace, the earth for the first foot was impregnated a good deal with fine charcoal in a powder, and there were also other hard lumps turned up and resembled the common furze branches. The earth, to the depth of 2 feet, appeared as if it had been before removed, but at the depth of 3 feet it assumed its natural appearance and I went no farther. In digging between 2 of the parapets at the southern end I also discovered a quantity of charcoal. I send a drawing of this hearth and a section also of the keep. [Signed] Charles W. Ligar, Ballymoney, 25 February 1834].

[View of] Craigbolie Fort and the rock of Binevenagh by J. Stokes.

Other Forts

Tamlaght Fort, which is situated at the base of the hill on which Craigbolie Castle stands, and also one of the forts in Duncrun, have been likewise described and drawn in connection with Craigbolie and forwarded to Dublin.

The other fort in the townland of Duncrun is called Dun Patrick. It is of an oval shape, measures 120 feet by 68, and the following drawing represents the hill on which it is situated. The parapets have been altogether removed and no traces of them are now to be seen.

Dun Patrick Fort, townland of Duncrun, near the ruins of the abbey [plan and section drawing giving heights of 40 feet and 10 feet with scale 80 feet to an inch].

Ballycarton Fort is formed entirely of earth, of a circular form, 112 feet in diameter. The parapet is 6 feet higher than the trench and the interior is covered with a growth of thorn and hazel. It is situated in the townland of Ballycarton, at the base of a hill called Dowland hill and 300 yards north east of the corn mill on the edge of the stream leading to the mill.

Caves

Under the house occupied by Matthew Cunningham in the townland of Gortmore is a cove or cave which is reported to extend 200 yards under the house and the adjoining field. Attempts have been made to explore it, but the candles went out from the damp and those who went in could not succeed in the dark.

In the townland of Duncrun, in the precipice of Binevenagh, there are 2 cavities in the rock: one of them is at the base of the precipice and is artificial. It is of an oval form and measures 15 feet by 12 and 6 feet high. The entrance is 3 feet high and 2 broad, but from the accumulation of earth at the entrance, it might probably [have] been higher than it is at the present time. The other is situated at a short distance north of the former and is of natural formation. It is at a height of 30 feet above the foot of the precipice, and the only way to it is by climbing up the perpendicular face of the rock, which is very difficult. It extends 18 feet into the rock, is 9 feet broad and with an entrance equal in height to the interior of the cavity.

[Ground plans and section drawings of caves]. Both of these caves are in the townland of Duncrun. Plan of the cave at the base of Benyevenagh precipice, which appears to be artificial [dimensions 12 feet wide and 15 feet long to the mouth of cave, 6 feet high, entrance 3 feet high 2 feet broad]; and plan of natural cave at about 30 feet above the base of the precipice of Binevenagh [dimensions 9 feet wide and 18 feet long, entrance 8 feet high, scale 2 feet to 1 inch].

Discovery of Human Bones

In the townland of Minearny and Lower Doaghs there are 2 sand-hills, one in each townland called the Bony hills. When the wind blows the sand off these hills, or the rabbits remove it, human bones become visible and soon turn into dust when exposed to the air. These bones are supposed to be the remains of the men who were killed in 1642 under the following circumstances.

Copy of part of a letter written by an officer of Lagan forces in 1642, published in James S. Reid's D.D., *History of the Presbyterian Church*, printed in Edinburgh in 1834: "From Strabane we marched up on the O'Cahan's country on the other side of Lough Foyle, and coming over against Derry, 4 companies of the Derry [forces] joined with us to relieve Lymavady Castle and Ballycastle, which had been 10 weeks before strongly beleaguered by great forces; and yet had sallied forth and killed many hundreds of the enemy, being commanded by a resolute young gentleman, Captain Thomas Philips, being gone about with 3 boats to bring provisions from Derry. That night we were welcome guests to the 2 castles who despaired of all succour. Next morning we advanced our march into the enemy's country, where at Magilligan we encountered the enemy: the O'Cahans, the Magilligans, the

O'Hagans and the O'Neals. We killed upwards of 500 of them and scattered the rest."

Coins

The following are coins found in the parish of Magilligan: [illustration of 2 faces of a coin].

Extract of Will

Extract of the will of Dame Blanch Bagnall, in the registry office of Londonderry, dated on the ninth day of February 1642, about 4 months after the massacre of the Protestants of Ireland commenced. "I, Dame Blanch Bagnall, of the city of Londonderry, being sick of body but, thanks be to God, of whole mind, do make my last will and testament in manner and form following, that is to say: first I bequeath my soul to Almighty God, my maker and redeemer in whose only merits, death and passion hope to be saved; and my body to Christian burial in some convenient part within the cathedral church of St Columb's in said city of Londonderry. Item, I give and bequeath unto the poor, robbed and distressed people of the parish of Tamlaghtard the sum of six pounds sterling, to be distributed among them by the religious care of my beloved son-in-law William Townham [Downham ?] Esquire and John Major, clerk, within half a year next after my decease." This was proved to have been the last will and testament of the aforesaid Lady Bagnall on the 1st of April 1642, by the oath of John Major and T. Baxter.

Modern Topography

General Appearance and Scenery

The general appearance and scenery of the parish of Magilligan has an air of retirement and seclusion peculiarly pleasing, and offers a striking contrast between the well cultivated plain and the bold headland of Binevenagh. The Inishowen mountains and Lough Foyle are seen from all parts of the parish with much effect, and near the Umbra the scene receives new features in the ocean and sand-hills of the rabbit warren.

Memoir Writing

Queries and Answers on Social and Productive Economy

[Answers by C.W. Ligar]

What coal is used? Answer: the principal fuel used in this parish is turf. A small quantity of coal is, however, used by the gentleman in the parish. Indications of coal have been found in the north-ern and southern parts of the parish, but has not been considered of sufficient importance to induce persons to dig for it.

Is there any illicit distillation at present? Answer: there has been considerable illicit distillation carried on up to the present time, although it has been generally relinquished by the respectable and wealthier class of farmers. It is said that about 30 years ago there were nearly 400 working stills in this parish. It was not then considered so disrespectable to be concerned in it as it is now. The smuggling on the coast is nearly extinct. At a former period it was very great, particularly in tobacco and brandy. [Insert addition by J. Bleakly: In one year 900 pounds was paid for still fines by the inhabitants of Magilligan about 30 years since].

What are the absolute numbers or the relative proportions of the various religious denominations? Answer: the absolute numbers of the various religious denominations are as follows: Established Church 560, Presbyterian 668, Roman Catholics 2,382, total 3,600.

What was the amount of emigration in 1833 and 1834 and to what places, specifying which of the Canadas? Answer: see tables for an answer.

What proportion or number emigrate annually for harvest work, and whither? Answer: some years not more than 10, at other times from 35 to 40 will emigrate to England and Scotland. The encouragement of late has been lessened by the number of resident Irish on the other side of the channel and very few are now likely to go over.

To what dispensary do the people resort, and could lists of cases for this parish be procured for 1833 and 1834 or even totals? Answer: not many applications are made to any dispensary by the poor of this parish. A few receive medical assistance from the Ballykelly and Newtownlimavady dispensaries.

What are the pecuniary emoluments of the clergy of the various religious denominations? Answer: the rector of this parish, the Rev. John Graham, has the following pecuniary emolument: tithes under the composition act 425 pounds, Glebe House and 37 acres of land valued at 36 pounds 15s 4d (the glebe land is held under the see at the yearly rent of 12s), [total] 461 pounds 15s 4d; deduct from this 15 pounds per cent, paid to landlords according to the late act of parliament, 63 pounds 15s, total 398 pounds 4d.

The Presbyterian minister, the Rev. Samuel Butler, has a contract of 60 pounds stipends and 50 pounds regium donum, [total] 110 pounds.

The parish priest, the Rev. Paul Bradley, received for the year 1834 70 pounds.

SOCIAL ECONOMY

Emigration in 1833 and 1834

List of persons who have emigrated from the parish of Magilligan during the years 1833 and 1834. [Table gives name, age, year in which emi-grated, townland of origin, religion, port emigrated to].

John Quinn, 19, Roman Catholic, in 1834, from Ballymagoland to Quebec.

Jane Melon, 23, Roman Catholic, in 1834, from Oughtymore to Philadelphia.

Nancy Melon, 25, Roman Catholic, in 1834, from Oughtymore to Quebec.

Jane Doherty, 18, Roman Catholic, in 1834, from Oughtymore to New York.

William Kelly, 20, Established Church, in 1833, from Ballyscullion to Philadelphia.

William Doherty, 22, Roman Catholic, in 1833, from Ballyscullion to Philadelphia.

Edward Doherty, 25, Roman Catholic, in 1833, from Ballyscullion to Philadelphia.

Michael Doherty, 24, Roman Catholic, in 1833, from Ballyscullion to Philadelphia.

Catherine McLaughlin, 20, Roman Catholic, in 1833, from Ballycarton to Quebec.

Patrick McCormick, 25, Roman Catholic, in 1833, from Duncrun to Philadelphia.

William McCormick, 23, Roman Catholic, in 1833, from Duncrun to Philadelphia.

James Kenedy, 20, Roman Catholic, in 1834, from Duncrun to New York.

John Doherty, 22, Roman Catholic, in 1834, from Duncrun to Quebec.

William Rudden, 24, Roman Catholic, in 1833, from Ballycarton to Quebec.

Catherine McLaughlin, 26, Roman Catholic, in 1833, from Ballycarton to Quebec.

Abraham Kilmary, 30, Roman Catholic, in 1834, from Ballycarton to Quebec.

Hugh Kane, 23, Roman Catholic, in 1833, from Claggan to Philadelphia.

Robert Smith, 23, Roman Catholic, in 1833, from Ballyscullion to Philadelphia.

Mark McLaughlin, 30, Roman Catholic, in 1833, from Ballyleighery to Quebec.

William Ferson, 24, Presbyterian, in 1833, from Ballymultimber to Philadelphia.

William Doherty, 24, Presbyterian, in 1833, from Ballymultimber to Philadelphia.

Maryanne Snell, 28, Established Church, servant at Bellarena, in 1834, to Quebec.

Samuel Tate, 28, Presbyterian, in 1833, from Woodtown to Quebec.

Thomas Tate, 20, Presbyterian, in 1833, from Woodtown to Quebec.

Thomas Paterson, 35, Established Church, in 1833, from Woodtown to Quebec.

James McNally, 30, Roman Catholic, in 1833, from Aughill to Quebec.

Margaret McNally, 21, Roman Catholic, in 1833, from Aughill to Quebec.

George Redgate, 25, Roman Catholic, in 1833, from Aughill to New York.

William McFeely, 24, Roman Catholic, in 1834, from Aughill to New York.

James Farren, 20, Roman Catholic, in 1833, from Aughill to Quebec.

Ellen Doherty, 20, Roman Catholic, in 1833, from Tircreveen to Quebec.

William Gilchrist, 40, Roman Catholic, in 1834, from Ballymaclary to Quebec.

Sarah Gilchirst, 41, Roman Catholic, in 1834, from Ballymaclary to Quebec.

John Gilchrist, 10, Roman Catholic, in 1834, from Ballymaclary, to Quebec.

William Gilchrist Junior, 8, Roman Catholic, in 1834, from Ballymaclary to Quebec.

Catherine Gilchrist, 12, Roman Catholic, in 1834, from Ballymaclary to Quebec.

Holland O'Brien, 25, Roman Catholic, in 1834, from Ballymaclary to Quebec.

Margaret O'Brien, 35, Roman Catholic, in 1834, from Ballymaclary to Quebec.

Margaret Tonner, 7, Roman Catholic, in 1834, from Ballymaclary to Quebec.

Margaret McCague, 24, Roman Catholic, in 1834, from Clooney to Quebec.

Ellen O'Kane, 20, Roman Catholic, in 1833, from Clooney to St John's.

Margaret O'Kane, 18, Roman Catholic, in 1833, from Clooney to St John's.

Nancy McCague, 22, Roman Catholic, in 1833, from Clooney to St John's.

George Doherty, 26, Roman Catholic, in 1834, from Upper Drummons to New York.

Nancy Doherty, 22, Roman Catholic, in 1833, from Upper Drummons to Philadelphia.

Hugh McTyre, 22, Roman Catholic, in 1833, from Upper Drummons to Quebec.

Betty McTyre, 25, Roman Catholic, in 1833, from Upper Drummons to Quebec.

Robert Smith, 24, Roman Catholic, in 1833, from Upper Drummons to Philadelphia. 2nd to 5th June 1835.

Townland Census

[J. Bleakly: alternative spellings from copy of 27th December 1834].

Ballycarton, 7 Protestants, 58 Roman Catholics, 8 Presbyterians.

Clagan [Claggan], 11 Protestants, 63 Roman Catholics, 2 Presbyterians.

Bellarena, 15 Protestants, 72 Roman Catholics, 15 Presbyterians.

Carrowreagh, 11 Protestants, 16 Roman Catholics.

Minearney [Minearny], 4 Roman Catholics, 3 Presbyterians.

Drumnahay, 8 Protestants, 62 Roman Catholics, 16 Presbyterians.

Oughtymole, 21 Protestants, 31 Roman Catholics, 32 Presbyterians.

Ballymultimber, 56 Protestants, 102 Roman Catholics, 29 Presbyterians.

Ballyscullion, 35 Protestants, 123 Roman Catholics, 15 Presbyterians.

Drumavally, 12 Protestants, 26 Roman Catholics, 22 Presbyterians.

Lenamore, 18 Protestants, 94 Roman Catholics, 20 Presbyterians.

Margymonaghan, 12 Protestants, 63 Roman Catholics, 10 Presbyterians.

Ballymulholland, 13 Protestants, 76 Roman Catholics, 6 Presbyterians.

Duncrun, 16 Protestants, 355 Roman Catholics.

Gort, 15 Protestants.

Milltown, 12 Protestants, 15 Roman Catholics, 13 Presbyterians.

Croaghan, 4 Roman Catholics.

Tamlaght, 2 Protestants, 63 Roman Catholics, 22 Presbyterians.

Ballyleighery [Ballyleighry] Upper, 43 Protestants, 75 Roman Catholics, 56 Presbyterians.

Ballyleighery Lower, 32 Protestants, 43 Roman Catholics, 22 Presbyterians.

Tircreveen [Tircrevin], 16 Protestants, 99 Roman Catholics, 106 Presbyterians.

Gortmore, 23 Protestants, 60 Roman Catholics, 44 Presbyterians.

Craig, 21 Protestants, 30 Roman Catholics, 33 Presbyterians.

Woodtown, 5 Protestants, 45 Roman Catholics, 21 Presbyterians.

Umbra, 14 Protestants, 14 Roman Catholics, 29 Presbyterians.

Avish, 9 Presbyterians.

Carnowry, 4 Protestants, 12 Roman Catholics, 45 Presbyterians.

Aughill, 39 Protestants, 25 Roman Catholics, 3 Presbyterians.

Clooney, 90 Roman Catholics, 19 Presbyterians.

Drumahorgan, 97 Roman Catholics.

Oughtymore, 74 Roman Catholics, 5 Presbyterians.

Ballymagoland, 84 Roman Catholics, 21 Presbyterians.

Drumans [Drumons] Lower, 7 Protestants, 2 Roman Catholics.

Drumans Middle, 5 Protestants, 1 Roman Catholic, 16 Presbyterians.

Drumans Upper, 3 Protestants, 85 Roman Catholics, 12 Presbyterians.

Upper and Middle Doaghs, 29 Protestants, 68 Roman Catholics, 1 Presbyterian.

Upper Doaghs, 3 Protestants, 67 Roman Catholics.

Lower and Middle Doaghs, 8 Roman Catholics.

Lower Doaghs, 3 Protestants, 11 Roman Catholics, 16 Presbyterians.

Ballymaclary, 44 Protestants, 139 Roman Catholics, 13 Presbyterians.

Benone, 5 Protestants, 23 Roman Catholics, 6 Presbyterians. Totals: 560 Protestants, 2,379 Roman Catholics, 668 Presbyterians.

There are in the parish of Tamlaght Ard Magilligan: 641 houses, 643 families, 1,687 males, 1,748 females, male servants 101, female servants 71, total 3,607.

Information obtained from the book which contains the census of the parish taken by Robert Ross, enumerator. [Signed] John Bleakly, 1st June 1835.

Analysis of Emigration

[C.W. Ligar] Table showing the emigration from the parish of Magilligan during the years 1833 and 1834. The parish consists of a population of 3,608: of that number 560 are of the Established Church, 2,380 Roman Catholics and 668 Presbyterians.

1833: total number of emigrants 31, of the Established Church 2, Roman Catholics 25, Presbyterians 4, males 22, females 9; to Quebec 15, Philadelphia 12, New York 1, St John's 3.

1834: total number of emigrants 17, of the Established Church 1, Roman Catholics 16, males 8, females 9, to Quebec 12, Philadelphia 1, New York 4; [overall] total number of emigrants 48.

Table showing the ages of the persons emigrating. In 1833: 2 males above 15 and up to 20 years of age, 3 females; 15 males above 20 and up to 25, 5 females; 3 males above 25 and up to 30, 1 female; 1 male above 30 and up to 35; 1 male above 35 and up to 40 1; totals 22 males, 9 females.

In 1834: 2 males up to 10 years of age, 1 female; 1 female above 10 and up to 15; 1 male above 15 and up to 20, 2 females; 2 males above 20 and up to 25, 2 females; 2 males above 25 and up to 30, 1 female; 1 female above 30 and up to 35; 1 male above 35 and up to 40; 1 female above 40 and up to 45; totals 8 males, 9 females.

Census Return

[Insert addition: Copy of the answers to the questions contained in the schedule to an act, 11th George IV, entitled <intituled> "An act for taking an account of the population of Great Britain and of the increase or diminution thereof."

[Table I contains the following headings: name and description of parish or townland, inhabited houses, number of families in occupation, houses building and uninhabited, families employed in agriculture, families in trade, manufacture and handicrafts, all other families not comprised in the 2 preceding classes, number of persons].

Parish of Tamlaghtard <Tamlaghtarde>: 629 inhabited houses, occupied by 643 families, 5 houses now building, 7 uninhabited, 449 families employed in agriculture, 93 in trade, manufacture and handicraft, 101 other families not comprised in preceding classes, 1,788 males, 1,820 females, 3,608 persons.

Parish of Aghanloo: 400 inhabited houses, occupied by 402 families, 6 uninhabited houses, 292 families employed in agriculture, 51 employed in trade, manufacture and handicraft, 59 families not comprised in preceding classes, 1,045 males, 1,114 females, 2,159 persons.

Parish of Drumachose: 501 inhabited houses, occupied by 516 families, 2 houses now building, 11 uninhabited, 353 families chiefly employed in agriculture, 111 in trade, manufacture and handicraft, 52 other families not comprised in preceding classes, 1,385 males, 1,467 females, 2,852 persons.

Parish of Newtownlimavady: 470 inhabited houses, occupied by 517 families, 2 houses now building, 37 uninhabited, 79 families employed in agriculture, 297 in trade, manufacture and handicraft, 141 other families not comprised in preceding classes, 1,106 males, 1,322 females, 2,428 persons. [Overall total of persons] 11,047.

Table II analyses occupations of males]

Parish of Tamlaghtard: 907 males 20 years old, 55 land occupiers employing labourers, 205 not employing labourers, 408 labourers employed in agriculture, 35 males employed in manufacture or in making manufacturing machinery, 100 males employed in retail trade or in handicraft as masters or workmen, 28 wholesale merchants, capi-

talists, bankers, professional persons and other educated men, 14 labourers employed by the 3 preceding classes and in other non-agricultural labour, 58 other males above 20 years (except servants), including retired tradesmen, superannuated labourers and males diseased or disabled in body or mind, 4 male servants above 20 years, 99 under 20, 72 female servants.

Parish of Aghanloo: 501 males 20 years old, 33 land occupiers employing labourers, 153 not employing labourers, 191 labourers employed in agriculture, 47 males employed in manufacture or making manufacturing machinery, 42 in retail trade or in handicraft as masters or workmen, 8 wholesale merchants, capitalists, bankers, professional persons and other educated men, 2 labourers employed by the 3 preceding classes and in other non-agricultural labour, 22 other males above 20 years old (except servants), including retired tradesmen etc., 3 male servants above 20 years, 28 under 20, 57 female servants.

Parish of Drumachose: 713 males 20 years old, 33 land occupiers employing labourers, 181 not employing labourers, 267 labourers employed in agriculture, 42 males employed in manufacture or making manufacturing machinery, 118 in retail trade or in handicraft as masters or workmen, 22 wholesale merchants capitalists, bankers, professional persons and other educated men, 14 labourers employed by the 3 preceding classes and in other non-agricultural labour, 27 other males above 20 years old (except servants), including retired tradesmen etc., 9 male servants above 20 years, 27 under 20, 91 female servants.

Parish of Newtownlimavady: 610 males 20 years old, 1 land occupier employing labourers, 6 not employing labourers, 97 labourers employed in agriculture, 1 male employed in manufacture or in making manufacturing machinery, 357 employed in retail trade or in handicraft as masters or workmen, 81 wholesale merchants, capitalists, bankers, professional persons and other educated men, 19 labourers employed by the 3 preceding classes and in other non-agricultural labour, 21 other males above 20 years old (except servants), including retired tradesmen etc., 27 male servants above 20 years, 22 under 20, 137 female servants.

The males employed in manufacture as shown in the above table are exclusively linen weavers. The families of gentlemen of property, clergymen and professional persons though holding land for their accommodation have been placed in the eighth column of the first table [all other families not comprised in the 2 preceding classes] and also the families of pensioners and widows who hold no land or have not sons engaged in agriculture or trade. All farming servants above 20 years of age, hired and living in farmers' houses for the purpose of labour only on their farms, have been put down as labourers as the term household servants has been considered to apply only to those employed inside the house, such as butlers, coachmen, footmen.

Legend concerning the McClarys

The people of this parish affirm that a castle was seen by several of the inhabitants of Magilligan on the Ton banks [insert footnote: a sand-bank at the mouth of Lough Foyle covered at high and low water, but at the latter there is a wash on it which marks its position. This legend had its rise most probably in the Fata Morgana which are very frequent along this coast], from the tower of which a flag was hoisted. A man named McClary, seeing the flag and being told that he would become heir of the castle if he could succeed in taking off the flag, immediately, without taking his eyes off the castle [insert footnote: if a person after beholding the castle takes his eye off the object he can no more behold it] mounted an excellent black race mare and galloped off towards it. He accomplished the desired object, but on returning 9 waves followed him: the first reached the hinder legs of the mare and changed them to white from black; the second wave reached the fore legs and turned them white also and so on until the ninth wave which covered the mare and changed her entirely from black to white. A voice was then heard from the castle uttering vengeance on the name of McClary and declaring that 7 smokes proceeding from the chimney of the McClarys should never be seen in Magilligan (that is, 7 families of that name should never live in the parish). From that time 7 families of the name have never been known to reside in the parish. McClary, it is said, placed the flag on Screen church.

Section of Memoir by John O'Donovan and George Petrie, with additions by J. Stokes [1835]

NATURAL STATE

Etymology of Parish Name

Tamlaghtard, or properly as it is written by Colgan, Tamlacht-arda, the ancient ecclesiastical name of this parish, signifies "the burial place of Arda", the territorial name of this district anterior to the introduction of Christianity. The appellation arda, which is the genitive case of the word aird, "a height or high lands", is evidently expressive of its peculiar ancient locality before its plain or lower district was gained from the sea, as it appears certainly to have been from the most conclusive evidences.

In the earliest historical notices of the foundation of the parish church, namely the Life of St Patrick by St Eimbin [Eimhin], it is called Domnach-airther-arda or "the church of the eastern height." The parish is now more popularly known by the name of Ard-Magilligan or Magilligan and is called by the Irish inhabitants *Parraiste-chlainne-Giollagain* or "the parish of the clan Gilligan." It is written Ard-meggiolagan by O'Donnell, prince of Tirconnell in 1520, and Ard-mic-Giolagan by Colgan in 1647. This name was undoubtedly derived from the district having been occupied from a very remote period by a tribe of the ancient Irish family of Magilligan, to one of whom at the Plantation of Ulster, the townland of Ballycarton was given as a native freehold and forfeited by Manus McGilligan in the rebellion of 1641. [Insert addition: A family of the name Magilligan is still living in the parish of Dungiven in the townland of Cashel. The native freehold of Ballycarton is at present held by [blank] Lane Esquire under the Marquis of Waterford].

Locality

This parish may be characterised as a secluded corner composing the north western extremity of the barony of Keenaght. It is bounded on the north by the sea, south by Aghanloo and Tamlaght Finlagan parishes, east by the parish of Dunboe in the barony of Coleraine and west by Lough Foyle, which separates it from Upper and Lower Moville parishes in the county of Donegal. It is about 5 miles long by 2 and a half broad and its boundary line is estimated to be 19 miles. Its contents are 13,142 English acres subdivided into 30 townlands and valued [blank] to the county cess.

NATURAL FEATURES

Surface and Soil

The parish is naturally divided into high and lowlands, the latter being perfectly level and the former rising in a chain of perpendicular precipices and constituting considerably the larger portion. These highlands are again divisible into the terrace-formed uplands connecting the plain with the perpendicular cliff of the mountain and the mountain tops each extending the whole length of the parish. This mountain top is partly covered with bog from 1 to 12 or more feet deep, and partly by a range of coarse pasture with a little coarse arable. [Insert addition: A range of coarse pasture extends along the brink of the Ballyliehery precipice].

Beneath the mountain promontories the uplands consist of rocky pastures, mostly reclining, and arable lands abounding with rocks and gravel. The lowlands are composed partly of sandy warrens adjacent to the sea and lake, partly of sandy arable within the border of the warrens; a portion of boggy arable upon a substratum of sand and of some remnants of bog lessening before the cultivators of the potato and oats. [Insert note: A peculiar natural feature of the low grounds is a beach of water-worn stones which can be traced throughout the parish running in an irregular line along the foot of the highlands. Between Bellarena and the glebe, the large rounded stones have been partially excavated to be broken up for mending the roads. This beach is generally covered to the depth of about 12 inches by the soil of the fields. The low grounds are not absolutely flat. Trivial eminences and slight undulations are to be met with. Between the Roe river and the point there occur alternately small risings and fallings in the ground. The former are always sandy, the latter or hollow places are filled with boggy soil. The latter are called "misk"].

A considerable proportion of the whole parish is either light, sandy ground easily disturbed by wind or rocky and mountainous lands of inferior value, but the remaining parts possess much fertility which, in the lower lands, is derived in a great measure from the temperature consequent on their contiguity to the sea level and in the higher lands from the protection generally afforded them from the east winds by their great mountain barrier.

It is worthy of remark, the more particularly as being the immediate cause of the selection of the county of Londonderry for the first of the series of the Ordnance maps of Ireland, from the length of base line which it afforded, there being nowhere else in the island so large a portion of level alluvial lands so compactly circumstanced as the lowlands of Magilligan and the conterminous plain of Myroe <Moyroe> in the parish of Tamlaght Finlagan. Of the former, about 1,000 acres of bog have been reclaimed within the memory of persons living. Some of the dry lands were then much moister and of considerably higher value.

Mountains

The basaltic mountain range which occupies so large a portion of this parish has several subdenominations but is collectively known by the name Binevenagh <Benevena> or *Beann Fhoibhne* i.e. "the mountain of Foivne" as it is written in the oldest Irish authority, the Dinnseanchas <Dionn-seanchus>. The greatest elevation of this mountain is 1,269 feet and the greatest height of the perpendicular cliffs 470 feet. Those bold precipices face the west. Towards their northern extremity they gradually decline in height and terminate in cliffs of from 400 to 470 feet. [Insert addition: They are subdivided into the Ballyliehery and the Gortmore precipices. They cease between these 2 townlands and are there replaced by more gradual slopes. Either of these are in fact one continued rock. The former, by its standing at the greatest height from the sea, is the most remarkable and being the only one visible to the adjoining parishes of Drumachose, Tamlaght Finlagan, Balteagh, is the most familiarly known. The Gortmore continues to Downhill. The perpendicular part of the Ballyliehery rock occurs at its greatest depth immediately under an Ordnance trigonometrical station which has been placed at its brink. It is there fully 480 feet deep. For an extent of 1 and a half miles it is now less than 350.

At the foot of this range of walls a series of rocky pinnacles arise, forming the other sides of a long and narrow valley. The manner in which the peculiar features of the valley can be most readily perceived is by ascending from the parish of Aghanloo. On approaching the beginning of the rock, a singular pinnacle appears at the foot with a square top and perpendicular sides resembling a tower. This natural tower is upwards of 50 feet high. It gives a grotesque aspect to the whole scene, which is soon exchanged for one of sublimity on arriving at the top of the ridge by which it is connected with the rock. The narrow valley already mentioned is then seen surmounted on the right-hand side by the rock towering in long perspective, covered at the bottom with debris and traversed by narrow and difficult paths. It re-echoes to a shout.

The left-hand side of this valley is steep and precipitous, and is generally about 100 feet deep. From its bottom the rock, including a steep, grassy declivity, rises to the altitude of 500 feet.

After proceeding for about half a mile it terminates, and the path then proceeds along the foot of the rock itself. Presently a low-browed door appears at the side of the path. This leads into the bowels of the precipice. It is the entrance to "the little cove of Ballyliehery" and will be described further on. The path then proceeds and the "great cove" soon appears. Its dark mouth can only be attained by a fearful exploit in climbing. The path at length concludes by proceeding up the precipice itself through a narrow defile called the Sheep Gate.

The most remarkable natural object at the Gortmore rock is a gulf called the Hell Hole, through which a stream of water runs over the precipice. The rock at Gortmore is more usually known as the Back Strand rock. The Merrick Stone is a remarkable pinnacle. The Robber's Cave is the name of a limestone cavern on that part of the coast.

Rivers

The Roe directly washes about a mile and a half of the southern border. The other waters are only 2 mill-streams, and the Big Drain, as it is called, which is the greatest outlet of the torrents descending from the mountain into the sandy plain and thence to the lough. This drain is a natural stream, and the failure of some parts of its banks in time of floods has not unfrequently produced inundations of great injury to the crops, an evil which the landlords Conolly Gage Esquire and Sir James Bruce, between whose lands it forms the mearing, have very laudably exerted themselves to prevent. [Insert addition: It is the mearing between Sir James Bruce and Conolly Gage. It has probably required attention from time to time. The chief branch of the Big Drain descends from the mountains between the Gortmore and Ballylieghrey rocks through a deep and narrow channel].

Drains and Water Courses

[Crossed out: Many lesser artificial drains are still required to discharge the mountain waters which give the country, otherwise level, something of a broken and impervious appearance, particularly when crossed from north to south, whereas the lines connecting the lake and upperland roads are numerous and of easy access in ways parallel to the drains].

Numerous mountain springs diffuse themselves through the whole sandy plain by percolation, whether seen or unseen, rising to the same general level and commingling at last with the waters on the shores.

In the long, dry summer of 1824 there was a great scarcity of good water in various places, which was not fully removed before the 1st of October. Water of some sort will, however, be found in all the lowlands in the direct seasons by digging nearly to the level of the sea, which is only a few feet below the surface. [Insert addition: The wells of the lowlands are chiefly near the seashore. Near Tamlaght 3 springs gush forth very close to each other. They are known by the name of the Three Sisters. Clerk's Well is remarkable for its great altitude and good water].

Woods

The general tradition, corroborated by names of places, sufficiently indicates that a considerable portion of the terrace lands of this parish was anciently under wood. At present, with the exception of modern plantations, there are only to be found a few ash trees, hazels, thorns, and in the uplands some gardens with apple trees. [Insert addition: One of the parishioners, a very old man, says that he recollects when the steep bank under the great cove of Ballyleihrey was wooded. The ivy that festoons the rock in many places has been propagated by the woods. Many alder trees still appear growing from its face. In the misks fossil timber is frequently found].

The modern plantations are the extensive demesne of Conolly Gage Esquire and about 50 acres on the side of Benevena planted about 1821 by that estimable proprietor, which are in a highly thriving state. [Insert addition: This 50 acres is almost wholly of larch and fir. There is some natural thorn and holly trees. Within the last 3 years Mr Gage has planted about 200 acres more also, with almost perfect shelter from every injurious wind. These situations are very frequent on the mountain and many of them are apparently capable of supporting good oak timber].

Bogs

Bog is abundant on the mountains. [Insert addition: That which occurs on the top of Ballyleighrey rock certainly has had an excellent fall for the drainage of its water. It, however, approaches in some places to within 60 feet of the brink and is there succeeded by a soft, grassy sward. It does not exhibit in its texture any remarkable appearances of twigs or fibres and is apparently about 4 feet deep].

NATURAL HISTORY

Birds

[Insert covering note: Whatever you write on this subject, put on a separate sheet that it may be stitched up afterwards].

[Insert addition: The lowlands in dry hot weather swarm with many species of insects, particularly of earwigs. The latter sometimes increase to myriads. Rats, mice and other small vermin also increase and multiply. As for the highlands, it is probable that many of the rarer British birds occur towards the bottom of the mountain. The top, particularly the rock itself, is a perfect rookery and contains not only crows but also a large kind of hawk commonly called the gled-hawk. Flocks of these birds perpetually soar around its weather-beaten front. They build in the innumerable chinks and crannies which occur among the rude basaltic columns. Their favourite place both for soaring and building is the brink and those parts which have been the most acted on and broken by the weather.

Eagles formerly haunted these places. In Mr Lane's tenure it is directed that he should preserve them. A rock on the Gortmore side, still called the Eagle rock, also testifies the same. They seem to have gradually deserted the place on the unwelcome increase of inhabitants in the plain below. The parishioners seem to be unaware of the temporary visit which it is said was paid to them some time ago by the 2 old eagles of Ballinascreen who, annoyed by the frequent robbery of their young, deserted, but only for a time, their home at Craigna-shoke.

Wild Animals

Foxes and badgers frequent the highlands. There are but few hares. It was formerly the practice to bring fox skins every year to the parish vestry and they were there paid for in order to encourage their extirpation. From the vestry book it appears that in 1748 8 skins were brought in, for which there was paid 16s; 1750 12 skins were brought in, for which was paid 24s; 1751 10 skins were brought in, for which was paid 20s; 1755 5 skins were brought in, for which was paid 3s; 1756 3 skins were brought in, for which was paid 8s; 1757 8 skins were brought in, for which was paid 16s; in 1759 7 skins were brought in, for which was paid 14s; 1760 4 skins were brought in, for which was paid 9s.

In this year it was ordered that everyone who brought a fox skin to the vestry should make affidavit that it was shot in the parish of Magilligan. 1761 7 skins were brought in, for which was paid 14s; 1762 10 skins were brought in, for which was paid 20s; 1763 6 skins were brought in, for which was paid 11s; 1764 11 skins were brought in, for which was paid 21s. In 1768 the price of each skin was reduced from 2s 1d to 1s 7d by ordering that the receiver should always give 6d to the poor. Upon the enactment of this ordinance, shooting of foxes ceased and no further mention of them is to be found in the vestry book.

The natural history of Binevenagh includes that of both Magilligan <McGilligan> and Aghanloo, as the same mountain stands in both parishes].

MODERN TOPOGRAPHY

Modern Buildings

This extensive parish has neither town, village, post office, fair or market, parochial court or pound for cattle, nor are any of these to be found in the parishes immediately contiguous excepting Dunboe. There are 5 or 6 hamlets which favourable circumstances might convert into villages, besides a number of places for the accommodation of bathers in the summer season. One of these, that of Mr S. Blair, is a kind of travellers' hotel. Dr Tyler, W. Moody and D. Cather Esquire of Newtownlimavady have built summer lodges near the shore and made other improvements. [Insert marginal query: Are not petty sessions held in Newtown? Answer: They are, but Drumachose is not an adjoining parish].

There is a Martello tower for 2 24-pounders at the point of Magilligan, which commands the entrance to Lough Foyle.

Bridges

In the southern extremity of the parish there is a neat wooden bridge resting upon stone pillars across the Roe. It is about 72 yards long. [Crossed out: There are also 3 small stone bridges across the drains on the way to Derry. The lesser drains are deficient in bridges, not having even a foot or bridle path across them, so that horsemen and the school pupils are in many instances obliged to travel a much greater distance than would be otherwise necessary]. There are 3 small stone bridges over the branches of the Big Drain.

Ecclesiastical Buildings

The ecclesiastical buildings are the parish church erected by Hervey, Bishop of Derry, in 1773; the

Presbyterian meeting house and the Roman Catholic chapel. The 2 former are of small size, the latter is of large proportion but unadorned architecture. It was built by the parishioners in 1773, the former chapel having become too small for the fastly [alternative: rapidly] increasing congregation.

Gentlemen's Seats

The gentlemen's houses are Bellarena, the beautiful seat of Conolly Gage Esquire; Castle Lecky, the country residence of Averil Lecky Esquire; and the Glebe House.

Mills

There is a flax mill belonging to C. Gage Esquire and 2 corn mills, all turned by water.

Schoolhouses

There are 3 schools, 2 of which are slated and of respectable size.

Farmhouses

The older farmhouses are generally large, unfinished and uncomfortable dwellings of brick or stone [crossed out: scarcely one of them being calculated to repel the cold and storms of a Magilligan winter; and of those, a considerable proportion being on dry, sandy ground are, in these times of their diminished value, getting out of repair]. Those lately erected are mostly on the recently reclaimed boggy lands, of less than the old houses and generally of stone.

In the uplands the poorer houses are of loose or uncemented stones; and in the lowlands of bog sods or mud [crossed out: which only became tolerably agreeable from continued use]. These bog houses last only 2 or 3 years before they begin to fail, but they are warmer than stone, cost only 2 or 3 pounds to raise them and sometimes less, and when the indweller has no other resource for fuel, he has in many instances resorted to a part of his own house walls. After they fail, more fuel is had and the residue forms good manure! The landlords are endeavouring to lessen the number of such habitations [crossed out: but the distance from stone or bricks causes buildings with those materials to be more expensive in the lowlands than the peasantry are usually able to bear]. [Insert addition: These houses are at present nearly extinct, perhaps wholly so. Many houses of stone and lime are to be seen in which the triangular apex of the gable is formed of bog sods. Pigsties and cow houses are also built of this material].

It is perhaps worthy of remark that in the lowlands nearly all the houses are built with one end towards the uplands and the other towards Lough Foyle, old experience having taught them that by this mode they were best protected from injurious winds. One of the few exceptions is the house of the Presbyterian clergyman, which is now nearly the oldest in the parish, and built, as it is said, in the year 1700.

MEMOIR WRITING

Memoir Writing

15 folios were intended, 18 May 1835 [initialled] by G. Downes.

ANCIENT TOPOGRAPHY

Ancient Monuments made by the Cruthen

There are no ancient sepulchral, or as they are generally called, druidic monuments remaining in this parish except a giant's grave at the Roe mouth, but there are several forts which may on historic date be referred to a period anterior to the introduction of Christianity. Of these, the most remarkable constitute a group of 3, 2 of which are situated in the townland of Duncreen or Dun Cruithen, and the third in the townland of Tamlaght and immediately adjoining. [Insert note: None of these is given in the Ordnance map? The one given appears to be Dunpatrick]. The relative position of these forts to each other and the similarity of their form and mode of construction leave no doubt of their being of coeval erection, and the name still retained in one of them, as well as in the townland in which it is situated, distinctly points to the Picts or Cruithnigh as the Irish call them, who held this district in the earliest historic times. From the *Tripartite Life of St Patrick*, said to have been written originally by St Evin in the 7th century, we learn that the name of Dun Cruthen existed here before the time of the Irish apostle; and Colgan adds in a note that this place appears to have taken the name Dun Cruthen signifying "fort of the Crutheni" from the Crutheni who (as appears from the second and third *Life of St Patrick*) reigned in the northern part of Ulster in the time of St Patrick.

It does not admit of doubt that the people called Picti by the Roman writers were called Cruithnigh by the Irish, the words synonymously signifying "painted people." The celebrated Duald McFirbis thus derives the word in his account of English and Irish families: "Cruithneach, a person who paints the forms of beasts, birds and fishes on his face (q.d. *cruth-eineach* i.e. "face painted"), which the cruithnigh did not only on their faces but upon their whole bodies. Caesar calls the Britons Cruithnigh (Picti) because they were accustomed to stain their faces with woad in order that they might appear terrible to their enemies."

Adamnan, abbot of Iona in the 7th century, always calls the Irish Picts Cruthnei in his *Life of Columba*, and the celebrated annalist Tigernach, abbot of Clonmacnoise in the 11th century, calls them Cruithne. [Insert note: Thus also the country of the Picts in Scotland is called by the most ancient Irish writers Cruithean-tuath or "the country of the Cruthnei or Picts." Other authorities might be added if it were necessary but these are sufficient, and it may be concluded with certainty that the ancient forts now to be described were the erections of that distinguished people].

Forts

These interesting remains are all of an oval form, the walls of earth faced with uncemented stone and generally about 7 feet in thickness. The principal of these forts, which is now generally known by the more modern name of Craigbolie or "the rock of the milking place", is situated about 200 yards from the bottom of the precipice of Binevenagh <Benevena>, on the border of Duncrun townland in Tamlaght-ard. It occupies the top of a steep and rocky eminence, the slope of which to the country opposite the acclivity is exceedingly precipitous, though smooth and regular. There is also a slope on the opposite side towards the precipice but which, though steep, is not more than 30 feet. Thus it will be seen that the position was naturally of great strength, and the plan of the fort as exhibited in the accompanying plate will show that considerable art was displayed in adding to its security, the 2 sides being protected by additional parapets, the approach in both these directions being along the ledges of small hills, that on which the interior of the fort stands forming one of the same chain.

The circle in the interior of the fort (F) is composed of a row of single stones of various sizes and irregular forms, varying from 12 to 16 inches. Such a foundation, it is obvious, could not have been designed for any defensive building but rather for a habitation, the upper part of which was roofed with pales, as [blank] describes the houses of the Britons. In the centre of this circle there is an oblong space 3 feet 2 inches by 2 feet which was evidently the fire hearth, the stones which now remain serving to keep the ashes and

fuel together. In digging within this enclosure, the earth for the first foot was found to be impregnated a good deal with fine charcoal in a powder, and there were also hard lumps turned up which resembled the common furze branches. The earth to the depth of 2 feet appeared to have been before removed, but a foot deeper it assumed its natural appearance. Charcoal was also discovered in digging between 2 parapets at the southern end. [Insert addition: About 2 feet from the hearth a large, round stone was found, apparently one of 3 that were used for slinging with].

Lesser Forts

Of the lesser forts, one is situated immediately below Craigbolie and about 200 yards from it; the other about 500 yards to the north west, immediately above the church of Tamlaght-Ard and distant about 200 yards. Both are placed in much less commanding positions than the principal fort. The former is scarcely elevated above the slope on which it stands and is only defended by a single parapet. This, like the larger fort, has in its centre a circle of a single row of stones. It is not known by any name. The third fort has a second concentric parapet. This fort is called Duncruin or Duncruithen.

There are also the vestiges of a similar oval fort called Dunpatrick, within 100 yards of the ruins of the ancient church of Duncruin and which occupied the whole summit of a green little hill. The walls or parapets have been entirely pulled down for cultivation, but report says that they were formed similarly in every [way] to those in its vicinity.

A careful examination was made in all these Pictish forts to ascertain if they exhibited any appearance of vitrification in their walls and none whatever were found. [Insert marginal note by T. Larcom: Mr Boyle said he had found 2 vitrified forts on the mountain. Did he mean these? Are there 2 others? He said he had seen pieces of vitrified matter. Pray enquire of him, Mr Stokes].

Coves in Ballyleighery

[Insert addition: The lesser cove of Ballyleighery is a chamber of about 12 feet by 3, and 6 feet in the highest part from the ceiling to the floor. The ceiling is arched and the floor is a mixture of stones and clay. Half-way in the side of the room is the door 2 feet high. The door stands exactly at the junction between the green bank and the wall of the precipice. On the left hand side of the door there is a hole about 6 inches wide. This has been horizontally perforated in the north east direction to the depth of 8 feet. The mouth of this hole is but a couple of inches from the side of the door. In the interior there is a cavity containing splinters of rock. [Insert query: Is this cove natural or artificial].

At the mouth of the large cove of Ballyleighrey there is an old tree. A difference of opinion exists among the parishioners as to the nature of this tree, and there are some who believe it to be a fruit tree].

Ecclesiastical Remains

There are remains of no less [alternative: fewer] than 3 small churches within this parish, all of which are of very great antiquity.

Tamlaght-Ard Church

The parish church of Tamlaght-Ard: this is of a simple, oblong form, 66 feet long and 21 feet wide. The masonry in the end walls which is of the original structure is large but polygonal. The side walls have been almost entirely rebuilt. The doorway has a slightly pointed arch and the east window is of the narrow lancet form. The latter is 10 feet high and 1 foot wide, and has a drip moulding springing from human heads. The material of both is red sandstone and the workmanship is good.

This church, having been allowed to fall into ruin after the Reformation, was repaired after the Plantation by William Gage Esquire, the bishop's tenant, ancestor to Mr Conolly Gage of Bellarena. According to tradition, it was afterwards burned by Sir Phelim O'Neill in the rebellion of 1641, but for this we have no historic authority. Archbishop King describes it as being in good repair in his time, and it was used as the parish church till the year 1773 when a new church was erected in a more central situation by the Bishop (Lord Bristol) and the old church given to the Roman Catholics for a parish chapel. A new chapel has been since erected within the cemetery and the old church is used as a schoolhouse.

Churchyard and Headstones

This churchyard contains a great number of headstones, but no tomb of much antiquity except one which is traditionally called the tomb of Bishop Aidan or properly Caidan. [Insert query by G. Downes: Is the "c" a spurious initial growing out of the final "g" of easbog? The Ness (waterfall) in Lower Lambeg thus borrows its initial from the final "n" of "an" *an*. (See next page where the reverse of this opinion is maintained)].

This interesting monument was in the form of an ancient church with a high, pyramidal roof, and is formed of chiselled red sandstones like the window of the church, with which it appears to be coeval. It is situated outside the east end of the church on a right line with the window, and is nearly buried in the accumulated graves on each side. A rude stone seat on a hill outside the cemetry is called St Aidan's Pulpit, and a holy well, springing from beneath a rock and shaded by a venerable ash covered with votive rags, is called Tober Easbog Cadan or the "well of Bishop Cadan."

Among the tombs of modern dates, a plain headstone marks the grave of Denis Hempson, the celebrated Irish harper, of whom some account will be found further on. The remains of the last minstrel of Magilligan and of its first saint reposed not inappropriately together. Though belonging to ages separated by more than a thousand years, they were both connected as end links of a chain with a singular and peculiar framework of society, now wholly broken up, but which had undergone but little change during the long period of time which had intervened between them. The remains of saint and minstrel never reposed together in a spot of more singularly romantic beauty.

Abbey at Tamlacht-Ard

Mr Sampson [crossed out: erroneously and without foundation] ascribes the foundation of an abbey at Tamlacht-Ard to St Columb. Had he referred to Colgan, he would have found the most direct evidence that this church, which was originally called Domnach Airther Arda, was one of 7 erected in the region of Kianachta by St Patrick after he had crossed Lough Foyle from the territory of Inishowen.

These churches, after the usual habit of the Irish apostle, were founded on the Sabbath day and dedicated to the Lord "for which reason" says the author of the *Tripartite Life* of the saint, they named them "dominicae." [Insert note by J. O'Donovan: In this Primate Usher concurs, and learnedly observes that the English words kirk and church are similarly derived from the Greek [crossed out: domnach or dominica signifies "a sacred edifice"]. "Domnach sive Dominica aedem sacram denotat non in Beati Patricii modo (quod in capite 91 Iocelinus innuit sed in nostra etiam vulgari loquendi consuetudine qua kirk et church a [Greek letters] kuriake [kyriake] hoc est dominisa [dominica] deductam eodem sensu usurpamus"].

This word "domhnach", which occurs in the names of so many places of ecclesiastic origin in Ireland, is now anglicised Donagh, Donny and not unfrequently abbreviated into Don as Donaghmore in Meath; Donnybrook near Dublin, Donshaughlin in Meath. Its most ancient anglicised form was Dovenagh, as in the charter of donation to Hugh de Lacy, anno VII Edvardi III. Donshaughlin is called Dovenagh-Sakelin, and in ancient records Donnybrook is called Dovenaghbrook]. [Insert note by T. Larcom: This will cover more appropriately in the orthography].

St Aidan or Cadan

That the Easboc Caidan or Bishop Cadan, whose memory is still venerated here as the patron saint, was the disciple of St Patrick to whom the church was given there can be little doubt. His name is now corruptly called in English Bishop Aidan, from the letter C at the commencement of his name not being distinctly sounded in following the c in Easboc, and hence he has been confounded by the Rev. Mr Butler in his excellent account of the parish with the celebrated Bishop Aidan, apostle of the Northumbrians. In Archbishop King's visitation book his name is more correctly written "Gaedan Tamlachtard alias Magilligin ecclesia St Gaedani." In the list of St Patrick's disciples given by Tirechan, a writer of the 7th century, this name occurs among the presbyters and is written Catanus [insert query: a remote ancestor of the O'Cahans ?]; and in the list of St Patrick's household given in the *Tripartite Life*, the saints Catanus and Ocanotus, presbyters, are stated to have been his 2 hospitalarii or butlers. "Sanctus praesbyter et Ocanotus presbyter duo hospitalarii sive hospitium ministri."

That the Catanus mentioned by these ancient authorities was the saint of Tamlaghtard is proved by the ancient poem written in the 12th century by Flan of Bute, and a prose tract enumerating the persons composing the family or household of St Patrick, both of which are preserved in the Book of Lecan. In these authorities Cadan is called cruimther Cadan or "priest Cadan" from Tamlacht Arda, and is described as being one of the "sagairt meise" or butlers of St Patrick.

Church of Dun Cruithen

This church was situated on a small hill about a quarter of a mile north of the church of Tamlacht

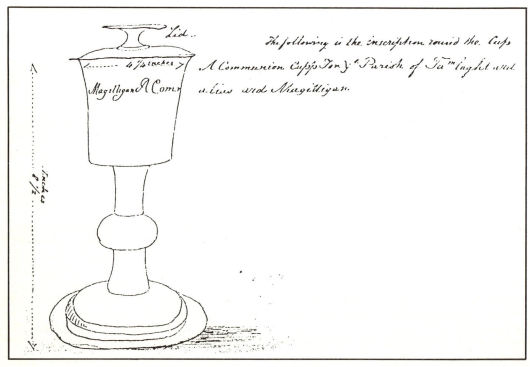

Communion cup from Magilligan

Arda; the foundations only can now be traced. It was a building of very small size, being about 30 feet long and 10 feet wide with a transept 20 feet long. On the side within this transept there is an ancient monumental slab 4 feet by 2, on which a cross is rudely sculptured. It is probably the tomb of the patron saint. According to tradition, an abbey was connected with this church. It was situated at the bottom of the hill but not a vestige of it now remains. A set of ancient weights from 1 to 30 lbs were found here a few years since. They were rounded, basaltic stones from the shore, inscribed with their weight in Roman numerals and probably of the earliest antiquity.

This church is expressly named in the *Tripartite Life of Saint Patrick* as one of the 7 erected by the saint during his sojourn in the barony of Kianachta, and over which he placed one of his disciples who was a bishop and named Broaidh, which Colgan latinizes Beatus. Nothing further is preserved of this saint's history. Archdall, on the authority of an erroneous conjecture in Colgan, supposes the church of Dun Cruithen to be the present Dunboe in the barony of Coleraine, but Colgan elsewhere corrects that error and assigns it to its proper place.

Church of Skreen

The church of Skreen or properly Scrin, from the Latin scrinium or shrine: of this church, as well as the former, only the foundations now remain. It was situated nearly 10 miles to the north east of Dun Cruithen. It was 30 feet long and 15 feet wide. It appears from the inquisition of 1603 that this church, as well as that of Tamlacht Arda, was then ruinous, but Archbishop King informs us that it was subsequently repaired by the bishop, rector and parishioners in order that the incumbent might occasionally officiate in it for the convenience of the parishioners of that part of the parish, the church of Tamlaght "being" as he says "in one corner of the parish, which is divided through the middle by a great bog so that the people could not go to church in winter without travelling 6 miles."

A monastery called Scrinium Sancte Columbae or the shrine of St Columb from a celebrated reliquary deposited in it, was founded in Ard Magilligan by that great church builder, but whether it was situated at the present church of Skreen or at that of Dun Cruithen is perhaps a point not easily ascertained. In the *Life of St Columb* compiled by Magnus O'Donnell, chieftain of Tirconnell in the year 1520, after speaking

of the shrine which he describes as a "noblessimus thesaurus" and one of the most remarkable of the sacred monuments of the sacred isle, he says that "the fabrication of that shrine was commenced a long time before the coming of Columba to those places, and as a tradition goes (while St Patrick was yet living) at a place called Duncruithne by the ancients." Hence it might be supposed that the church for which it was originally designed was that in which it was afterwards preserved, particularly as it is nowhere related that it was transferred to any other. To this it may be added that Colgan thought that the Scrin Columbkilla and Dun Cruithne were but different names of the same place.

In opposition, however, to this conclusion it may be objected that the church called invariably Skreen or Scrin Columbkille is distinct from that called Dun Cruithen, and that it is altogether opposed to probability that the shrine was preserved in any church but that to which it give a name; but Colgan, it is evident, was imperfectly acquainted with the topography of this district and O'Donnell does not distinctly say that the church of Screen and Duncruithen were the same. There appears therefore better evidence for the supposition that though this celebrated shrine was originally in its unfinished state preserved in the church of Duncruithen, it was afterwards removed to the present church of Screen which St Columb is said to have founded. Archdall erroneously connects an historical event with this church which evidently relates to the church of Ballynascreen in the barony of Loughinsholin. The veneration paid to the great reliquary appears to have been the origin of the grant of the whole of this beautiful parish to the church.

The great inquisition of the 10th of November 1603 found that "the ancient inhabitants of O'Cathan's country granted to St Columb and his successors Ard-Magilligan, containing 12 quarters of land where 2 chapels now destroyed were erected; and the *Life of St Columb*, above referred to, states that "moved by the miracle of the completion of the shrine and other miracles, Aidus, son of Ainmarech, King of Ireland, granted to God and Columba the land in which they were wrought, called at this day Ard Meggiolagan and inferior to no ecclesiastical territory in all Ireland at this day 1520."

Conla the Artificer

The antiquary will regret that this monument of the arts of the 5th and 6th centuries has been involved in the general fate of nearly all such remains in the British islands. From O'Donnell's *Life of Columba* we learn that the name of the artificer who commenced "this noble and well-executed work" was Conla, surnamed the artificer from his super-eminent knowledge of his profession; and Colgan, in a note on this passage, observes that the excellence of this artificer has given rise to many proverbs familiar to the Irish: for when they wish to praise a good artificer or brazier, they say "Conla himself is not a more excellent tradesman." Likewise, when they wish to represent anything as irreparable or impossible to be mended, "Conla the brazier could not mend it."

Screen Church and Shrine

O'Donnell states that this shrine was in existence in his time, and the extraordinary veneration paid to it will appear from the following extract from an account of the parish written by Mr Beck of Magilligan in 1683 and preserved among the manuscripts in the library of Trinity College: "In the said parish are the ruins of an old church called the Screen church, which is thought to be vulgar from shrine; in which, before the Reformation, was kept several of popery relics <relicks> as the shrine, a picture that they used with the picture of the Virgin Mary, and hand bells which the priests used in some ceremonies. This is called Columbkille's church, which is counted among them the great saint of the north parts. And on the 9th day of June yearly, which is Columbkille's day, the Irish come there to perform some devotions and will creep on their knees several times about the same church. The use is to this day continued but nothing to what is was before the rebellion, for they they would come from the furthest parts of Ulster and Connaught, a great sort, 500 horse and more as I have been told by their priests. I have likewise been told that this parish Magilligan was a sanctuary and that no man might be taken out of it (if escaped thither) for what offence whatever, but this was before the British inhabited here."

Traditions connected with Screen

The customs above alluded to are now wholly abrogated, and but few traces remain of the peculiar feelings connected with those times. Among the latter may be noticed the traditions of St Columb's frequent residence here, of his blessing the ferry boat to Greencastle [Donegal], since which it is believed that none have been ever lost,

and of his cursing Bunowen river in consequence of which no fish can live in it! Among the local traditions there is one connected with a high, sequestered and almost inaccessible spot on the side of Craig precipices, affording, however, a considerable tract of green pasture land called Mary's Meadow. It is said that this Mary, at a time when the country was in the hands of enemies and all the other inhabitants had fled or perished, got herself and her cow up into this solitary recess, in which she lived on the milk, coming down every night to provide water for her companion, and supported till the enemy were beaten from the lands and their occupation was resumed by their former possessors.

Section of Memoir by J. O'Donovan and G. Petrie, with additions by J. Stokes

MEMOIR WRITING

Memoir Writing

[Insert covering note: Much of this is very good, but it was done early and grounded in a great degree on an excellent Irish Memoir by Rev. Mr Butler, the Presbyterian clergyman. I wish only that it had been our own, [initialled] T.A. Larcom].

HISTORY AND SOCIAL ECONOMY

Early Inhabitants

From the notices given in the preceding section, it will be seen that this parish was peopled at the earliest period of which we have historic records by the Cruithne or Picts, the ancient inhabitants of the great portion of modern Scotland. In subsequent ages this race, being either expelled or amalgamated with the Scoti or native Irish, all traces of them were eradicated, long prior to the Plantation of Ulster.

From the traces of cultivation which appear on the mountain side, 200 feet higher than modern industry has reached, it may with probability be inferred that the parish was not thinly inhabited in those distant times, but what the amount was, there are no data now remaining to enable us to ascertain. In the wars of the native chieftains of the north with Elizabeth, the parish must necessarily, as tradition reports, have been nearly depopulated, and on the Plantation of Ulster a number of families of English and Scottish race were fixed among the survivors on the unoccupied lands. The rebellion of 1621 brought still greater desolation in its train, and Magilligan became once more desert. But few of either race escaped its destructive effects, and of the Irish clan from whence the popular name of the parish is derived, not one is now to be found either in it or the adjoining districts.

Plantation Period

After this unhappy period, the lands were again thickly peopled partly by persons of English race and by Scottish settlers, the descendants of those Picts who were perhaps their earliest occupiers; and the numbers of the latter were, it is said, increased considerably by others of the same stock during and after the rebellion of 1745 in Scotland. A century since, the inhabitants were almost wholly of Scotch or English origin and all professed the reformed Episcopalian and Presbyterian religions.

Immigration from Inishowen Peninsula

By slow degrees, however, these peculiar characteristics of the inhabitants have become less and less visible. The wasteland required humble and laborious hands to reclaim them; male and female servants were necessary to assist the farmers; smugglers, illicit distillers and paupers settled in the mountain wilds. From these and other causes the population in the central parts of the parish has increased twentyfold in the memory of persons now living, and Magilligan has once more become the abode chiefly of native and Roman Catholic Irish.

Of these settlers within the last and present generation, the larger portion have passed over from the opposite shore of Inishowen in Donegal, a fact of which a sufficient proof is found in the prevailing family names being those of the ancient clans which inhabited that wild and nearly insular district. Thus, of the name of O'Dogherty, there was in 1824 no less than 54 families, amounting to 313 individuals; and of the name of McLoughlin, 14 families and 221 persons. Of the settlers who have thus recently fixed themselves in Magilligan, it is only just to add in the words of the Rev. Mr Butler "that they are fast rising into the possession of lands and houses and with these also into moral and religious respectability."

Census Returns

The returns of the census under the population act of 1821 gave an aggregate of 1,626 Protestants and 1,562 Roman Catholics, making a total of 3,188; but from a more accurate investigation made by Mr Butler, it appears that the returns made to the baronial constable must have overrated the former and greatly underrated the latter. The amount of each as given by Mr Butler's census taken in 1824 being: Protestants, families 233, individuals 993; Roman Catholics, families 398, individuals 2,034; total families 631, total persons 3,047.

According to the parliamentary census of 1831, this parish contained in that year houses 641, families 543, male inhabitants 1,788, female inhabitants 1,820, total inhabitants 3,608. Of these, 449 families were employed in agriculture and 43 in manufacture and trade.

Celibacy in Protestants

The causes already alluded to as effecting a change in the population of Magilligan still exist to a considerable extent, and others have more recently arisen of equal influence. Among these Mr Butler notices the prevailing disposition to celibacy existing in the 2 Protestant communions, a cautious feeling in which those of the Roman Catholic faith do not participate. A more potent cause, however, is to be found in the readiness of the one to emigrate in the hope of bettering their condition and the unwillingness of the other to leave their natal soil, as long as it will afford them the humblest means of existence. This cause is in more or less active operation in every other part of the country, and may ultimately produce a nearly complete obliteration of the character of the rural inhabitants produced by the Plantation.

Landlords

Of the 2 lessees, Conolly Gage Esquire and Sir James Bruce Bart, who hold the parish under the bishopric in nearly equal portions, only Mr Gage resides within its bounds. The residence of the other is in the adjoining parish of Dunboe. Among the farmers who hold under these intermediate lessees is to be found the next class in point of respectability, the parish being subdivided and sublet in about 270 farms varying in size from 3 to upwards of 300 Cunningham acres, a very few farms only being held directly from the see. The native freehold of Ballycarton is held by [blank] Lane under the Marquis of Waterford. [Insert note: The freehold of Ballycarton was granted by Lord Waterford's ancestor to the ancestor of Mr Lane as a reward for his services in a contested election].

Farmers' Diet

The condition of the better class of farmers is still frequently comfortable and independent, though generally inferior to what it was in former years. At that period the food of such persons and their servants was generally better than with the average of the same class in the north of Ireland. Beef is now more rarely seen at their tables [insert query by T. Larcom: and mutton I suppose; reply by J. Stokes: not any mutton], but pork is still in abundance as well as fish of various sorts and, in much of the parish, rabbits for the 3 winter months. Geese are also common at the tables of some farmers and ducks and barn-door fowl more generally. From the abundance of rabbits during the season, it is not uncommon for the farmers' servants to stipulate that they shall not be exclusively fed on them, and the following jingling grace is often repeated by those persons, the servants, before Candlemas Day.

> "For rabbits hot, for rabbits cold
> For rabbits young, for rabbits old
> For rabbits tender, rabbits tough
> We thank the Lord we've had enough."

Farmers and Lifestyle

The houses belonging to the higher farmers are comfortable and frequently present good furniture, the remains of times more opulent or ranks more respectable. Their dress is perhaps too costly for their rank. These observations must be understood as applying chiefly to the Protestants who have been long settled here. Those of the Roman Catholic faith, however liberally they may occasionally spend at merrymaking, as marriages, baptisms, are accustomed to live much more frugally both in food and dress, and it is this circumstance, coupled with their amor patriae, that enables them to hold lands on terms which would not give most Protestants subsistence and even sometimes to accumulate property on farms which Protestants had previously abandoned. [Insert query by T. Larcom: This contradicts [earlier section on] farmhouses: which is correct? Answer: Above relates to the new farmhouses, earlier reference to those that are older, perhaps to those of the Catholics].

Between the class now alluded to and the labouring cottiers there are necessarily many intermediate grades, whose varied habits of life it would be tedious to detail. The comforts of the farmer of 3 or 4 acres must obviously be very limited and the condition of the labourer poor indeed who has to support a family on 10d a day, in addition to his own food. According, however, to their degrees of industry, the very poorest get, occasionally, supplies of shell fish, flounders, herrings and cod fish; and milk, butter and eggs are obtained plentifully by the majority of the people and in some degree by nearly all.

Use of Tea and Tobacco

With all classes and ages, the use of tea gains ground whilst that of tobacco is decreasing among the juniors; but still there is, says Mr Butler, more money spent on this foreign weed than would pay for the education of all the children of the poor and provide the most necessary medicines for the sick. The writer knows no place where it is in such general use with the general population. It is a legacy of the smuggling times, when money was very plenty and tobacco almost gratuitous to those who paid no duty. "Those times also left other and worse legacies which shall be nameless."

Furniture

The inventory of the poor man's furniture is easily taken: usually 1 or 2 plain bed frames, which have seen much service, with coarse bedding including chaff or straw and the extra beds wanted supplied by shakedowns of straw or bracken upon the cold floors and raised daily unless when a sick person lies on one of them; a pot or two, a water jug, a few low stools to sit on and generally one or more spinning wheels and a reel; a tea chest or other cheap box and perhaps a small table and a few articles of delph ware.

Fuel

Turf is still the only fuel used in Magilligan, but it cannot very long meet the wants of the increasing population; happily, however, coal can be obtained at low rates from the lough in the summer season. [Insert addition by J. Stokes: Mr Butler seems to forget that there is plenty of mud and chopped straw at hand].

Diseases

The people of Magilligan are usually healthy and there are no diseases peculiar to the district. Rheumatism, the effect of the bogs and imperfectly-drained mountain sides, is that from which they most generally suffer. Pulmonary affections sometimes occur in a certain district and may be attributed to the same cause. Gravel complaints are not uncommon when sufficient care is not taken to procure water free from stagnancy or the admixture of blown sands.

Mr Butler remarks that "were cleanliness more attended to by the poor, were the fermentation of manure removed a little farther from the doors, were greater care taken to procure substantial aliment than tobacco and ardent spirits and were the hearsay remedies of every pretender to medical skill disregarded, the diseases of Magilligan would be very few indeed."

Longevity

Instances of longevity are numerous. There are now living many persons above 70 [insert note by T. Larcom: nothing short of 80 (at the least) should be noticed], some above 80 and a few much older. Not many years since, in a line of by-road called the Black Row, from a range of blackthorns, there were 15 persons alive at one time, the average of whose ages was 90 years! Daniel McCurriston could run well at 102 years and died aged 112. Henry McLaughlin died aged 113.

Population, Character and Disposition

In speaking of the genius and disposition of the poorer classes, it is obvious that no general character can be given that would be applicable to the descendants of such diversified ancestry, living without any town as a common centre of association and among whom the English, Caledonian and old Irish customs must all partially have influence.

It may, however, be said generally that some truly estimable characters are to be found among all those distinct races, and if they are not more numerous, great allowance should be made for the want of an enlightened ancestry, the introduction and long-continued practice of smuggling and illicit distillation, the paucity of means, until lately, of procuring a moral and religious education, together with the absolute want of a place of Roman Catholic worship at no very remote period, and of Presbyterian till of late years. It is consolatory, however, to know that the character of the population generally is improving.

Morality

The prevailing vice of drunkenness, though still a serious public evil, is confessedly on the decrease and *fornication*, a frequent vice of the last age, is now but little known. "How little" says Mr Butler

"the imputation of this last vice hurt the feelings of some in the preceding age may be estimated from the answer given by an old woman to a clergyman who remarked to her that her daughter could not well be admitted to suckle another's child who was not married. "Hoo sir, mony's the bra' wean oor Bess had, and ne'er was married."

Illicit Distillation

[J. Stokes] Illicit distillation is at present carried on to a very great extent. This is owing to the absence of revenue officers and police.

Amusements

Among the Irish population intemperate drinking at funerals and indulgence in the savage pastime of cock-fighting has been greatly diminished through the influence of the priesthood, but nightly dances and gatherings for mere amusement are still too frequent among a population not sufficiently educated to indulge in them safely, and the substitution for such customs of manly sports by daylight under the direction of moral and respected persons would be of great advantage to the population generally. [Insert note by G. Downes: rather contradictory [in relation to morality].

Superstition and Tradition

Superstition cannot be said to exist here in any very high degree and party spirit, though too common, has not hitherto assumed that savage character that tends to violence and blood.

Provision for Poor

Charity is here, as it is in most other parts of Ireland, a prominent feature in the character of the people, though the collections at the church, the chapel and the meeting house, with a few pounds annually, the interest of 200 pounds bequeathed by one of the Gage family, constitute the only funds for the support of the destitute together with Mr Lather's [Leather's] legacy of 100 pounds. Yet the want of more ample means is but little felt in a district where the poorest or the vilest scarcely ever apply in vain to the poor cottager for lodging or to the farmer for food. In 1821 there were 55 families apparently belonging to the parish, subsisting on charity either wholly or in part; the number this year exclusive of strangers is 43. In 1821 many strangers received the charity.

[Insert note by J. Stokes: It appears from the

vestry book that in 1773 21 badges were delivered to the poor. In 1817 it was again resolved that the poor of the parish be badged. No badge was given without the recommendation of 3 respectable persons from each townland. Charity to beggars not of the parish was prohibited, and it was further ordered that it should be extended only to poor housekeepers. 2 days in each week were appointed for almsgiving or "helping" as it is called, namely Tuesday for the "upper end" and Friday for the "lower end of the parish"].

In 1703 the Rev. John Lather, rector of the parish, bequeathed 100 pounds to the poor. In 1798 Hudson Gage bequeathed 200 pounds. This forms a fund of 18 pounds a year which is distributed at Christmas.

[Insert note by T. Larcom: Tithe 425 pounds].

Education

At the commencement of the present century the people of Magilligan had but little facilities for obtaining education. In 1747 the chief parish school was at Ballymaclara. In 1748, 5 pounds were given for the repairs of a schoolhouse in the "upper end" and in 1755, November 1st, a schoolhouse was ordered to be built at Claggan. In 1775 the vestry assessed for schoolmaster 2 pounds, schoolhouse in the "upper end" 2 guineas and also "lower end" of the parish 2 guineas. This may be cited as an instance of what was common from the earliest preserved records.

In 1814 and the 2 succeeding years there was no schoolhouse worthy of the name. In 1816 a subscription was commenced by Mr Butler for a schoolhouse of stone, and by the assistance of Mr Conolly Gage, the rector Mr Knox and some of the wealthier farmers a respectable schoolhouse was built and some others partially encouraged. The same gentleman, aided by Sir James Bruce Baronet, afterwards erected a second schoolhouse on a smaller scale, suited to its locality and a third has been subsequently added. There are also 3 other schools without any endowment. The number of children receiving education in 1824 was about 430, viz. 35 of the Established Church, 95 Presbyterians and 280 Roman Catholics. The number in 1834 is not more than 260.

The salaries of the teachers vary from 10 pounds downwards, in addition to some trifling emoluments from the parents which are, however, but badly paid. The charges are 1s 3d to 5s per quarter but usually 1s 8d to 2s.

The Presbyterians have a circulating library and a person to teach psalmody.

Table of Schools by J. Stokes

[Insert note by T. Larcom: To be superseded by tables of the parliamentary form].

[Table gives townland in which situated, when first instituted, religion of teacher, number of pupils subdivided by religion and sex, remarks as to how supported].

Drumnahy, 1630, 1 Protestant teacher, 60 males, 20 females, total 80; parish schoolhouse, it was formerly under the Kildare Street Society.

Claggan, 1755, 1 Protestant teacher, 65 males, 15 females, total 80; this was formerly supported by an assessment on the parish and also by the Kildare Street Society.

Ballymclary, 1734, 1 Catholic teacher, 40 males, 20 females, total 80; this has lately been brought under the new Board of Education. This school is very unpopular in the parish, as well as its supporters.

Gortmore, 1833, 1 Protestant teacher, 13 males, 12 females, 25 total; supported by the Kildare Street Society.

Ballyleighery, 1828, 1 Protestant teacher, 10 males, 10 females, total 20; supported entirely by the peasantry. [Total number of pupils] 260.

The state of education in this parish has been much injured by the destruction of the Kildare Street Society and by the clandestine means believed to be used in the introduction of the new board. Support from Kildare Street is at present only nominal or next to it.

PRODUCTIVE ECONOMY

Stock Holdings

[J. Stokes] There are about 2,000 head of black cattle. The breed of sheep have declined to about 200 head. Goats are apparently extinct. The parish was formerly much resorted to for the sake of drinking Magilligan <McGilligan> goat's whey.

Fishing

The cottiers of this parish and of Tamlaght Finlagan are chiefly fishermen. The seas of this coast abound with cod fish, trout, salmon, grey lords, black soles, flukes, herrings and oysters. The several banks are from 3 to 15 miles from the shore. Deep sea fishing is chiefly practised. The Londonderry fishermen have no piers or any proper places for shelter for their boats. The greater number of these are without sails, open and small. It is not uncommon for them to row out 16 miles from the shore in these frail vessels. Cod fish is in season the whole year round except June and July and May, salmon are in May and June. Grey lords, black soles and flukes accompany the herring shoal which comes in from July to September. All white fish are generally salted. Cod fish are sold at the shore for 5s per dozen; 6s is the average market price. Herrings at the shore are sold at the rate of 6d for 20, market price 10d. Salmon is sold at market for 2d ha'penny per lb. All inferior fish are very cheap.

There are no local regulations among these fishermen, no general salting houses or any other encouragement.

Extracts from Draft Memoir by G. Petrie

SOCIAL ECONOMY

Poem or Song

[J. O'Donovan's hand, possibly a translation ?].

The sun now having far advanced his course
Upon the cloudless sky and pouring down
A flood of heat upon this nether world
Soon changed the chilling aspect of the
   morn.

The myriad drops of clear and pearly dew
That like bright eyes had glistened to his
   beams
While in the morn he smiled with milder ray
Now fled before his fervid, scorching glare.

PRODUCTIVE ECONOMY

Rearing of Rabbits

[Insert addition: The rabbit warrens for which Magilligan has been so long celebrated should probably have been noticed with more propriety in the first section, but they constituted so large a portion of its productive economy that it was deemed more expedient to reserve an account of them for this place]. These warrens are situated in the northern portion of the parish and occupy about 3,000 acres, the chief part of which is in the dry, sandy lands, but a few spots also of them are in the rocky mountain side which appears to be their most natural situation.

"The conies are but feeble folk, yet make they their houses in the rocks." Proverbs 30. 26.

In the 17th century, when Magilligan was thinly inhabited, the warrens occupied the greater portion of the parish, extending says Mr Beck, a distance of 10 miles from Solomon's Porch to the Roe foot or properly mouth, and at this period the warrens were abundantly stocked with juniper shrubs now destroyed.

These warrens are held in all proportions, from a few burrows to hundreds of acres, and constitute the staple production of several large farms. The holders of such grounds are about 70 in number, but there are also a number of others who hold smaller spots fed on by rabbits but on which they get but a divided pasture with cows, horses or more generally numerous flocks of sheep. The species cultivated here is of the small, grey kind, yet at times there appears a few of black, white and mixed breeds.

Economy and Management of Rabbit Warrens

The rabbits are taken annually to an extent varying with the favourableness of the season and the skill and care of the cultivators. It is said that from 3,600 to 3,700 dozen is the usual annual amount sold of made skins, as they are called. That is, when any particular deficiency is found, 2 such skins are counted only as one to the buyer, and those very defective are called racks or libbocks and sold to pedlars for very trifling sums. If then the number of halves and libbocks, together with the various small portions stolen and otherwise disposed of than at the public sale be taken into account, it may be assumed that the average take, as it is called, will be from 48,000 to 50,000 single rabbits annually.

The rabbit skins, which are said to be the best in Ireland, for many years sold from 10 to 16s per dozen and produced from 2,000 to 2,500 pounds annually. But for the last 30 years they have been gradually declining in prices and do not now bring more than 3s 6d. Besides this, however, the flesh produces probably as much as pays the outlay on their account. As many of the rabbits as the inhabitants can conveniently use are retained for domestic consumption during the time of taking them and the rest sold to carriers of them to Coleraine, Derry, Dungiven and other towns in which they are likely to find a market. In 1683 their usual price was 2d per couple in Magilligan and 3d in the neighbouring towns; subsequently they rose to [blank] and their present price is [blank] per couple.

Sale of Skins

The mode of sale of the skins is by public advertisement annually made, and 2 men called casters are sworn to administer impartial justice between seller and buyer. The purchase or purchasers first bargain for the price per dozen for all he needs and pays for them in ready money in Coleraine, after the casters have first determined the number of made skins delivered by each individual. The refuse of the skins is converted into glue.

Rabbit Husbandry

In rabbit husbandry, the smaller warrens unconnected with others are generally the most productive, acre for acre, as the rabbits have the advantage of more good feeding in neighbouring cultivated lands and pastures. No exact calculation can be made of what an acre of ground is worth for them, it being dependent on so many circumstances. In some spots where the feeding is abundant and the skill of the owner distinguished, the acre might produce occasionally several pounds; but in other cases 10 acres might not produce the same amount. And whenever the lands are capable of raising frequent crops of grain and potatoes, it seems an error to encourage many rabbits, or rather to have any large bounds of continued warren. The multiplicity of their holes and mining operations open the ground, already too dry, to sun and winds, whence much of the better materials are lost by evaporation and the accumulation of vegetable mould prevented; but where the white sands approach the surface, there is perhaps no remedy and the land had better be given up to them.

Burrowing is by the oldest right of prescription the rabbit's own profession, and the young ones from trying it in sport soon learn to earth the ground in good earnest. But lest they should not choose the precise grounds which the farmer wishes them to occupy, or lest they should be too tardy in their operations, those who desire to have rabbits occupying new grounds plant them by the aid of a rabbit spade, which consists of a long handle of wood shod with a long and narrow groove of iron, pointed to cut and hollow the sand, whence it acts at the same time as spade and shovel and fetches the sand or mould underneath from a long distance. By this means artificial holes are made, and after closing up the top of the hole with a strong sod, the materials that had been taken out are laid on the top and nothing appears but these artificial hillocks and a few mouths or entrances elsewhere left by the spade. Here rabbits elicited from the vicinity willingly enter and complete the necessary operations, being predisposed to enter where they see fresh mould raised.

Historical Notice about Rabbits

From a notice in Young's *Tour in Ireland* in 1776,

it would appear that the average number of rabbits taken has been nearly the same for the last 50 or 60 years. He gives the average as 3,000 dozen, but adds that there had been killed the year previous, 1775, 4,000 or 5,000. Supposing it to have been the latter number, the aggregate of single rabbits killed in that year was probably upwards of 60,000.

Agriculture and Crops

Oats, barley, potatoes, rye also in the lowlands and flax in the uplands are the crops usually cultivated. According to the soil the rotations are something as follows: potatoes, barley, oats and then pasture for some years; or on lea lands: oats, potatoes, oats and pasture or oats twice or more, then pastured. In very dry lands rye or potatoes and rye, then pasture till well swarded. In 1825 there were 1,800 acres of the parish under crop and in 1833 [blank].

In the uplands there is soil good enough for wheat, yet it would not succeed well except in dry years, from the excessive moisture of the climate.

Clover is sown in the uplands in small quantities. In the lowlands the soil is not suited to it but would, in a great part, be well adapted to grass, fiorins, vetches, peas, carrots and turnips. Yet these cannot be cultivated whilst cattle roam at large in the winter and "biped depredators take such liberties in the summer." Potatoes are usually put in by the back of the spade, in the mode called kibbing.

Irrigation and Manures

Irrigation is but little used, being suited only to a few spots. The highlands are usually too steep and the lowlands too flat and porous to be drained at pleasure. Top dressings are in great use, and the effect immediate: they are from ashes, sheep fold manure, and one object of them being to rot the swards, they should be put on the ground only in winter, or if on meadow lands, immediately before the rise of vegetation in the spring. Burnt ashes is valuable for oats in all places not previously exhausted and especially on moist lands. The manures commonly used in Magilligan are from the stable, cow house, sheep fold, fermented bog or the seaweed and crag of the shores. Lime is rarely used as a manure, crag succeeding but less and with less injuries to the following crops.

Farming Implements

The farming implements in general seen in Magilligan though improving are still very imperfect. Ploughs in several cases begin to be directed by reins, but they are generally made of the worst construction. Carts are becoming common, but from the want of a road in one part of the parish, slide cars are still necessarily used. Except in the barn of Conolly Gage Esquire there is neither roller or scarifier, straw-cutting instrument or thrashing machine in the parish.

Rents

No accurate statement can be given of rents, as the lands are set by holdings, not by acres. No rent is charged for turf bogs.

Wages

The wages of men servants is about 3 pounds yearly and half that amount to women. Labourers receive 10d a day with food in summer and something less in winter. Coleraine and Newtownlimavady are the markets.

Cattle

The stocks of cattle in Magilligan are inconsiderable, those of the mountain grazing excepted, and of course that of C. Gage Esquire, which is good. The prices latterly obtained have offered but little inducement to the rearing of good cattle. Sheep are the most numerous of the small cattle and may be seen on almost every farm on the plain and some on the uplands, from 3 to 3 score. The breeds are various but improving and the wool very fine.

Cows are occasionally injured by the sandy quality of the soil. If the grass be short and though their flesh is apt to be in good condition, the supply of milk and butter from each cow is not abundant except on a few fiorin farms. In a few instances the bull has been called into requisition for the cow and evidently for the advantage of the proprietor. Oxen are used in draught only by C. Gage Esquire.

Horses and other Stock

The breed of horse is generally too small but otherwise not dispicable, and it is not uncommon for poor fishermen and carriers to have one, who have no cow. The swine are generally of a bad description. The goats once so numerous in the uplands are now reduced to a few, which are chiefly confined to 2 localities in the parish.

Linen and Woollen Manufacture

Respecting manufactures in Magilligan, but little can be said. Linen weavers are not numerous, and they are nearly all ill-taught and badly supplied with looms and situations. There are a few exceptions and one of these works diaper.

The flax crop is inconsiderable, being almost confined to the upperlands where it is usually coarse or at leastly coarsely spun. 3 or 4 hanks of yarn in the week is the usual work of the spinners generally, whereas in Down and Antrim multitudes spin much finer yarn from 6 to 8 hanks weekly without any laborious efforts. Too commonly also, the spinners are obliged to purchase in Coleraine and Newtownlimavady small quantities of flax and to return these to sell their yarn, by which the poor consume a large portion of their time. No double wheels are used and but little is done in the way of preparing yarn and employing weavers as a source of internal employment. At whatever time this may be thought of, the upperlands will afford its very best water and accommodations.

A few woolsorters or persons skilled in the spinning and weaving of wool are very much wanted in this parish, as it abounds with wool of a fine quality and makes a certain coarse manufacture very much used. But the home-made goods look so badly compared with those purchased in the neighbouring towns, that even the poor are ashamed of them for a dress and begin to purchase abroad. About as many stockings are made in the parish as are required for domestic use, but none are exported.

Manufacture of Bent Grass into Carpets

The manufacture of bent grass into carpeting has been exclusively followed [alternative: established] and has been productive of considerable profits.

Shipping

Since the decline of smuggling and distillation, there has been but little use for ships and the only vessels belonging to this maritime parish are about 6 or 8 small boats of 1 or 2 tons each; nor would the lea shore be favourable to boats of a better description unless some wharfs were erected. The fishing of the inhabitants extends only to flounders, cockles near the coast and for a short time annually, the employment of a few boats in catching herrings in the lough; but there is a considerable carrying trade of fish taken by the Inishowen fishermen, usually codfish and sold at the point of Magilligan.

Plans and Section Drawings

Drawing and Plans of Burrows

[Plans of 5 types of burrows, showing location of mouths]: 1, a single planted burrow; 2, a double planted burrow; 3, a double burrow; 4, plan of a certain very old burrow; 5, a certain burrow of 3 years imitated; 6, a burrowing spade.

Nos 1, 2 and 3 represent new burrows made with a rabbit spade by grooving out the sandy soil at the crossing points, which are afterwards covered with strong sod and the excavated mould; nos 4 and 5 are specimens of the endlessly diversified natural burrows.

Illustration of Water Table and Druims and Misks

[Section drawing showing water table] Percolation of the water in the lowlands through the sand: the upper line represents the surface, the lines "TO TO" horizontal levels of the tide at low water, at which depth water will be found anywhere in the lowlands, but it is pure and fit for use only where found together. The water percolates from the springs S S S in the rock X S O by the dotted line towards the tide at whatever height that stands, and if passed from W in a well when lower than T, it is stagnant.

Druims and misks in the lowlands: [section drawings] direction of the coast on Lough Foyle showing how much old arable land lies now covered with light sands. The figures 1 to 12 denote the old stratum of wrought vegetable mould, the letters A,B etc. the present surface; H O is the lake at low water.

In figures 8 and 9 the letters DD etc. mark the eminences called druims, M M the flat lower parts or misks which appear from the Roe mouth to the Back Strand; the first with very little vegetable mould, the other with a depth of surface soil which is here imitated. They were formed originally by the waves as ordinary sand banks.

Notes for Memoir by G. Downes and J. Stokes [c.1834]

Early Improvements

In addition to what has been stated in the report respecting former times, it may be observed with reference to the present that there are in the parish 42 families of the name of McLoughlin and 57 families of the name of Doherty.

Obstructions to Improvement

These arise out of the secluded situation of the parish, the want of a sufficiently remunerating price for agricultural produce and perhaps the want of a suffiently active and enterprising disposition in the parishioners themselves.

The ancient customs which continue to militate against improvement: by the exertions of Sir James Bruce and Conolly Gage, the ancient custom of rundale is now almost entirely unknown. The system of subdivision is also kept down and efforts are constantly making by the proprietors to enlarge the farms of the parish.

Local Government

The resident magistrate is Conolly Gage Esquire, who is non-stipendiary. As for residence, firmness and popularity, he possesses all the three.

The usual force of constabulary police, who are stationed at Newtownlimavady, is (see parish of Drumachose). There are no revenue police nor officers. The water guard amounts to: there is no water guard. There are no peculiar jurisdictions.

The petty sessions are not held in the parish but at Newtownlimavady (see parish of Drumachose). The number of outrages committed since 1830 is nothing. Concerning their increase there is nothing to be said, as the parish is profoundly quiet. About 20 years ago a riot took place at the burial of an Orangeman. Also the house of William Cust, Oughill, was robbed within that period.

The perpetrators have been properly punished. The outrages have been committed with reference to party at the time when they were of more frequent occurrence.

Combinations

No combinations have been resorted to for any purpose.

Illicit Distillation and Smuggling

Illicit distillation is at present carried on to a great extent but it is diminishing. Since it was put down in Inishowen, it has increased in Magilligan, but Conolly Gage thinks he has reason to believe that he has succeeded in putting it down almost entirely in his own estates in this year, 1834.

There is no smuggling carried on. Illicit distillation is chiefly carried on by the poorer cottiers, who almost always succeed in hiding their liquor by burying it whole in the sand and then drawing a cart over it so as to give it the appearance of a beaten track.

Respecting insurances: There are none.

Dispensaries

The parish is very healthy and seldom are there any applicants to the dispensary. Sore throat is the most conspicuous disease.

Schools

The introduction of day schools into this parish was so early that, in order to trace the gradual effect they may have brought, it is necessary to go back several centuries. If they have produced any more improvement in the character of the parishioners, it has only been by being accompanied with religious instruction. The effect produced by those of more recent introduction i.e. the Sunday schools is more marked. This is universally the opinion of practical men with respect to other parishes besides Magilligan. The people are anxious for information and knowledge.

Poor

In 1703 the Rev. John Leather, rector of the parish, bequeathed 100 pounds to the poor. In 1798 Hudson Gage Esquire bequeathed 200 pounds. This forms a fund of 18 pounds a year, being 6 per cent raised by interest. Mr Leather's 100 pounds is at present lent to the Honourable and Reverend Arthur Pomeroy, on his bond to Sir James Bruce and Conolly Gage. The interest is punctually paid by him and distributed publicly about Christmas by the rector and parishioners. Hudson Gage's interest is in the hands of Conolly Gage, the interest paid and disposed of in the same manner. There is no building of any kind for the poor, aged and infirm.

The collections made at the several places of worship are divided among the poor.

Habits of the People

The usual number in a family is 5 and a half. The earliest age for contracting matrimony is [blank].

The amusements and recreations are dances, common playing and a yearly fair held on the Wooden bridge and on the road near Mr Graham's. On the bridge they spend the day in drinking and eating and dancing. It owes its origin in part to a fiddler called McNamara, who first introduced the assembly on this bridge, it being a better place

for dancing than the road. It is held on the 13th and 14th of July.

Superstitions and Legends

In the parish of Magilligan there is the same superstitious legend about our Saviour and the bottle as there is in the parish of Banagher.

Emigration

Emigration does not prevail to a great extent, the annual number being about 20. The seasons at which and the places to which they emigrate are: the summer months to the United States. They are chiefly of the labouring class and tradesmen. The annual number of nearly 20 has continued for the last 3 years. None have returned. Some individuals visit home occasionally and return to America in the following spring.

The number that go annually to get harvest or other work is small. They do not take their wives and families with them. As to renting ground and sowing potatoes for winter, it is sometimes done and sometimes not. Many of the families beg.

Remarkable Events

The name of Dennis Hempson, the last of the old Irish harpists, is so popular that the following elaborate particulars respecting him will be found generally interesting: refer to a small tract written by Mr Sampson, which I forward to Lieutenant Larcom.

In addition to Hempson, the only remarkable person to whom this parish has given birth was Cushy Glenn, a noted robber who was shot near the Murder Hole in Dunboe by a native of Drumachose whom he was attempting to rob. This occurred in 1799.

PRODUCTIVE ECONOMY

Manufacturing and Commercial

There are a few linen weavers, who are badly provided with looms and localities. Among the exceptions, one works diaper. He lives in the townland of [blank]. There is also a coarse woollen cloth manufactured. A sufficiency of stockings for home consumption are knit, but no more.

Bent grass (botanically called agristis stolonifera) is made into carpeting.

Fairs and Markets

There is no fair nor market. The markets usually frequented by the parishioners are those of

Coleraine and Newtownlimavady. The commodities in which they deal are (in addition to rabbits and rabbit skins) mattings, woollen and linen cloth, with the usual agricultural produce.

These are brought to market in Newtownlimavady and Coleraine. The produce of the spinning wheel and loom is all consumed on the spot, bought up by dealers.

Originally there was a fair at the Back Strand. It was removed to the road near the Glebe House, but has now degenerated into an amusement fair on the Wooden bridge held on the 14th July.

Landowners

The great proprietors are Sir James Bruce and Conolly Gage Esquire, of whom the latter is resident. All the parish except Mr Lane's farm is churchland.

Leases and Tenures

They are not generally held by lease and the tenure is 19 years. They hold direct from the landlords. The average rent of the best land is from 30s down to 16s, of middling from 16s to 2s 6d and of the worst from 2s 6d to 6d. The rent is paid wholly in money but is accompanied by duty work and other customary service.

The farmers are generally comfortable. They farm wholly for the purpose of subsistence.

The quantity of land let in conacre is considerable but is diminishing. It is given to a great extent by Conolly Gage and by the large farmers.

They [fields] are not well shaped in the hilly ground. There are few regularly-enclosed fields. In the flat, their boundaries are generally the drains.

Local Taxes

The local taxes or cesses to which tenants are liable are the same as in the other parishes.

Farm Buildings

The farm buildings are sometimes good and commodious. The houses of cottiers are always bad. They are erected and kept in repair by the tenants.

Soil and Manures

The lime used is quarried at Craig and also brought from Sir James Bruce at 1s 4d a barrel.

Burning the ground for manure does prevail with a view to the reclaiming mossy ground. It is done in Tamlaght and Duncrun more than in any other townland of the parish.

Horses

The number of horses put in a team is generally 2.

Breeds of Cattle

The following improved breeds have been introduced: Ayrshire and a few Durham cattle by Conolly Gage. His sheep are partly Leicester and partly Scotch, black-faced. With these he has stocked the top of the rock. He has some good horses.

Cattle Dealing

There are no professed dealers in cattle. Jobbers buy them up and drive them to the markets of [blank], where they are sold for about 6 pounds.

Crops

Green feeding is not extensively practised. The following vegetables: turnips, clover and vetches are principally used. Field peas are sowed occasionally. Mr Gage does it judiciously and extensively.

Uses made of the Bogs

The bogs are grazed at summer and harvest. They are principally on the top of the mountains. The fuel is consumed wholly in the neighbourhood. None is carried to any place extraparochial.

The people have free right to turbary but not to grazing. Respecting mines and mineral deposits, there are none at present known.

The bog wood is used for fuel, roofing houses, candlelight. The turf is made into charcoal for the smith's forge.

Drainage

Respecting the means used and the difficulties: each farm in the flats is bounded by an open drain 6 feet wide and 3 and a half feet deep. Along the sides of the mountain French drains are used. On the top the bog is drained in those parts worked upon by the turf cutters, by the manner in which they take out their fuel.

Planting

The modern plantations are the extensive demesne of Conolly Gage Esquire and about 50 acres which he planted on Binevenagh <Benyevenagh> about 1823, and which are in a highly thriving state. There are no nurseries for young trees. The prices of the several descriptions are [blank]. Mr Gage's plantations consist of almost every description of tree in his demense on the lowlands, and of Scotch fir, larch fir, oak and ash on the mountain side.

The aspect and nature of the soil of Mr Gage's plantations may be thus described: the demesne is a dead flat, having a soil of clay and sand. The aspect of the mountain is moist and the soil a stiff clay, very hard in dry weather.

The trees which thrive best in reference to different soils, aspects, slopes and exposures are as instanced in Mr Gage's plantations: Scotch firs interspersed with oaks on the hills and exposed places, larch firs with oaks and ash in the hollows and sheltered glens. Mr Gage has planted 70 acres since 1816. He procures his seedlings from Messrs Dickson of Edinburgh and plants them out when 2 and 3 years old. They are injured by the north and south west winds. Easterly winds have no effect owing to the shelter of the rock.

Respecting the consumption of timber and its exportation and growth, it may be stated that the carpenters generally procure their timber from Newtownlimavady or Coleraine. For inferior kinds of work they purchase wood at moderate terms from the plantations of Downhill and Bellarena.

Sea Coast

The seaweed is burnt for kelp which is sold at [blank].

General Remarks on Physical Features

The flatness of the lowlands of Magilligan and the advantages which would ensue not only to that parish but to all the others of its vicinity from an increased facility of communication with the city of Londonderry naturally suggests the idea of a railroad from Londonderry to Newtownlimavady. Next to the line already made in the kingdom, no place appears better adapted for such an attempt [than?] <for> the ancient beach of Lough Foyle, above which it could be laid in a line already surveyed and drawn out, as it were, by nature. The banks of the Foyle present every facility for carrying it up to the Waterside of the city, and the central situation of Newtownlimavady presents itself the natural depot for the agricultural produce of many miles around.

The highest point to which cultivation has been carried among the rocks is at the altitude of [blank] feet above the sea, in the townland of [blank]. The position of the cultivated land does not offer much general facility for either drainage or irrigation. The climate is not unfavourable and

there is shelter from every wind among the hollows and ravines of Benevenagh. That mountain is very well adapted for both planting and sheep-walks.

ANCIENT TOPOGRAPHY

Plan of Ancient Enclosure

Ground plan [triangular shaped, 35 feet 6 inches by 35 feet 8 inches by 35 feet 3 inches, 6 feet between wall and ground with orientation] of ancient enclosure on the hill behind Castle Lecky House, parish of Magilligan, scale 20 feet to an inch. Walls very indistinct and surrounded by many rocks and stones.

Miscellaneous Discoveries

There are ruin, ruins, old castle and giant's stone near Castle Lecky, in Craig and Aughil. What are the particulars respecting them? Answer: A plan sketch of the old castle has been taken. It seems to be nothing military, but it is similar to the Picts' House of Duncrun.

Near the townland of Ballymatimber, on the left hand side of the shore road, workmen were cutting turf in May 1834. They found 3 feet below the surface, and in the sand, a wooden vessel about 8 inches across the mouth and 12 to 14 across the bottom. It was 20 inches long and made of stones of what appeared to be oak, bound with one spiral hoop from the bottom to the top. This as well as every other part of the vessel was fastened with pegs, no iron being anywhere visible. The bottom was inserted as it usually is in modern vessels.

Church or Abbey of Duncruithen

The original report states that "not a vestige of the abbey connected with the church of Dun Cruithen" remains. Yet the Ordnance map gives in Duncrun "ruins of an abbey." Is the building only 30 feet by 10 with a transept 20 feet long, which would be rather the dimensions of a church than of an abbey? Is the transept to be considered as consisting of what, in architectural language, is usually described as the north and south transepts with the intermediate part of the nave, in other words, is the building cruciform? How wide is the transept? Answer: The church of Duncruithen is called "abbey" by mistake on the Ordnance map.

Ruins at Magilligan Point

Are the ruins at Magilligan Point near the Martello

tower worthy of notice? Answer: not worthy of notice.

Giant's grave and ruins near Ball's Point north west of Roe mouth, worthy of notice? Answer: Not worthy of notice; "giant's grave" is a name which the parishioners have for the old sea beach of the lough, beginning at Ball's Point and proceeding through the parish.

SOCIAL ECONOMY

Smuggling and Illicit Distillation

The original report mentions the decline of smuggling and distillation. What is their actual state? Whiskey is imported from Inishowen; is there any ever exported thither? Answer: Its actual state of distillation is at present one of far greater extent than is supposed by the proprietors of the parish. From the great extent of flat, sandy ground there are great facilities for hiding, and many of the parishioners are so circumstanced that it is nearly impossible to detect them. It is, however, on the decline owing to the reduction of the duty and a change in the habits of the people. Still, there is nothing else drunk by the tenantry of the parish. It is consumed among themselves and also exported and sold in the neighbourhood of Newtown-limavady in large quantities.

Letter to George Petrie from the Reverend John Graham, 1833

MEMOIR WRITING

Letter to George Petrie

My Dear Sir,

According to promise I gave you my own corrected copy of Butler's *Statistical Report of the Parish*, which will, I think, be an useful document for you. Mr Boyle called on me a few days ago and I gave him some other materials for you.

If those enormous work[s] for similar documents for Donegal and Tyrone survive, I think I could procure them; and if they would get the bishops, which they might do, to engage clergy through the island to give you similar materials, this opportunity which may not recur for a century might be used to elicit a development of the circumstances and rich resources of the land, men [?] etc., which might most beneficially accomplish what Smith in 1743, the Dublin Society in 1807 and Shaw Mason in 1814 attempted in

vain. Write soon to me and believe me, I be ever most truly yours [signed] John Graham, Magilligan Glebe, October 11th 1833.

PS Make what use you please of these documents.

Statistical Report [following the North West Society's Questionnaire] by the Reverend John Graham, 1833

NATURAL STATE

Name and Extent

In old writings *Mac-Ileogain* as the territory of Inishowen on the opposite side of Lough Foyle was denominated *Kinel Eogain*; why in either case is not recorded. A family of this name is said to have lived in this parish and enjoyed the native freehold of *Ballycarton* until he forfeited it by rebellion in *1641*, when the parish suffered severely.

Latitude: the latitude of the centre of this parish has been calculated to be 55 degrees 81 inches and the longitude 6 degrees 50 inches, which are short of these given in the maps of Ireland.

Contents: by the old maps this parish contained 10,800 acres, Cunningham measure; by the commissioners of tithe <tythe> composition it was ascertained in the 14th July 1827 to contain 9,961 acres 2 roods 30 perches of the same measure; and by the late Ordnance survey [blank]. Its contents are rapidly decreasing by the action of the ocean and Lough Foyle.

Population

According to the census in 1821 this parish contained 1,626 Protestants and 1,562 members of the Church of Rome; but the Rev. Mr Butler, who wrote a valuable account of the parish for the North West Society for which he received neither remuneration, thanks or the slight favour of being made an honorary member, thinks that in this calculation the number of Romanists has been underrated: a more recent examination gave, he says, the number of Protestants families to be 182, that of all the rest 428. According to the parliamentary census of 1831, this parish contained in that year houses 641, families 643, male inhabitants 1,788, females 1,820, total inhabitants 3,608. Of these, 449 families were employed in agriculture and 93 in manufacture and trade.

NATURAL FEATURES

Soil

In the highlands, as the ground on the breast of the mountains are called, the soil is heavy clay mixed with basalt in progress of decomposition. In the lowlands, on the parts of the parish which the sea has abandoned, the soil is alternately sand and bog in what are called druims <drymms> and misks, from the Roe to the ocean.

Mountains

Binevenagh <Benyevenagh> mountain (that is "the frightful promontory" as 2 *Celtic words signifies)* is a prominent feature of this romantic parish. Some say it is 1,100 feet above the level of Lough Foyle, others more. It appears to have formed one half of a mountain in which a disruption was made by volcanic fires. Under the *basalt stone* which contain numerous air holes to prove it has once been in a state of passion, there is the usual lead or *limestone*, the residuum [of] which fell to the bottom of the boiling mass and uniformly occupies the bottom of all these exhausted volcanoes. The front of the majestic mountain opens towards *Lough Foyle* in a bold and striking elevation above the subjacent places, which is quite flat and level as a drum head. It commands most extensive views not only of the most conspicuous parts of the counties of Donegal, Tyrone and Antrim, but of the Scottish Isles and some of the mainland of the northern portion of Great Britain.

Climate

The climate here is, as might be expected, more moist but not so cold as that of inland counties. Gibbon says *the severity of weather is tempered by a vicinity of the ocean*. This is the case here, where the snow seldom rests many days on it except in the very depth of winter and the severest seasons, when old Binevenagh is shrouded in snow and gleams forth upon Lough Foyle, a pale mountain of light on which the moonbeams cast their yellow, [?] shadowy, melancholy lustre and the silence of death pervades this "darkness visible."

Waters

Lough Foyle and the River Roe: The former divides this part of Londonderry county from the county of Donegal, the latter separating it from the tract of Aghanloo and Finlagan parishes commonly called *Myroe*.

NATURAL HISTORY

Plants and Trees

Osiers, alders and furze with a small number of *white and blackthorn, hazel and bramble bushes* are almost the whole of the *shrubs*, except those in the demesne of Mr Gage of Bellarena.

Trees: There is a scarcity of trees except at Bellarena, and crag through the whole of the parish. A few *ash* trees are scattered through it and remain full-grown and some of them decayed, in proof then, if timber were planted and protected here, it would grow as it does elsewhere and did here in former times.

There are some few *apple trees* in the clay lands on the breast of the mountain and an orchard in the townland of Tamlaght. Fruit trees of all kinds as well as timber grow well in the gardens and demesne of Conolly Gage Esquire, though situated on what is called the lowlands and consisting of the older matter of bog and sand called misk and druim <drym>, here of which the whole of the flat, alluvial soil of the parish from the Roe to the ocean consists.

Characteristics of the People

Magilligan has its full proportion of animated nature: earth, sea and water teem with living creatures. Here we have one active mass of life with all its enjoyments and sufferings. Of men, women and children we have already given an account: their capabilities great, their foibles few and those arising chiefly from ignorance and old habits, but far indeed from being as offensive as they are in other places; rent, tithe and taxes paid cheerfully, hospitality exercised in proportion to ability and often beyond it; no beggar refused alms in any house that has a potato to spare, no lodging refused to the wanderer in the habitations of the poor.

Animals

The *horses* are of a middle size and hardy, but too great a proportion of them kept; the *cows*, of a good kind, thriving well but come from other pastures apt to die of the mourle, a disease indicated first by bloody urine and supposed to be caused by the water which is impregnated with lime that forms the substratum of our basaltic mountain. On post mortem examination, the faeces of the animal are found in an indurated, dry state in the intestines. Nature seems to have designed these lands for a sheep-walk. This animal thrives remarkably here.

Goats and Health

[Word obscured] [are ?] common [here ? but we have] few or no mules, and goats, [for whose ?] milk [our mountain ?] was once so famous as to attract numbers of consumptive persons to come here and drink it, are seldom to be seen. A large house called Montsalut was once established here in the townland of Craig, an ordinary [word missing ?] kept in it and, for half a century, was a fashionable resort in summer and autumn, but these days are passed and we hear as little now of *Magilligan goat's whey* as we do of the *Lucan Spa.* "Everything in the world changes and *passes away.*"

Rabbits

Pigs once paid the rent of the cottager here and are still a rich resource to him. *Rabbits* once produced from their skins alone *1,500 pounds a year;* are now fallen so in value that a dozen of skins which would bring upwards of 10s 30 years ago may now be had for 3s 6d. Their flesh is a great article of food here, so that servants some times stipulate that they shall not be entirely fed upon them during the season which lasts from October to February. "*Rabbits hot, rabbits cold, rabbits young, rabbits old, rabbits tender, rabbits tough, of rabbits I have got enough*" is the cry of the servants long before Candlemas Day.

Fowl

Geese are plenty here; *turkeys*, not being scarce, has the difficulty of rearing them and expense of feeding them on oats prevents their being reared in any considerable quantity. Ducks of a large side [size ?] are plenty, particularly on the banks of the *River Roe* where they fatten and grow rank by feeding on what the river affords them. *Hens* and *chickens* are abundant and cheap.

Vermin and Insects

Tho' out of place here and although they should be mentioned before the fowl, we should notice other animals useless in appearance and perhaps noxious: and these are *rats, mice, cats, weasles, ferrets, dogs, foxes, hares, fleas, earwigs, the grubworm and the minnow worm.*

The *rats* are great enemies to the rabbits and in some parts of the upper end of the parish have nearly extirpated them. Cats are here in great numbers, some of them wild, and from their nature probably find occupation and food from great quantities of rats which are known to excess

far from the habitation of man and live on the sea wrack and other food which they can find on the banks of Lough Foyle or the shores of the ocean.

We have some weasles here, but no ferrets though the latter have been frequently used to catch rabbits. There are a great number of dogs here.

NATURAL FEATURES

Water

The *Roe* washes and bounds about 1 mile and a half of this parish on the southern border of it, as the *ocean* and the Foyle enclose it on the north eastern, northern and western sides of it. The other waters are: 2 small mountain streams for mills and what is called here the *Big Drain*, which divides the lowlands into 2 parts, one held by Sir James Bruce Bart and the Messrs Reynolds, Ross, Church and Nolan; and the other by Conolly Gage Esquire *(with the exception of the native freehold of Ballycarton, held in perpetuity by Benjamin Lane Esquire)*, both these parts of the parish being the estate of the see of Derry. The numerous mountain springs diffuse themselves through the whole of the sandy and boggy plain called *"the lowlands"*, whether seen on the surface or not rising to the same level and at last passing off into the lough at the Fore Strand.

Water of some sort is found in all the lowlands in the driest season by digging wells sunk to the level of low water mark on the shore, which is only a few feet below the surface. A usual expedient is a *stout barrel* inserted in the top of the running sand, having been previously perforated with holes in the bottom of it. It is occasionally cleansed out and scalded to prevent the taste of the decaying timber from being communicated to the water, which at least is unwholesome.

NATURAL HISTORY

Mines

From the frequent appearance of iron in stones and intermingled with earth, and from the impregnation of several springs with it, there is a general idea of mines of that valuable metal being in the mountain or at the foot of it. Iron has been seen melted in some of the great fires of clay made in the hilly lands for the purpose of obtaining ashes for manure.

Coals

After storms *coals* have been found in small quantities on the shores of *Magilligan* and from certain indication of them, in the townland of *Tircreevan*. The late Earl of *Bristol*, then Bishop of Derry, had the places on which these marks were discovered *searched to the depth of 50 feet*, without more success than the discovering of the appearance of small portions of a *bad kind of culm*.

The *limestone* here has a large proportion of *flint* in it if got near the north bay; less in the south side of the parish. *Spar* has been found in the rocks in small quantities. The seams of clay are in some places increased with *marl*.

Botanical Observations

The spontaneous vegetable productions will be found in the breast of *Binevenagh* and the flat land under it, more numerous and diversified than perhaps in any other parish in Ireland.

Centuries ago, when herb doctors prevailed much and were in full sway among the credulous Irish, many of them came here annually from distant parts of the island in search of plants nowhere else to be found, and such was their ascertained superiority in feeding *bees* that *Magilligan honey* in the earlier part of the last century, particularly that made in the townland of Tircreevan, brought the highest price of any that was sent to the market of *Dublin, Derry or Belfast*.

A list of most of these will be found in the census made by the Rev. Mr Innis to Bishop Nicholson in the year 1725, respecting the natural history in the parish of Magilligan. It is preserved in the *Anthologia Hibernica*. It has been originally published with other writings of same author among the [? past papers] of the Royal Society.

Rabbit Warrens: Ferns and Grass

The *rabbit warrens* so extensive in our lowlands, once so profitable and then decreasing, abound with male *fern*, a plant which protecting the rabbits, sheltering them from cats and rain, serves other useful purposes. *Horses*, if accustomed to eat it when young, require little other food. When the fern is full-grown, it makes a substitute for *kelp* and is sometimes burned in large quantities for this purpose. It serves for beds for cattle when straw is not to be had, and for some cold lands it makes manure. A portion of it laid above and below flax in the dams when it is steeped tends much to preserve the colour of that useful article. *Fern* is put under hay ricks and corn stooks to preserve the grain and straw from the dampness of the earth on which they are built. They are put over the holes in which *potatoes* are kept to cover them from the superincumbent mould, which otherwise would cause inconvenience or injury by intermingling with them. The poor use these *ferns* for an inner coat of thatch when they can, saving much straw by so doing. They often use them for *fuel*. So valuable is the [?] darkened ferns, better known here by the name of brackens.

On some of the *rabbit warrens* the *bent grass or basquz* is plentiful. It was introduced here, according to tradition, for the purpose of preventing the blowing of the sands, which it does to a considerable degree. The seed is sufficient to propagate it, but the usual mode of extending it on these hillocks of sand is by dividing the roots and transplanting them in any season except that of its greatest vigour, when it grows luxuriantly, if properly planted. That is here used earlier, and with sufficient care, a large portion of growth irrecoverably lost by the action of winds and waves on these strands might have been preserved. It is now used for *besoms* <beesoms> and for *matting*, which latter forms a kind of *carpet* much used in churches and on staircases and in many rural parlours. It has for these purposes been introduced not only in Derry and Belfast and almost all the towns of Ulster but of late into the metropolis.

Mosses used in Building and Upholstering

The *mosses* with which some of the Magilligan rabbit burrows abound are very beautiful, and some of them might be rendered valuable by their being worked *(after cutting of the roots and drying the moss)* into French beds, sofas or armchairs; forms admirable stuffing. Moss is useful here in filling up [the ?] interstices between joints and check the sound rising from one storey of a house to another. For this use it must be *(previously wet being put on to the space it is to occupy)* pressed in large quantities under heavy weights. It may be wrought up with fresh *lime* without *sand* to make a good substitute for slates in covering of houses. It is very abundant in Magilligan.

Herbs and their Uses

The plant called *mother thyme*, also to be found in these warrens, looks very pretty on the ground and from the peculiar niceness of its aromatic flavour, the medicinal values of it have been highly esteemed. A small portion of the herb well dried is deemed to be a great improvement of *congou tea* and all the *weak teas*. Even one ounce or half of this quantity is sufficient to impregnate an entire pound of tea.

Dyeing Plants

The plant called *crotter or crotwell* is supposed to be that which in *dyeing* gives the fine imitation made of the *red* colour of *turkey shawls*. In this process human urine is said to be used in very large quantities to colour with the herb *strawell*, with which the ancient Irish were in the habit of colouring their linen of a saffron hue. Both these herbs are found here.

The *souroy or field sorrel* affords the dyers the basis of a fair *black colour*, and the *saggan or flag* are used as materials for a deeper black colour *intermixed* with brown. The root of the soft briar affords a nice brownish colour for [?] the clothing made of a mixture of linen and wool called *droggets (a name given in Ulster to the offspring of Protestants and members of the Church of Rome, and very characteristic of them as links to connect discordant portions of our population, a link which operates in disarming civil dissension, and will be found at last to amalgamate us into one united people and, by the influence of Christian education, may in the ensuing ages bring us all into the knowledge and love of Christ as our only refuge from eternal ruin into happy operation, in an island blessed with the highest capabilities of rendering its cultivators happy).*

Ink made with galls and a strong decoction of *flag* root is particularly *bright and tenacious*.

Other Herbs and Grasses

Couch grass, now so valuable for *bonnets*, might be obtained here in great quantities from the sandy grounds as might *rye (a grain nearly as heavy as [?] lead and very nutritious)* and *barley straw* for the same purposes.

Docks (commonly called dockins) are not too plentiful, notwithstanding the industry used to eradicate them. The *seed* of them has been found of use to *horses* of delicate chest and broken wind. *Sow thistle* is common here and eaten with avidity by *horses*.

The lately-famed *fiorin* would soon advantageously occupy our moist lands were it not disturbed by the plough and spade in spring and the poaching of cattle in winter.

Of the other native plants, some of the most noted and useful are: *watercresses*, which make a good salad; *water hemlock*, so powerful in discussing swellings on the human body; *rape and bush vetch*, both good *esculents* for cattle; *lesser*

centaury; bog myrtle (a substitute for *Peruvian bark); lesser centaury; geraniums and poppies*, differing more in strength than species from those in the *East Indies*. An amateur might fill a *volume* with a description of the external appearance and uses of the plants of this district [insert note: to be continued if accepted].

Predatory Animals

Foxes: about 80 years ago foxes were so numerous and troublesome in this parish that in the years 1747, 1748, 1749 and 1750 2s were voted in the parish vestry at Easter for each skin of them produced there. They are now nearly extinct, but 1 or 2 of them have been lately seen in the townland of Craig.

The last wolf said to be seen in the province of *Ulster* was started about 90 years ago upon *Binevenagh mountain* in this parish and hunted into the woods near Dungiven, where he was killed.

Hares and Mice

There are but few hares found here. *Mice* are here in great numbers and very mischevious in corn stacks and in houses. *White mice* have lately been numerous in some parts of the parish. They are of a very beautiful kind.

Insects

Fleas are here in myriads. They will occasionally be found in the rabbit warrens, far from houses in thousands, so as to astonish them who see them. Nor can the habitations of man be kept free from them if sand be not carefully excluded, which it seldom is. A small, reddish insect resembling a *bug* is common in the dry, sandy grounds.

Earwigs are in their season so numerous as to be a [next words illegible] in the windows, beds, and the wearing apparel of the inhabitants [but have never ?] been found to create more inconvenience than the horror of their appearance, from the popular error that their propensity is to enter the ear and feed upon the brains of man.

The grubworm, so destructive to corn, is unfortunately a busy intruder on the hilly and boggy sands, bad especially on the former. Seaweed of the kind called *crag* is a partial remedy against them, and early sowing is frequently a safeguard. Rolling the lands after a shower tends to get rid of them, as does *salt* mixed with the seed corn and spray.

Fishes

These are chiefly *flounders and cockles* and at particular seasons *herrings*, but far from the shore; and *oysters*, those on the opposite shore at *Greencastle* large and of a fine flavour, those off the Myroe <Myoe> shore smaller and comparatively *insipid*. We sometimes get *turbot* and *haddock*, but these are generally brought to us from other places, as are *codfish* which we have in great abundance and fine condition from the fisheries off the mouth of *Lough Foyle*.

Wild Fowl

There are a few *eagles* in the mountains and *hawks* of all kinds. *Barnacles* are found in great numbers on the shore of Lough Foyle. 36 of them have been taken in one net during a winter night. The fowl is not much inferior to a goose in size and feathers. They assemble with as great regularity as troops at a review, often times in a line a mile long just near the water, and the noise they make is sometimes terrific.

Ravens are often very destructive to rabbits here and to young poultry. The want of trees almost excludes crows: great flocks of them often pass over the parish and there is a rookery in the centre of it at Tamlaght. They sometimes annoy the farmers by lighting on their newly-sown fields; but there is an idea afloat that the injury they do never can be felt in harvest and that they do more good by devouring worms than by eating grain.

We have a few *plover* on the mountains and *some partridge* visit arable lands. *Wild ducks, teal and widgeon* are plenty on the shores. Swans visit us in hard winters, and now and then we see a solitary *crane or heron*. The *shelldrake and duck* are a beautiful species of their kind and sometimes when their nests are found in the *rabbit warrens* where they breed, the young are brought to the houses and brought up with other ducklings. They are frequently then domesticated but are apt to disappear in obedience to the instinct which keeps them wild. They are often sought here as [?] commodities and are frequently sent as presents by the Magilligan folk to their inland friends.

Extracts from Fair Sheets by J. Bleakly and T. Fagan, May to July 1835

MODERN TOPOGRAPHY AND PRODUCTIVE ECONOMY

Flax Mill in Duncrun

[J. Bleakly] The fall of water upon this wheel is 19 feet. The mill is 14 years built and of stone and lime, slated and wrought by a stream proceeding from 2 springs. The cog or pit wheel is 8 feet 10 inches in diameter. There are 4 rollers of wood. This mill can work all seasons of the year. Information obtained from Thomas McCluskey and John Doherty, proprietors of the mill.

The road leading from this mill (called the Curragh Lane) through Duncrun is 18 feet broad in the clear, made and kept in repair at the expense of the county.

Bleach Green in Duncrun

A flax mill is where one of the old houses of the bleach green formerly stood. Information obtained from John Doherty and John McLaughlin.

Corn Mill at Bellarena

The cog wheel is 10 feet in diameter, the horizontal wheel is 10 feet in diameter and drives 2 pinions. Each pinion drives one pair of stones and each pair of stones has one hopper. This mill can work all seasons of the year and can shell and grind together 5 cwt of oatmeal per hour.

Corn Mill at Craig

This mill is single geared, has one pair of stones and one hopper. This mill is built of stone and lime, slated, to which a corn kiln is attached with a metal head and is situated about 120 yards north east of Castle Leckey on the road leading from Bellarena through Magilligan to Coleraine. Information obtained from Edward McCoristin, occupying tenant, and John Moody, farmer. 19th May 1835.

Bridge at Tircreveen

The bridge over Tircreveen burn has one arch 27 feet in the span, the breadth on the top is 12 feet. The wall is 100 feet long, 2 and a half feet high and 18 inches thick. This bridge divides Tircreveen from Ballyleighry.

Roads

The road leading from Mr Graham's Glebe House to Castle Leckey across Tircreveen bridge is very hilly and is 21 feet broad, of stones and gravel, in tolerable repair, made and kept in repair at the expense of the county.

Bridge over the Big Drain

The bridge over the Big Drain has one arch 12 feet in the span. The wall is 130 feet long and 18 inches thick. The breadth of the bridge on the top is 18 and a half feet, in good repair except a little at the top of the wall. The road leading to this bridge is 2 feet [wide], of stones and gravel, made and kept in repair at the expense of the county.

Wooden Bridge

The Wooden bridge is situated on the River Roe and divides the parish of Magilligan from the parish of Tamlaght Finlagan, and measures across the river 189 feet 6 inches and is 16 and a half feet wide. There are 12 piers, built of stone and lime; 8 of these piers are built from the bottom of the river and serve to support the bridge. The other 4 piers are placed one at each corner of the bridge. Each of these piers measure from the ground to the capstone 6 feet 10 inches in height and 3 feet broad on the face. There are 3 flags of cut stone each 3 inches thick, with a spherical ball of stone on the top. Each of the inside piers are 5 feet high and 3 feet on the face in width. The capstone is 6 inches thick. The wooden pailing, which is painted white, is 3 feet 9 inches high. The road leading to this bridge is 21 feet in the clear. All the above made and repaired at the expense of the county. Information obtained from Mr Benjamin Lane, Ballycarton.

Bridge at Duncrun

The bridge at Duncrun near the wall of the church has one arch which is 12 feet wide. The bridge is 19 feet broad on the top and the wall is 84 yards long and 3 feet high. A splendid spring is situated between the bridge and the mountain, on John Doherty's farm. The stream which passes through the arch of this bridge has its source from this spring, which is the chief spring of the townland.

The road leading to the above bridge is 21 feet broad in the clear and in good repair. The above bridge and road is made and kept in repair at the expense of the county. 18th May 1835.

Ferry Boats

There are 2 ferry boats on the water near the round tower, viz. a large one for conveying cattle, the other a smaller boat for passengers. Sir Arthur Chichester, the proprietor of Greencastle, receives the benefit of these boats and is the proprietor of them. The one half of the money goes to Sir A.C. and the other half to the boatmen. Cattle cargo and passengers are boated over at all seasons of the year. The prices are as follows: 6d for a person of respectable appearance and 3d for a poor man; a

cow or horse 1s 8d, a sheep or pig 3d, a sack of potatoes containing 5 bushels 6d.

Roads

The road leading through Gortmore near Castle Leckey is 24 feet in the clear, in good repair and at the expense of the county. 23rd May 1835.

Tower at Lower Doaghs

The tower at Lower Doaghs was commenced in 1812 and finished in 1817 and is 166 feet 10 inches in circumference above the basement, which is sunk 16 feet deep. The walls are 11 feet thick above the basement and 13 feet below, of cut stone procured at Ballyharrigan in the parish of Bovevagh, the lime at Downhill. Also an excellent spring inside the tower, 16 feet from the surface and level with the tide. Architects Henry and Mullins, Dublin. 29th May 1835.

Church at Duncrun

The parish church of Magilligan is situated on an eminence about 150 yards from the road. Inside the church is 11 single pews, each 9 by 3 and a half feet and 3 double pews each 9 by 6 feet 8 inches. The communion table occupies 11 and a half by 6 feet at the north end of the church. The pulpit and reading desk is at the west side of the church. The aisle is 7 feet wide and flagged. On the south side, at the entrance of the inner door, is a marble font on a fluted pillar of cut freestone 4 feet high. There are 3 Gothic windows on the east side and 1 Gothic window on the east end. The door is on the west end and 4 and a half feet wide. The outside of the church is 72 by 30 feet. There is no gallery in this church. There is a very good bell in the steeple. The church is 52 years built, the supposed cost 700 pounds, 150 pounds of which was raised off the parish, the rest by subscription. Information obtained from the Rev. John Graham, rector of the parish, and Mr John McCurdy, farmer. 26th May 1835.

Roman Catholic Chapel

The additional part is 16 by 5 and a half feet and in the rear <rere> of the altar. The altar is 12 by 26 and a half feet, ornamented by a large painting of the Resurrection. A small pew, which is the only one in the chapel, at the north end of the altar is 6 and a half by 3 and a half feet. There are 2 doors on the front or west side of the chapel with 2 fronts of cut freestone, one at each door, inside the house. There are 4 windows in Gothic style on the east side. The additional part has a large window on the east end. The sum at present expended on the chapel is 575 pounds. Information from the Rev. Paul Bradley, parish priest. 22nd May 1835.

Presbyterian Meeting House

The Presbyterian meeting house is situated in the townland of Margymonaghan; was built by subscription in 1803 and cost 205 pounds. The edifice is 52 by 25 feet outside with 34 seats inside; each seat would contain 6 persons. There are 5 windows on one side and 1 window on the end, with a door on the side and one door on the end. Previous to the erection of this meeting house, the Presbyterians used to go to Dunboe and Ballykelly meeting houses. The principal contributers of the Established Church towards the erection of this meeting house was Sir Hervey <Harvey> Bruce and Marcus Gage Esquire. The latter also gave 1 rood of ground on which the meeting house stands. From Mr John McCurdy, Mr John Moody and Rev. Samuel Butler. 27th May 1835.

Expense of Magilligan Bridge

[Remainder by T. Fagan] The expense of erecting the above bridge was 500 guineas, which sum was defrayed partly by the county and partly by the late Mr Gage of Bellarena. Flat boats carrying glar shells can come up the Roe to Bellarena at spring tide. The Roe is navigable for small, light boats at spring tides up to Ballycastle. The floods in the Roe does no injury to any part of the parish of Magilligan. Information obtained from James McGeehan, John Dunlop, John Millar, John McGuiness and others. 8th July 1835.

NATURAL FEATURES

Depth of Bogs and Bog Timber

The mountain bogs in this parish vary from 1 to 5 feet deep. There is no timber got in those bogs unless fir roots. The flow bogs in the lowlands in this parish vary from 2 to 16 feet in depth. There are yew and oak trees got in those bogs. Information obtained from Charles Begley, farmer and rate agent, John Moody, Patrick McLaughlin and many other farmers. 9th July 1835.

SOCIAL ECONOMY

Magilligan Bridge and Annual Dance

Magilligan bridge was commenced to be built in May 1799 and finished 14th July 1800. After the bridge being finished on the evening of the afore-said date, there was a dance introduced on the bridge by the carpenters, masons etc. which continued to a late hour on the following morning and from that period to the present a dance is held on Magilligan bridge annually on the 14th of July, where hundreds of the youths and all of both sexes assemble to enjoy themselves at drinking, dancing. It is also well supplied with liquors, bread, fruit, gingerbread. This dance is locally called the "bridge dance" and the assembled multitude only separate with a desire for breakfast on the following morning, exchanging promises to meet at the same place on the ensuing 14th July.

Wooden Bridge and Fair

The Wooden bridge is situated on the River Roe and divides the parish of Magilligan from Aghanloo. This bridge was erected in 1800 [queried] and cost 500 pounds, 300 pounds of which was taken off the county, the other 200 pounds was granted by Conolly [spelling queried] Gage Esquire of Bellarena. This bridge is still kept in repair at the expense of the county. The fair on this bridge commenced in 1800 and still continues. This fair originated from a fiddler named McNamara who assembled a few persons on the 14th of July, being the day after the fair on the road near the Rev. John Graham's, from whence they adjourned to the Wooden bridge as the best place for dancing, where the day and part of the night is spent in drinking whiskey, eating fruit, cakes and dilsk. Tents are erected at these fairs, where the people sit and drink. NB None frequent these fairs but Roman Catholics. Information obtained from Mr Benjamin Lane, Henry Abraham and John Dunlop. 24th December 1834.

Origin of Kilmary's Fair

There is a pleasure fair held annually in Magilligan on the 13th July locally called Kilmary's fair. This fair originated in the following manner: William Kilmary, formerly a resident landholder in the townland of Clagan, and who was a good player on the bagpipes, regularly attended a pleasure fair annually held at the Back Strand near Downhill during the greater part of his life. But when arrived at old age and not able to attend it at the Back Strand according to custom, he took out his bagpipes opposite his dwelling in Clagan on the 13th July, which was the date on which the aforesaid fair was and still is held, and played on the pipes for hours for young and old of his neighbours and all who stayed with them. In a few years the neighbouring people assembled into hundreds to hear Kilmary playing the music on 13th July. Spirit tents was also introduced and became so numerous that about 20 years ago there was no less than 36 whiskey tents counted at one fair in Clagan. Clagan fair commenced about 70 years ago. This fair was dedicated to the aforesaid Kilmary and has since been locally called Kilmary's fair. Informants James McGeehan and Charles Begley. 6th July 1835, [signed] Thomas Fagan.

Note on Place-Names by S. Butler, June [1834]

NATURAL STATE

Origin and Meaning of Place-Names

Derivation of the names of the townlands of Magilligan or Tamlaghtard parish by S. Butler, minister.

Aughill "the field with the high rocks in the end of it."

Avish "the pleasant place."

Ballycarton "McCartey's town."

Ballyleighry "the pasture town having a field of view."

Ballymaclary "McLary's town" (a family still existing in it).

Ballymacgowland "the town of the smith's son."

Ballymulholland "Mulholland's town" (a family name).

Ballymultinner "the town with the dwelling house on the sea."

Ballyscullion "the town belonging to the young man."

Bellarena "beautiful sand" (formerly Ballymaryn "the market town").

Benone, it should be Bunowen, "John's mouth or bottom John Cahan."

Carnouvy "Nouvy's leap" (a family name still in the place).

Carrowreagh "the king's quarter or the quarter of viewing."

Claggan "the small stones" (clacheen).

Clooney "the valley field or field of retirement."

Craig "the rock."

Croghan "the stacklike hill."

Doaghs "black sandy fields by the shore."

Drumnahay "the back or ridge of the horses."

Drumnahorgan "Harrigan or Harkin's ridge" (proper name).

Drummans "the backs or ridges."

Drumavally "the town back."

Duncrun "the round (that is Gibbon's) fort" (it was a monastery founded by O'Cahan; Columba's Throne colloquially).

Gort "the part of the glebe where clergy put their horses."

Gortmore "the great fort or glebe common."

Lenymore "the great heathy meadow."

Margymonaghan "boggy field market."

Minearney "the middle erenach or bard's town, else west middle."

Milltown "town of the mill."

Oughtemore "the great breastlike place."

Oughtymoyle "the breastlike projection" (bold breast).

Scotchtown "a place of Scotch settlers."

Tamlaght "the burying place" (gives name to the parish Tamlaght Ard being "the high burying place").

Tircrevan "the foxes' district."

Umbra "the shady place" (a name like most of the rest very appropriate).

Woodtown "town of the wood" (formerly Killymorgan that is "Morgan's town", a proper name of a family).

A few of the above names might possibly be referred to other derivations. The above seem to me the most probable and with a few exceptions they are certain. June 17th, [signed] S. Butler, Presbyterian minister of the parish.

Extracts from Fair Sheets by J. Bleakly, January to May 1835

ANCIENT TOPOGRAPHY

Fairy Bush in Clooney

In the townland of Clooney there is a fairy bush of holly which was seen on fire several times by night.

The Merrag

The Merrag is a rock situated in the townland of Craig which serves as a sundial for the inhabitants of the lowlands. [Insert marginal note by C.W. Ligar: This has not been mentioned in the Memoir].

Earthquake in the Townland of Gortmore

The people in this parish affirm that about 35 years ago in the townland of Gortmore in this parish, a number of large stones (some about 3 ton weight) were removed from their bed in the earth (in great frost and snow) and jumped about 30 yards up the hill. At the same time, the roof of Cristy Eaton's house was taken off with a large hawthorn bush and about 40 yards of a clay ditch blown down by a south east wind. Bridget Quigley seen the rock foot on fire, convenient to these stones and on the same night; supposed to have been an eruption occasioned by fire. The largest of these stones is to be seen at the Witch hill on Matthew Cunningham's farm. Some of the effects of this earthquake was felt at the Umbra about 1 and a half miles in a north east direction.

Cave at Matthew Cunningham's House

It is also affirmed that a cave is at Matthew Cunningham's house in the townland of Gortmore, which extends about 200 yards under the road and field adjoining the house. Several attempts have been made to explore this cave, but from the dampness of the atmosphere the candles were extinguished and those who went in to explore the cave could not succeed in the dark. The cave is now closed up at the mouth. Information obtained from Matthew Cunningham and John McDonnald, farmers. 23rd May 1835.

Ancient Coins and Plough Irons

Daniel McClary in the townland of Lower Drummans, in digging his farm found 3 small coins about the size of a farthing, 2 of brass and one a copper farthing of George II. One of the brass coins had on it: Tom Waddle, Colerane; the other brass coin had on it George Wilson. [Insert marginal note by C.W. Ligar: Not been mentioned in the Memoir].

Also very ancient plough irons were found by Daniel McClary about 14 inches under the surface on his farm in the townland of Drummans about 12 years since. [Insert note by C.W. Ligar: Not been mentioned in the Memoir]. The coulter was of an unusual shape, the sock wanted the feather or wing. Another plough iron was found by Joseph Conn in Lower Doaghs last spring, 1834, and of the same dimensions. From Daniel McClary and Joseph Conn. NB The characters on the above coin is almost illegible.

Mary's Meadow and Glassagh Spring

[Insert marginal note by C.W. Ligar: This has not been mentioned in the Memoir]. This is a secluded spot which produces a most luxuriant soil and is situated between 2 rocks at the Windy hill

south east of Castle Leckey. [Insert note: This is called Windy hill from its exposure to the northern blast]. A female named Mary (from which the meadow takes its name) used to convey her cow to this meadow in order to preserve her from the army who went through this parish in search of food during the siege of Derry.

Glassagh spring: this spring is situated near the base of the Windy hill and to which Mary used to resort with her cow to drink. Mary was the only Protestant in the parish at that time. The cow was her only support during the siege.

Tubberdonagh Spring

Tubberdonagh spring is situated in the townland of Gortmore and is called Sunday's Well, as the people used to resort thither on Sunday in order to perform stations. It is affirmed by the people that the primitive custom (immersion <immerging>) of baptisms was performed at this well. Information obtained from Mr John McGurdy, Mr John Moody, Charles McDonnald and William Boyle, farmers.

Fort at Ballycarton

A fort comprised entirely of earth is situated at the foot of Dowland hill and 300 yards north east of the corn mill, and at the edge of the stream leading to the mill. This fort is circular and 112 feet in diameter. The parapet is 6 feet higher than the trench, which is a quagmire. The centre of the fort produces blackthorn, a small rose tree and brushwood of hazel. This fort is of clay and undisturbed. 14th May 1835.

Tamlaght Fort

A fort of earth and stones in the townland of Tamlaght, situated between Binevenagh <Benevenagh> rocks and John Bullion's house and on his farm: this fort is oval and 48 by 30 feet. The parapet is 8 feet high, the fort interspersed with brushwood of hazel and undisturbed i.e. has never been tilled. A good spring with a fairy bush growing over it is about 200 yards from this fort. There are also 6 fairy bushes at John Bullion's house. 18th May 1835.

Duncrun Forts

In the townland of Duncrun, and between the church and Binevenagh about 300 yards east of the church, is a fort of earth and faced with stone,

Coins from Magilligan

oval shaped and 120 by 50 feet. The parapet in the highest part is 10 feet, with a trench which is 6 feet broad at the bottom. The parapet is 4 feet broad on the top. At the upper part is a very deep trench with a double parapet. This has been tilled some years ago as the shape of ridges appear, and quite free from weeds or brushwood of any kind.

Another fort of earth in the townland of Duncrun called Downpatrick Fort is situated on a hill about 140 yards south west of the church, and is of an oval shape, 68 by 120 feet and about 10 feet high on one side and [?] 48 feet high on the other. This fort was also tilled some years ago as the ridges appear and is situated in the midst of a corn field at present, and on James McLaughlin's farm and on the estate of Conolly Gage Esquire.

Ruins of Screen Old Church

This old church was situated in the townland of Craig and is said to have been a chapel of ease for this part of the parish, and supposed to have contained a number of manuscripts at that time. The ruins is on the east side of the road about 20 yards from the bridge and measures inside the walls 18 by 21 feet, grown over with briars and blackthorn.

Screen Church

McClary succeeded in placing the flag on Screen church and from which the church took its name.

Bishop Aidan's Chair

This stone chair, a natural formation of rock, is situated in the townland of Tamlaght and about 100 yards west of the Roman Catholic chapel and is 6 and a half feet high, 2 feet 8 inches broad at the back. The seat is 2 feet 4 inches broad at the front and 2 and a half feet broad at the side. The seat faces the north with a slope towards the west.

Tale of Craig Mill

This mill was burned at the war [insert note by C.W. Ligar: The miller does not know what war, it is most likely in 1641], the meal chest being burned; but a quantity of shelling was saved which at the ensuing season was of great use to those who found it, as many at that time were in a state of starvation.

Deer Horns

A deer's horn was dug out of Mrs Lee's farm in the townland of Drummans, 2 feet 4 inches long, on which 5 branches which indicate the animal as being 5 years old, each branch being 1 years growth. Several deers' horns are at present in the parish of Magilligan and all nearly found in the lowlands. Many are found with part of the skull attached and of a pale colour. Information obtained from Daniel McClary, farmer. [Marginal drawing of deer's antler].

A large horn of a deer was found in the townland of Drumnahay by William Fleming and on his farm (see specimen procured by J. Bleakly).

Coins

Some small pieces of coin were found in the townland of Umbra about 18 months ago by Hugh McClary and on his farm. [Insert note by C.W. Ligar: He has given them away to different people]. From Hugh McClary, Rev. Samuel Butler and David Connell. 28th May 1835.

Witch Hill

The Witch hill is a small (supposed to be), artificial hill in the townland of Gortmore, at the rock foot on Matthew Cunningham's farm. At this hill some of the large stones removed thither by the supposed earthquake are to be seen. Also on the top of this hill is a stone which was supported by 4 other stones which served as pillars, in the shape of a table but now lying almost flat in a hole on the top of the hill, the hill of an oval shape [insert footnote: is 36 feet high from the basement].

Miscellaneous Discoveries

About 40 years ago on John McCurdy's farm in the townland of Ballymaclary, and about 20 inches under the surface in sandy soil, was discovered the skeleton of 7 human bodies.

About 4 years ago a quantity of silver coins of Elizabeth were discovered in the townland of Ballymaclary, on Thomas Church's farm.

Part of the townland of Minearney on Edward Doherty's farm is called the Boney hill from a quantity of bones being found on this hill.

Old Abbey or Castle in Duncrun

There was an old abbey or castle at John McLaughlin's house and about 100 yards from the flax mill in the townland of Duncrun, in which a number of weights of water stones were found from 4 to 25 lbs weight, one of which may be seen at John McLaughlin's house and marked thus: XIIII. An old axe, an old flesh fork with some old silver coins and a quantity of grain supposed to be barley, all were found about 10 years since by John McLaughlin in a corner of the old ruins.

Ruins of an Old Church

The ruins of an old church and graveyard is visible on a beautiful hill at the trigonometrical station in the townland of Duncrun. The ruins of the old church is 42 by 20 feet inside the walls. In the centre of the ruins was a standing stone and which is now lying flat on the ground, and is 6 feet long and 2 feet broad at the head and 1 foot at the foot, with a cross which is quite visible on the stone. Information obtained from John McLaughlin, farmer.

Holy Well

In the townland of Tamlaght, about 20 yards east of the Roman Catholic chapel, is a holy well called Elspiaiden's Well, called after a Bishop Aiden. The bishop's grave is at the east end of the old church. A stone chair is also to be seen and a bookcase of stones which was broken about 12 years since by John Connell, James McCorry and William McConnell whom, it is said, have had no good luck since they broke this chair.

Old Church

The old church still remains in the graveyard with the new Roman Catholic chapel, and where mass was celebrated before the new chapel was built. Divine service was also performed by the Episcopalians before the new church was built in Duncrun. It is said Bishop Aiden used to preach in this church. The edifice is still standing but in a state of dilapidation. Nothing remains inside but part of the old altar. Information obtained from John Connell. 22nd May 1835.

SOCIAL ECONOMY

Remarkable Man: Dennis Hempson

Dennis Hempson, the blind, two-headed harper: Dennis Hempson lived in the townland of Ballymaclary in this parish, and was called the two-headed harper from large lump which was on the side of his head. Dennis Hempson's harp is now at Downhill House and is 270 years old. The body of the harp is of sallow on which is carved the following inscription (but almost illegible):

> "The time of Noah I was green,
> Afterwards was not to be seen,
> Till Cormick Kelly raised me up to that degree,
> The queen of music you may call me."

Dennis Hempson played on this harp for Charles, the Pretender of Scotland:

> "The King shall enjoy his own again,
> and also the white cockade."

Dennis was taught to play on the harp by Bridget Kelly. At a consort in Belfast, Dennis obtained 12 pounds. Dennis is 25 years dead. Information obtained from Mr John McCurdy, Mr John Moody, farmers, and Dennis Hempson's daughter, Catherine McKeever. 25th May 1835.

Remarkable Characters

James Conn and Dennis Hempson <Hamson> were the only remarkable characters in this parish. The former was born in the townland of Ballymagoland in this parish and was remarkable for his strength: was known to lift a pair of large cartwheels, newly shod, and raise them with one hand above his head and also to break new horseshoes into pieces with his hands. James Conn's ribs on both sides were grown together in one bone without any fleshy substance between them. [Insert marginal note by C.W. Ligar: Has not been copied into the Memoir].

Weddings in Magilligan

Weddings in Magilligan among the lower order of farmers and cottiers: when a couple purpose to get married, the friends of both parties meet at the intended bride's residence, where the match is made up over a bottle of whiskey (as there is no good luck in a dry bargain). A day is appointed for the wedding, when the intended bridegroom will invite a number of his male companions and, after each drinking a glass of whiskey, will repair to the bride's residence, where the cordial is repeated and where the bride with her party (dressed in white if it can be procured) waits to receive the bridegroom with his party, from whence they repair on foot (observing to place the bride and bridegroom's friend in the front, the bridesmaid and the bridegroom next in order) to some appointed [place] to meet the clergyman.

After the happy couple are united, they repair with their party to the bride's residence where the remainder of the day and night is spent in feasting and dancing. When the bride is seated at the table, a cake (sometimes of oatbread) is brought and broken on her head and distributed among the guests. This is called the bride's cake. Before the party disperse, they form themselves into a circle and run round the room. The bride standing in the centre with her eyes muffled, a stocking filled with oatcake is put into her hand which she throws. The person the stocking first strikes will be the first married. If the marriage is extraordinary, the wedding is announced by lighted torches, cheering, firing of musquetry and playing of musical instruments. Information obtained from Mr John McCurdy, John Forsythe, John Moody and William Boyle, farmers. 27th May 1835.

Fishing Tragedy and Superstition

About 65 years ago a number of fishing boats went out towards the Tons on a Saturday [insert footnote: this is called Black Saturday to the present day], in the month of November, when a tremendous hurricane arose which upset the boats and all the crew (except one man, William Maginnis) apparently perished in the waters. It is said that 65 widows were left on that day to lament the sad fate of their husbands. The only surviving person was William Maginnis, who was saved by means of an oar which he seized, by means of which he reached to shore on the Umbra. After ascending the banks he beheld his companions with folded arms walking about and quite unconcerned. It is supposed that they were not drowned

but taken off by the inhabitants of the enchanted castle. William Maginnis lived in Inishowen.

The Ton Banks is a most dangerous place for ships on their voyage to and from Derry, and on which many ships have been wrecked. Information obtained from Charles McDonnald and William Boyle, farmers.

NATURAL FEATURES

Fish in Drains of Magilligan

[Crossed out: The few fish which are in the drains of Magilligan are principally flounders and eels. These drains are nearly dry in summer].

Names of English and Scotch Settlers

English settlers: Gage, Lane, Reynolds, Chase, Church and Moorehead; Scotch settlers: Moody, McCurdy, Caldwell, Conn, Allison, Clarke, Flemming and Sinton. These came over in the reign of James I.

Prevailing Names

The most prevailing names in the parish is Doherty and McLaughlin. These are Irish settlers and came to this parish in the capacity of herds and servants to the English settlers. The Irish settlers came from Inishowen. Doherty means "oak habitations." From William Fleming, John Forsyth, Rev. Samuel Butler and John Moody. 28th May 1835, [signed] John Bleakly.

Fair Sheets by J. Bleakly, January to May 1835

PRODUCTIVE AND SOCIAL ECONOMY: TOWNLAND DIVISIONS

Clooney Townland

In this townland there are 32 horses, 52 head of black cattle, 49 sheep, 6 turkeys, 30 geese, 52 ducks and 60 hens. The soil of this townland is light moss under clay in some places near the mountain, the other a sandy soil, a subsoil of sea sand. The depth is various. Method of draining is by open drains from 6 to 8 feet wide and [there] are mearings between each farm on the flat.

Manures are farmyard on the mossy land, a top dressing of ashes from moss for oats, compost for potatoes. Moss and sand left to sour in a pool at the cabin door answer well for rye on sandy ground, next year potatoes on manure. Burnt ashes sold for 2d per carload and 4d per cartload, hire of a carthorse and man 2s 6d per day. Sea wrack is also used as manure, drawn from the shore of Lough Foyle 2 or 3 miles, forces early potatoes on sandy soil. About 40 cars would give a light top dressing to lea land. Compost would require 3 times as much. Sand upon moss when repeated raises couch grass and would render the land unproductive. Once in 6 years is enough to apply ashes.

Rotation of crops: lea top dressed with ashes early in the season and let lie on the ground from January to February or March, then ploughed. Barley does well on a mixture of heavy earth and sand on the third crop. Other rotation is in February or March if the season is dry, then rye on moss or rye on sand and oats on moss, then 2 years' lea, sometimes grazed for 7 years. Little or no flax: when sown, is put down after barley. No wheat: soil too light and mossy. Quantity of seed to sow on an acre: barley about 3 and a half bushels, sown in May, early; dry soil will produce about 84 stone, wet 140 stone, reaped in August about the middle. Oats about 5 bushels to sow an acre if weak or poor and 4 bushels if strong, produce about 4 or 5 boles of 12 bushels each bole and 3 stone to each bushel; potato <potatoe> oats on [crossed out: dry land] potato grounds, [?] angish on dry land; blanter reaped in the end of August or beginning of September. Rye about 10 stone to sow an acre, produce about 4 barrels of 5 bushels to each barrel of 4 stone to each bushel. Potatoes from 24 to 34 bushels to sow an acre, produce from 8 to 10 bushels for each bushel sown, sold from 8d to 10d per bushel. Planted in April and May and dug out in October and November.

Irish and Scotch breed of black cattle. Every 10 acres of good land is supposed to feed 1 horse and 2 cows. The pigs have a little of the Dutch breed in them, the poultry all Irish breed. Information obtained from John Moody, William Doherty and Abraham Moody, farmers. Dated 7th January 1835.

Clooney Townland

Clooney: Sir James Bruce, proprietor, churchlands. There are 13 farmers in this townland, viz. John McCallian holds 32 acres, Cunningham measure, pays 18 pounds 10s; William Doherty holds 22 acres, pays 16 pounds 5s; Patrick Doherty holds 22 acres, pays 16 pounds; George Doherty holds 18 acres, pays 16 pounds 17s; James Gilland holds 18 and a half acres, pays 16 pounds 16s; William Begley holds 17 and a half acres, pays 17 pounds; Daniel Macallian holds 14 acres, pays 11

pounds 10s; Miss Kane holds 13 acres, pays 11 pounds 10s; Matthew Quinn holds 14 acres, pays 11 pounds 10s; Edward Gillespie holds 7 acres, pays 6 pounds; John Kane holds 7 acres, pays 6 pounds; Archy McKaig holds 7 acres, pays 6 pounds; John Moody holds 10 and a half acres, pays 8 pounds 17s 6d.

The following is a list of those who pay county cess, with the amount paid by each: William Begley pays 1 pound 15s 8d; Rose Canning pays 8s 5d 3 farthings; George Doherty pays 1 pound 11s 5d 3 farthings; John Doherty pays 1 pound 9s 3d 4 farthings; William Doherty pays 1 pound 9s 1d; James Gilland pays 1 pound 13s 6d ha'penny; Elizabeth Kane pays 1 pound 1s ha'penny; John Kane pays 9s 11d 3 farthings; Daniel Macallian pays 1 pound 2s 1d ha'penny; John Macallian pays 1 pound 19s 11d; Archibald Makeag pays 12s 8d ha'penny; John Moody pays 17s 10d ha'penny; Michael Quinn pays 1 pound 2s 1d ha'penny, total 15 pounds 13s 4d ha'penny. Information obtained from John Moody, William Doherty, farmers, and John Forsythe, applotter of county cess. 7th January 1835.

Gortmore Townland

There are 6 farmers, 1 farm above 50 acres, 1 farm above 30, 2 farms above 20 and 2 farms above 10 acres. Rotation of crops: 1st top dressing with sea sand for potatoes, 2nd barley, 3rd potato oats, 4th flax, 5th oats again. This rotation is for the middle part of the townland. For the lower or flat part, 1st oats with top dressing, 2nd potatoes, 3rd and 4th oats top dressed with ashes if possible. On the upper part of the townland, 1st potatoes, 2nd barley, 3rd oats, 4th oats. There are 2 lime kilns. Mrs Forsythe has planted about half an acre of wasteland with larch and alder trees, the larch about 8 years planted, the alder about 7 years planted. Nature of the soil: a blue clay. The trees are thriving remarkably well, north west aspect. There are 19 horses, 2 asses, 12 sheep, 54 head of black cattle, English, Irish and Scotch breed, 40 pigs. John Moody has Berkshire pigs, 22 turkeys, 6 geese, 60 ducks and 60 hens. John Moody has on his farm Scotch firs, larch, spruce, ash, beech, sycamore and alder planted by [blank] Lynam, who also built Gortmore House. Age of trees from 30 years to 1, seem to thrive pretty well. John Moody has sowed naked oats the last year, seems to be very productive; the first who cultivated this sort of oats in this parish. Implements of husbandy very good. From John Moody and Abraham and James Moody. Dated 10th January 1835.

Tircrevin and Ballymulholland Townlands

Tircrevin: There are 5 looms, 4 of which are at work. Fuel very good, cut turf procured in Tircrevin mountain, 2 lime kilns. Rotation of crops: 1st oats, 2nd manure and plant potatoes, 3rd flax laid down with clover and grass. Size of farms varies from 3 acres to 20 of arable. 12 sheep; when sheep are kept they are sent to Tircrevin mountain; 34 horses, 51 head of black cattle, Irish breed, 34 pigs, 1 turkey, 12 geese, 36 ducks and 60 hens, 1 Friesland <Freezeland> hen. Cottiers keep horses for hire to farmers at 1s 8d per diem and fed, 2s per day without food. Information obtained from John Fleming, John Caldwell and William Doherty, farmers.

Ballymulholland: There are 2 farms above 50 acres and 3 farms above 20 acres. Order of crops: 1st oats, 2nd potatoes, 3rd oats again, then let out for pasture 2 years. There are 14 horses, Scotch and Irish breed, 100 sheep, 60 head of black cattle, 20 pigs, 15 turkeys, 30 geese, 50 ducks and 51 hens, all Irish breeds except 3 shell ducks, the property of William Ross.

Ballycarton Townland

Rotation of crops: 1st potatoes, 2nd barley, 3rd barley and clover, 4th wheat or oats. Only one farmer, Benjamin Lane Esquire, 8 cottiers. Soil on the upper part stiff clay, on the lower part a dark, sandy loam. Subsoil of the upper a stiff clay, lower, red sand. Has had no meadow these 10 years, pasture about 45 acres, Cunningham measure, 1 farm above 50 acres. Mr Lane pays rent for the half of the River Roe. There are 5 horses, 30 head of black cattle, no sheep, 15 pigs, an orchard with apples, cherries and gooseberries and currants. The orchard is let each year at 11 pounds per annum. Tenure of holding, lives renewable for ever. Manures are farmyard, compost for the clay soil made of moss, sand and lime; about 80 loads of compost to an acre for potatoes and turnips. Sand is only applied every third or fourth year. Markets for produce in Newtownlimavady and Coleraine.

One corn mill, water wheel undershot, 14 feet in diameter and 2 in breast [breadth]. The people are not bound to this mill. Sometimes the grain is purchased in the markets and ground and the oatmeal stored; toll thirty-second grain. Could shell and grind 16 sacks of 20 stone to each sack in the day if water enough; 1 man and the miller to attend. Metal works, pit wheel 120 cog, 9 feet in diameter, spur wheel 14 cogs, stones 1 pair, 4 feet 8 inches in diameter, would grind from 10 to 12 barrels of shelling in 11 hours. From Benjamin Lane, proprietor, dated 19th January 1835.

Ballymaclary Townland

Churchland, Sir James Bruce, proprietor: there are 7 farmers in this townland viz. John McCurdy holds 36 acres 3 roods 35 perches, William Campbell holds 28 acres 2 roods 16 perches, Thomas Church holds 34 acres 1 rood 30 perches, Thomas Blair holds 96 acres 2 roods 5 perches, James Dughan holds 300 acres 1 rood 5 perches, George Canning holds 28 acres 1 rood 12 perches, Magee and Collins holds 42 acres. Tenants at will, former leases 21 years and clause of renewal for 10 years expired in 1831.

Manures: animal; 7 or 8 head of black cattle folded or closed up from the 1st June to the 1st November will make manure sufficient for half an acre of potatoes. Barley or turnips: 12 sheep folded for the same time on 20 perches of ground will manure it for potatoes. The scourings of ditches and drains mixed with domestic cleanings is used for potatoes. The poor collect the sea wrack along the shore of the Foyle and spread it on the sandy soil for potatoes. Mr McCurdy has tried clay on sandy soil but with little or no success. If compost, 1 or 2 carloads to manure a perch (Cunningham measure). 100 loads per acre of shelly sea sand applied to the stiff clay improves it very much for oats and flax. Burnt ashes from bog applied to stiff clay is found to be superior to the shelly sand for potato oats. Sea wrack by itself produces wet potatoes. Rotation of crops are 1st oats, 2nd potatoes, 3rd barley, 4th oats, 5th, 6th and 7th pasture. Dated 19th January 1835.

The manure is generally applied on the potato crop. No wheat in the townland; the uplands produce good wheat on clay loam. Potatoes mostly lazy beds; when set in drills, 20 bushels produce 400 bushels; 32 bushels to set an acre in lazy beds, produce 300 bushels. In drills the potatoes are much larger. The prices fluctuating: for the last 4 years the average price was about 8d per bushel. The failure of the potato crop was felt much on the flat part of Magilligan.

From 10 to 12 stone of barley to sow an acre sown in April will produce about 1 ton and 2 cwt, reaped in the month of August. Rye, about 2 and a half bushels to sow an acre of 4 stone per bushel, sold from 9d to 10d per stone. Sown early in February, the produce will be about 24 bushels. Flax not sown: the soil does not suit.

Remains of oak and yew are found in the bogs

in a growing position. Breed of cattle: Sir James Bruce has introduced a cross breed of cattle, Devonshire and Ayrshire shorthorns, and are much better for milk and butter. Information obtained from John McCurdy and William Campbell, farmers.

Woodtown Townland

There are 3 farmers, viz. John Forsythe holds about 53 acres 1 rood, Edward Diamond holds about 43 acres 2 roods, James Tait holds about 44 acres 3 roods.

Drainage not much practised; Mr Forsythe has introduced French drains. Manures are compost, sea sand. The sand is drawn about 1 mile distant, no charge. About 70 or 80 cartloads to the acre on any part except the flat for potatoes, on mossy about 60 carts per acre for potatoes; sea sand on the clay 160 cartloads to the acre, on clover lea for barley or oats about 6 or 7 cwt, owing to the necessity of drawing up the hills. Rotation of crops are: 1st potatoes on stubble, 2nd barley on the upper part and oats on the lower, 3rd flax, 4th barley or potatoes, 5th oats or wheat on the flat part, wheat on the flax land, flax on the barley and barley on potatoes; 6th wheat or oats on flax land, flax on barley land, potatoes with manure. Wheat 13 or 14 stone per acre [barrel ?] to sow per acre, produce 6 to 8 barrels of 20 stone per barrel; barley 13 stone to the acre sown in April produces from 10 to 18 barrels of 21 stone; oats 20 to 24 stone per acre, produce 8 to 10 barrels of 18 stone, reaped in September, 3 stone per bushel. Oats sold at 8d to 9d ha'penny per stone; potatoes in drills from 16 to 20 bushels per acre, in ridges from 28 to 32; produce from drills 300 to 400 bushels.

There are 3 kinds of flax, viz. American, Riga and Dutch. American and Dutch are the cleanest, Dutch the largest. The Riga flax seed is as large as the Dutch but very dirty. 3 bushels of America flax seed to sow an acre, Riga 4 bushels to sow an acre, Dutch 3 and a half bushels to sown an acre. Price of America flax seed 4 pounds 15s per bushel, price of Riga 2 pounds 7s 6d per bushel, price of Dutch 4 pounds 4s per bushel. 2 barrels in the hogshead generally sown, the [beginning ?] of April. Produce of American 2 and a half cwt per acre, Riga 2 and a half cwt, Dutch 5 cwt, all clean, scutched. Market price at Newtownlimavady 2 pounds 10s for American, Dutch 3 pounds 15s per cwt.

10 horses, 33 head of black cattle, 100 sheep, 4 goats, 16 pigs, geese, turkeys, a few ducks and hens, old Irish breeds. The south wind most

injurious. Mr Church of Ballymaclary has a few French hens, black with white ears. Information obtained from John Forsythe and James Tait, farmers.

Benone Townland

There are 3 farmers, no leases; when granted 21 years was the lease. The leases expired in 1831 (November). A great portion under rabbit warrens. Drainage is performed by making small drains, some 3 feet deep and 3 feet wide, the water falling into the Benone river.

Manures are 1st compost of sand and stable dung, 2nd a compost of sand and scouring of ditches, 3rd sea wrack, a little used, brought from the shore at Magilligan Point, a distance of 4 miles for the trouble of gathering. Compost about 480 cartloads to the acre for potatoes; 320 carts of unmixed stable dung is equal to 480 of compost. Compost is used only once in 7 years.

Rotation of crops: 1st potatoes on lea with compost, 2nd barley, 3rd oats or rye or flax then let out 4 years for pasture. Method of planting potatoes is either by topping and spading, or by ploughing, harrowing and kibbing. The ridges are called lazy beds about 6 feet broad. Horses 8, black cattle 24 head, sheep 112, pigs 9.

About 250 acres under rabbit warrens, commonly a sheep-walk. The expense of sea wrack is that of man and horse. The sea wrack produces early potatoes but very wet, and is gathered principally by females who also collect the shellfish. Information obtained from William Mulholland and John Magee. Dated 20th January 1835.

Clooney Townland

William Begley holds 18 acres 3 roods 2 perches, value 17 pounds 12s 2d ha'penny; James Gilland holds 19 pounds 2 roods 28 perches, value 16 pounds 18s 1d ha'penny; George Doherty holds 19 acres 24 perches, value 17 pounds 3s 6d; John Moody holds 10 acres 2 roods 22 perches, value 9 pounds 11s; Miss Kane holds 12 acres 3 roods 28 perches, value 11 pounds 11s; Daniel McCallian holds 14 acres 3 roods 29 perches, value 11 pounds 18s 10d ha'penny; Michael Quinn holds 15 pounds 34 perches, value 11 pounds 17s 3d; John McCallian holds 31 acres 3 roods 14 perches, value 20 pounds 16s 6d ha'penny; John Doherty holds 22 acres 2 roods 16 perches, value 15 pounds 2s 3d; William Doherty holds 22 acres 1 rood 35 perches, value 17 pounds 13s 7d; [blank] McKeagh holds 8 acres 8 perches, value 6 pounds 16s 7d ha'penny; Edward Gillespie holds 7 acres

3 roods 21 perches, value 4 pounds 5s; John Kane holds 8 acres 1 rood 15 perches, value 4 pounds 14s 7d ha'penny; total 213 acres 3 roods 10 perches, value 164 pounds 7d.

Craig Townland

There are 2 farms above 50 acres, 1 corn mill, the property of Sir James Bruce, rented by Edward McCarriston, 1 loom. Rotation of crops: 1st potatoes, 2nd barley, 3rd oats, then potatoes again. Sometimes barley is laid down with clover and grass seed. One kiln for corn. 52 sheep, 77 orchards, hedgerows of ash and sycamore, 10 horses, 20 head of black cattle, 9 pigs, 24 geese, 16 turkeys, 12 ducks, 36 hens, Irish breed. Enclosures badly shaped except on the lower part. 7 cottiers. Information obtained from John Coyle, the only farmer.

Aughel Townland

No looms, 30 head of black cattle, 14 horses, 21 pigs, 40 geese, 50 ducks and 40 hens, no turkeys, Scotch and Irish breed of black cattle. Churchland, no lease, rent of the best land 30s per acre, middling about 17s per acre and worst about 5s per acre. Rent paid in cash, farmers tolerably comfortable; 2 cottiers and 11 farmers. Information obtained from John Moody and John Campbell, farmers.

Aughtimore Townland

One loom, 11 farmers, 15 horses, 30 head of black cattle, 10 pigs. No farm above 100 acres, 1 above 10 acres, rest under or about 10 acres. Order of crops: 1st potatoes, 2nd oats or barley laid down with clover and grass seed and let out for 2 years. Land of best quality about 15s per acre. One goose, 1 turkey, 40 ducks, 30 hens; hens are killed at seed time. The best of the land is bad. From James Doherty and William Crampsie, farmers. Dated 23rd January 1835.

Drumahorgan Townland

No looms, 90 sheep, 11 horses, 60 head of black cattle, 14 pigs, no turkeys, 24 geese, 50 hens, 50 ducks, 4 farmers, 3 farms above 30 acres and 1 farm above 15 acres. Rotation of crops: 1st rye, then let out for 2 years as part of the townland, will carry nothing but rye. In the mossy part: 1st potatoes, 2nd barley, 3rd corn. In the middle part a sort of soil called till, the bottom under this till like marle. From James Dermott and James Crampsie, farmers.

Ballyleighry South Townland

In this townland there are 14 farmers, 39 horses, 110 head of black cattle, 35 sheep, 3 goats, 30 pigs. Rotation of crops on broken lea: 1st oats, 2nd oats or potatoes with a mixture of bog and ashes, 2nd [sic] sand, 3rd ashes of burnt turf, 4th sometimes shelly sand for clover, ashes and bog procured in the townland of Duncrun about 1 mile distant. Ashes at 2d per cartload, bog free, shelly sand drawn from the shore at Benone 3 miles distant. Only 3 loads can be drawn in the day in summer. Hire of a cart, man and horse 2s 6d. About 240 cartloads of manure to the acre for potatoes and about 120 cartloads of ashes for potatoes. This mixture is used every third year, the sand and ashes every 7th year.

Rent of the best land below the road about [?] 1 pound per acre, 12s 6d above the road for arable and 2s 6d worst pasture up to the rock. Tithe about 2s 6d per acre. The tithe is now reduced to 1s 6d per acre. Drainage not much practised.

Rotation of crops are as follows: 1st oats, 2nd potatoes, 3rd oats or barley, 4th flax, 5th oats, 6th potatoes. Another rotation: 1st oats, 2nd oats, 3rd potatoes or turnips, 4th barley or oats, 5th flax, 6th oats laid down with clover, white; 6 bushels of 3 stone per bushel of blanter to sow an acre; less of potato oats: in bog about 12 stone of potato oats to an acre to be sown at the end of March. Produce of blanter 4 and a half bows, equals 54 to 60 bushels of 12 bushels to each bow. 84 bushels is the produce of an acre of potato oats, [?] angish oats not considered profitable. Potatoes are red Downs, seedlings, blacks, cups and Mullans, set in ridges, kibbed in the month of May, produce about 200 bushels. About 16 lbs of clover to sow an acre put down with barley or oats; 4 bushels of barley to sow an acre, produce from 8 to 9 barrels. Flax: Dutch 32 gallons to sow an acre, 10 gallons per bushel at 12s 6d per bushel; sown in April, produce 640 lbs of clean, scutched flax, best crop. Information obtained from Thomas Eaton, publican and John Coldwell, farmer.

Umra Townland

Only 2 farms; rent of the best land arable 1 pound per acre, middling 15s and worst 5s per acre, about 40 acres in the 2 farms. Rotation of crops are 1st rye, 2nd potatoes, 3rd barley let out for pasture for 3 years. 2 horses, 6 head of black cattle, 4 pigs, 4 goats, 2 ducks and 6 hens.

Soil: clay, red on the side of the mountain, lower part sandy, very poor. 2 good houses, 2-storey high, built of stone and lime, built by the present owners, David Cather [no other name given], for a summer residence during the bathing season, not occupied at present. A few ash and sycamore for ornament and shelter.

Manures are lime for the clay ground, on the sandy soil farmyard manure with a compost of sea sand and wrack for early potatoes, which are planted about the 1st February on the sand banks. Vegetables, viz. cabbages, beans and peas, are put down so early as 1st February. Plenty of limestone in Carnowry rocks. The farmers who have no limestone on their farms generally buy from Sir James Bruce at Downhill for 1s 4d per barrel. Head proprietor Sir James Bruce; churchlands. Information obtained from John McDermott and Hugh McClary, farmers.

Oughtymoyle Townland

One linen weaver, 2 woollen weavers. Conacres or rood ground are let by farmers to cottiers who live under them at 8 pounds per acre. The farmer gives the cottier ground for his manure. Those who set potatoes in this way receive only one crop for their manure. This system is not much practised. In the conacre system if the potatoes do not look well, the cottier will throw them upon the farmers' hands, thereby losing his seed and labour. The conacre potatoes are seldom allowed to be taken away until the rent is paid, which is generally before Christmas. Cottiers generally pay 1 pound 17s 6d for a house, garden and cow's grass; must pay a trifle for a permit to cut turf; have also a place for their manure. Sometimes cottiers pay their rent by work, at 6d per day with food and 10d per day without food, 8d per day in winter and 10d in summer. Enclosures pretty well shaped on the flat but badly fenced.

The mearings between each man's farm are drains about 6 feet wide and 4 and a half or 5 feet deep. Herds are kept constantly with the cattle. Ditches cannot be made as the soil is so sandy. Oats, barley and rye are taken to Newtownlimavady for sale; expense 2s 6d per day for man, horse and cart. Farmers generally send their own men and horses to market. Turf is generally procured at the mountain; only 2 loads per day can be brought. Turf is never brought from this parish to Newtownlimavady for sale.

Carpenters generally get their timber from Newtownlimavady or Derry.

Sea fowl are shot for food and feathers: the barnacle, wigeon and teal. The Roman Catholics make use of the barnacles on Fridays and other days when flesh meat is prohibited, as they say it consists of fish principally.

Rotation of crops: 1st potatoes, 2nd barley, 3rd oats or rye. Little or no flax: the soil does not suit, too sandy. 7 farms in the townland, viz. 1 farm above 50 acres, 1 farm above 40, 1 farm above 30 and 2 farms above 10 acres.

17 horses, 30 head of black cattle and 60 sheep. Average rent of the best land 1 pound per acre, middling 15s and worst arable 10s per acre. Information obtained from farmers John Linton and William McGranaghan. Dated 29th January 1835.

Margymonaghan Townland

Conolly Gage Esquire, proprietor; average rent of the best land 30s per acre, middling 15s, worst, not heathy mountains, 2s 6d per acre. The tithe composition valuators valued 200 acres 1 rood 8 perches of heathy mountain land, the property of Conolly Gage Esquire, so low as 3d per acre. All the parish is churchlands except the townland of Ballycarton which belongs to the Marquis of Waterford, now occupied by Benjamin Lane Esquire. Conacre or rood ground let by Mr Gage, John Donald and David Connell at 8 pounds per acre, some less according to the quality but from the bad payments usually made, this system is in some degree diminishing.

The farmhouses of the Presbyterians are the most comfortable. The Roman Catholics in all parts of the parish are very poor, their houses mere cabins built of sods and very dirty. Bog is scarce on Mr Gage's estate, plenty on Sir James Bruce's estate. No regular sheep-walks in the parish. Mr Gage has tried sheep on the mountain this year.

The barnacle is sold at from 1s to 1s 8d per pair; widgeon 8d to 10d each. The curlew is also shot for food and feathers. The most cottier tenantry are in Duncrun and Ballylieghrey.

The reason of the cottier tenantry being so numerous in those townlands is because the farmers are poor and the bog more convenient. On Mr Gage's estate in this parish there are 3 farms above 100 acres, 8 farms above 50, 4 farms above 20 and the rest under 20 acres; grazing farm exclusively in the townland of Croaghan stocked by Mr Gage. Information obtained from Charles Begley, agent to Mr Gage.

Tamlaght Townland

No looms, no woollen weavers, only 3 farmers. 2 farms above 50 acres and 1 farm above 10 acres; 13 horses, 32 head of black cattle, 6 sheep, 16 pigs, 12 geese, 10 ducks, 15 hens. Rotation of crops: 1st corn on lea with ashes, 2nd potatoes then corn again. In the upper part: 1st corn, 2 crops, then 3 years in lea. Convenient to the shore: 1st potatoes on manure, 2nd barley on rye, 3rd oats and rye, very little wheat. About 17 stone of barley to sow an acre at 10d per stone, sown in May, produce about 10 barrels of 21 stone to 21 stone to the barrel. From 21 stone to to 31 stone to the acre of oats on clay ground; 4 bushels of potato oats on bog land after potatoes at 8d ha'penny to 9d per stone; 21 stone to the barrel sowed from the end of March to the 1st of May, produce 6 to 8 boles of 12 bushels per bole, 3 and a half stone to the bushel. Potato oats reaped early in October, other description of oats in the middle or end. Nature of the soil on the upper part near Binevenagh, light loamy, good for grazing in wet weather but stiff or bound up in dry weather; the lower part light crofting ground, lower a subsoil, a stiff clay. Ashes procured by burning the bog.

Drainage: a small patch of swamp by French drains and the upper part of the land drained by the march ditches. Manures: a compost of sand for the clay. Price of sand in Cleggan, the mere trespass. Turf is brought from the mountains; only 1s is paid by the tenants for liberty to cut the year's turf on the mountain. The quantity of manure is put on according to the nature of the soil: shells for stiff land used once for potatoes on stubble or clover land on clay moss, and ashes on stubble ground on clover land, sand and ashes. Rye on the sandy hills, wheat not sown as the soil does not suit.

In 1815 Conolly Gage Esquire planted fir, ash, larch and hazel (in Leggalane). Sold occasionally to the tenants to make ribs for roofing houses, about 8d or 10d per pole of 8 feet long. Scallops at 6d per 1,000 sold at Coleraine and Newtownlimavady. Informants John McDonnell, David Connell. Dated 31st January 1835.

Gort Townland

The soil of this townland is considered to be superior to any other in the parish, chiefly owing to the existence of a bleach green which was in this townland many years ago.

Bellarena Townland

The soil of this townland along the river is a marshy clay; interior to this the clay is stiff; farther off from the river a sandy soil. The green feeding of Bellarena is turnips, potatoes, beans, carrots and mangle wurzle. Shells are raised in Lough Foyle and spread on lea 1 year before it is broken. Mr Gage purchased lime at Keady mountain at 10d per barrel of 3 bushels. Glar is got in the

lough and put on sandy soil for wheat. Drainage by tiles is practised by Mr Gage. The arch is formed by the tile and covered on the top. Drainage is not extensive as the land is sandy and does not require it [marginal diagram showing a tile drain]. Most exposed to west winds. Mr Gage keeps a boat to draw his manure from the lough. Compost is made of lime and the scouring of ditches is put on light, sandy soil.

The plantations of Bellarena are of oak, ash, beech, fir, sycamore and elm; sycamore and beech thrive best. Mr Gage sells timber for roofing houses at 10d for 16 feet of 4 inches in diameter. Hazel is natural, is sold at 2s 6d per 100 for hoop rods for baskets. Those sold for scallops are 6d per 100. Information obtained from J. Craig, steward to Mr Gage. Dated 12th February 1835.

Mr Gage's Farm

The potatoes on Mr Gage's farm are red and white Downs, blacks, kidneys, Miller's thumbs, English reds, Lammas apples, seedling blacks, posies and Northland wonders. Of English reds, about 24 bushels to sow an acre, black kidneys 24 bushels, red and white Downs 24 to 26 bushels. Produce of red and white Downs from 350 to 450 bushels off an acre, black kidneys from 300 to 400 bushels, English reds from 350 to 400: sold at present at 10d per bushel; Northland wonders from 460 to 600 bushels. Carrot seed from 4 to 5 lbs to the acre in drills about 27 inches asunder, produce about 2 tons 2 cwt.

The stock on Mr Gage's farm are as follows: 25 horses, 8 for the farm and 4 for the carriage and 4 for the saddle, with some young ones, 113 head of black cattle, 17 sheep, 6 pigs, English, Irish and Scotch breed. The poultry are geese, turkeys, ducks and hens with some shell duck and peafowl. Has a threshing machine, 4 horsepower, cog wheels of metal, can thresh about 2 bows of 24 bushels in an hour; cleans at the same time it threshes. 5 or 6 men to attend the threshing machine. The implements of husbandry are 4 iron ploughs and 1 moulding plough, 1 plough for pairing, 6 harrows, double on hinges, a machine for sowing turnips, can sow 2 drills at a time; spades, shovels, rakes and forks, pickaxes, turf spades, hoes, 10 carts, 2 grub harrows, commonly called scarrafiers, 9 tumbling carts.

Duncrun Townland

There are 22 farmers in this townland, many of them very small farms. The manures are ashes, sand, lime and farmyard manure from 120 to 160 cartloads to the acre, put on boggy ground for oats. Compost is mostly put on for potatoes, from 140 to 160 loads per acre. Crops are 1st barley, 2nd oats, 3rd wheat, 3 potatoes or flax after wheat; sometimes 1st potatoes on lea, 2nd oats, 3rd oats or 4th potatoes. About 30 bushels of potatoes to plant an acre, set in April and May, produce of an acre of potatoes 240 bushels; barley 4 bushels to sow an acre, produce from 8 to 10 barrels. Information obtained from John Donald and George Doherty, farmers. Dated 16th February 1835.

Milltown Townland

In this townland there are 3 farmers, 2 farms above 20 acres and one 20 acre farm with 2 cottiers to each farmer. Churchland property, no lease. The last lease expired about 19 years ago, Conolly Gage Esquire, proprietor. Rotation of crops are 1st oats, 2nd oats, 3rd oats or flax, 4th potatoes, 5th flax. 36 bushels of potatoes to sow an acre in broad ridges commonly called lazy beds. Oats from 6 to 7 bushels to sow an acre at 10d per stone, sown from March to May, produce from 3 to 4 bows per acre. Barley from 4 to 4 and a half bushels to sow an acre, sown in April, produce 4 bows of 12 cwt, cut at Lammas, 29th September. Nature of the soil in the upper part a light, hazely, middle clay, lower part mixed with sand. The manures are farmyard, compost of farmyard manure and moss used for clay soil. No lime, yet plenty in the parish, no use from want of turf. The sand is procured at Carroreagh, 2 miles distant. Ashes is sold at 3d per load on the field when burned. Clover 16 lbs to sow an acre, sowed 2nd or 3rd day after the barley. Flax is sown in April, 4 bushels to sown an acre, produce 6 to 7 stooks to the cogue of a quart⌐
scutched flax to the but and 9 ⌐ ⌐ogue. Scutched flax sells from 2 pounds 10s to 3 pounds per cwt.

There are 45 acres planted in 1831 with oak, ash, beech, larch and Scotch fir. For the last 3 or 4 years the above timber was sold for ribs for houses. There are 7 horses, 15 head of black cattle and 6 pigs and poultry. Information obtained from William Robinson and James McGeehan, farmers. Dated 17th February 1835.

Drumnahay Townland

Only 2 flax dressers in the parish; are paid 10d per score of 20 lbs for hackling at his (the hackler's) house. Travels as far as the Back Strand, where at constant work could hackle and dress two score in the day. Sometimes hires a man and pays him 10d

per day. The throngest season is from Hallowtide to Candlemas; has often cleared 9 pounds in the half year.

Gort Townland

In the townland of Gort there are only 2 houses, 1 horse, 1 cow, 2 pigs, 6 ducks and 3 hens. Order of crops are 1st potatoes, 2nd barley, 3rd oats, 4th potatoes again with manure. Manures are a compost of sea sand, farmyard manure and clay. The sand is got in Claggan for the drawing. Clay soil, part of this townland belongs to the Glebe. County cess for the last year (1834) amounts to 16s. No wood in the flats of Magilligan, as the trees would not thrive. When the roots reach the quicksand, the trunk begins to die away. From Robert Clyde and John Donald, farmers.

Duncrun Townland

There are 22 farmers in this townland, many of them very small farms. The manures are ashes, sand, lime and farmyard manure from 120 to 160 cartloads.

Shoeing Horses

In Magilligan, blacksmiths charge 1s per set for shoeing horses and 6d per set for removing. The iron is found by the owner of the horse. From John McCann, hackler and John Moody, dated 18th February 1835.

SOCIAL AND PRODUCTIVE ECONOMY

Amusements

Shooting at a target is practised on certain days, ·. Christmas Day, [?] old series and new series; New Year's Day for geese, turkeys, ducks, hens and sometimes shoes. Dancing on the Wooden bridge on the 14th July is one of the greatest amusements practised by the Roman Catholics. Card playing, common playing and dog-fighting, horse racing and cock-fighting was a common practice in Magilligan but is now decreasing as the people must apply themselves wholly to industry in order to meet the demands of the landlord. Throwing the stone, leaping and ball playing is practised in summer after working hours.

Schools

Margymonaghan night school, Michael Lane (a Roman Catholic), teacher, only one quarter teaching. House built of brick and sods, thatched, a room in a dwelling house; 7 boys at 1s 8d per month, a pay school; Protestants 3, Presbyterians 1, Roman Catholics 3, males 7, total 7. Night schools are seldom taught longer than the winter quarter. Information obtained from William Park, John Moody and John McCurdy, John Donald and Michael Lane. 9th January 1835.

Margymonaghan, Michael Lane (a Roman Catholic), teacher, a pay school, annual income of teacher 10 pounds; a room in a dwelling house, built of brick and sods, thatched. Of the Established Church there are 4, Presbyterians 6, Roman Catholics 4, males 45, females 9, total 54. Connected with no society at present, about a year ago received 2 pounds from the Kildare Street Society. Information obtained from Michael Lane, teacher.

Gortmore school, William McCracken (a Presbyterian), teacher, a pay school. Annual income of teacher 10 pounds, schoolhouse built of stone and lime, slated, cost 38 pounds, ample accommodation for 100 children, schoolhouse built by subscription. Of the Established Church there are 2, Presbyterians 41, Roman Catholics 4, males 31, females 16, total 47. Connected with no society, supported by the parents of the children. House built by subscription. Information obtained from William McCracken, teacher.

Ballyleighery, Hugh McGeehan, teacher, a Roman Catholic. Pay school, total annual income of teacher 8 pounds. Schoolhouse built of stone and lime, thatched, cost 4 pounds 7s, built by subscription. The Kildare Street Society gave 3 pounds for repairing the house. Of the Established Church there are 11, Presbyterians 8, Roman Catholics 32, males 37, females 14, total 51. Connected with no society, supported by the children alone. Information obtained from Hugh McGahan, teacher.

Ballymaclary, William Doherty, teacher, a Roman Catholic. Pay school, total annual income of teacher 16 pounds, viz. 10 pounds from the National Board and 6 pounds from the children. Schoolhouse a small, thatched cabin, cost about 10 pounds. Of the Established Church there are 11, Presbyterians 3, Roman Catholics 81, males 70, females 25, total 95. Connected with the National Board. Information obtained from William Doherty, teacher.

Margymonaghan night school, Michael Lane, Roman Catholic, teacher (see former report). Information obtained from William Ross and William Doherty, farmers. Dated 10th January 1835.

Drumnahay, Samuel Eason, a Protestant, teacher. Annual income of teacher 14 pounds,

viz. 12 pounds from the rector and 2 pounds from the children. The parish schoolhouse built of stone and lime, slated, cost 42 pounds, the Kildare Society gave 3 pounds 10s. Of the Established Church there are 10, Presbyterians 9, Roman Catholics 21, males 31, females 9, total 40. This school has decreased since 1832, chiefly owing to the want of funds. From Samuel Eason, teacher. Dated 16th February 1835.

Income of the Rev. Mr Porter

Mr Porter's income is as follows: 75 pounds Irish currency regium donum, 30 pounds from the congregation and 50 pounds for the clerkship of the synod, making a total of 115 pounds. Mr Porter's congregation is considerably increased, chiefly owing to his religious principles. Information obtained from the Rev. Mr Porter and Abraham James Moody.

Remarkable Man: Denis Hempson

This old harper died in 1807 upwards of 100 years old. He bequeathed his harp to Sir James Bruce of Downhill where it <is> remains to this day. Information obtained from John McCurdy and John Forsythe, farmers. Dated 7th February 1835.

Remarkable Characters

Denis Hempson, the harper who lived in the townland of Ballymaclary, was called the "two-headed harper" from a large tumour which grew at the back of his head; is said to have played the harp for Charles Stuart <Stewart> of Scotland, the Pretender, in the year of '46. Died in 1807 aged 100 years. Dated 16th February 1835.

Paddy Cushy Glen, a noted robber, lived at the Back Strand, afterwards removed to the Murderer's Hole on the road between Newtownlimavady and Coleraine, was shot by James Hopkins for attempting to rob him about 34 years ago. Paddy Cushy Glen had a brother called James Cushy Glen, who was executed in Derry for stealing 3 bullocks, the property of Mr Hughy.

Wages of Farm Servants

Male servants in winter (labourers) have 6d ha'penny per diem with diet, in summer 10d per diem with diet. Male servants in the farmer's house have from 50s to 55s per half year with board and lodging, female servants within doors from 15s to 1 pound 5s per half year. Wages are regulated according to the quantity of yarn they engage to spin: most commonly 10 cuts per day of

5 or 6 hanks yarn; and milk the cows, make the beds, sweep the house and fetch 2 goes of water. Servant maids provide and keep in repair their own wheels. Cost of a common wheel from 14s to 16s, a castle wheel from 18s to 1 pound, cost of reel 5s. It is not unusual for male servants in a farmhouse to purchase oatmeal and store it till summer and sell it out on credit in order to make money. From John Linton and John Moody, farmers. Dated 20th February 1835.

Linen Trade

The quality of the yarn of this parish is from 3 to 7 hanks out of the pound of flax, the 3 to 4 hank yarn for warp and the 5 to 7 hank yarn for weft bleached a little; this will make 13 hundred webs, 1 and a half hanks of tow yarn out of the lb. Of this, 8 hundred webs are made for coarse working-shirts, half bleached at home. Sacks are commonly made from tow yarn twilled. Dated 9th January 1835.

A weaver will weave 6 yards per day of 8 hundred linen and receive 3d per yard for weaving. The weaver is paid 1d out of the shilling for weaving 13 hundred webs. A 13 hundred web of 52 yards long will be put in and out in one month. Flax not a common crop as the soil does not answer; flax is generally bought rough at market of Newtownlimavady and Coleraine.

Rabbit Warrens

The season for catching rabbits commences the 1st of November and ends the 12th February. The carriers give 6d per couple for the bodies and sell them in Newtownlimavady at from 8d to 10d per couple. The carriers are obliged to return the skins to the farmers, who sell them to the merchants of Coleraine who take them to England. The skins are bought at auction at so much per dozen from [?] 15s in 1815 to 5s 5d in 1834. The carriers give 6d per couple for the bodies.

Method of selling the skin at the end of the cribbing season: on the 12th of February the merchants or commissioners appoint a day (next Thursday, February 19th 1835) and assemble at some house near the warrens, either by person or proxy, when the skins are disposed of by auction. One man generally buys the whole lot. In 2 or 3 days after the skins are brought to Coleraine or Newtownlimavady, where 2 persons are appointed to count and examine them; the carters are paid by the farmers half per dozen. The skins are then sent to England. The warrens are measured off something cheaper than the arable and are only used as grazing pasture for sheep and cows and affording bent grass for making mats, baskets. The warrens are becoming less productive owing to the invasion of rats and the desire to catch the rabbits to excess, not leaving enough to continue the stock from anxiety to make up the rents. Dated 22nd January 1835.

Corn Storage

It is a common practice for servant-men to purchase oatmeal or corn to make it and store it till summer when oatmeal is dearer. Dated 26th January 1835.

Bent [Grass] Manufacture

The bent [grass] manufacture is extensive in this parish. The grass of a year's growth is cut on the warrens in the month of August, must be cut low and laid on the sand to dry like hay for about 8 days, then fit for plaiting <plating>; is performed by boys and girls. Matting for halls etc. are made in the following manner: the bent is made into strands of 7 streaks. Sometimes 13 [?] strike plait are joined latterly to make a stripe [strip ?] of 30 to 31 yards long and 8 inches broad and sold at market at 1s per yard in Coleraine, Belfast, Antrim and Derry and all over the province and some to Dublin, but could not compete with the Dublin rush mat. When the matting is made, it is sold for 20d to 2s per web of 30 yards to 31 yards.

In August a man could cut about 2 stooks of 12 sheaves per stook in the day. A stook will make 3 webs. Each sheaf makes one strand. A man will make a good day's work if he can plait one web in the day. The strands are sown together with 3 plat strings made of bent. A boy or girl is kept to sew and trim them. Matting for the doors etc. are made 2 and a half feet long and 2 feet broad; sells for 3d at the market. A man will make 8 of these mats each day. The above are the only things manufactured of bent except besoms and beehives, besoms 3d to 4d. The bent is bought growing on the warren at the rate of 6d per stook. From Thomas Magee, manufacturer. 27th January 1835.

Rabbit Catching in the Warrens

The rabbits are taken in a trap made for the purpose. Rats are also taken in those traps; sometimes hawks or other birds of prey are taken also in those traps. Dated 28th January 1835.

Rent Arrears

The tenants of Sir James Bruce are always half a

year's rent in arrears. When a year's rent is due, only the half is demanded.

Grey Flannel Production

After the sheep-shearing, which is generally in the months of May and June, if a farmer wishes to make grey webs or flannel, in order to have it done expeditiously a number of females are invited from various parts of the parish. The girl who arrives first at the house is called the bride. The wool is washed, dried and picked, then mixed and greased. Cards are provided and the females are set to work, some to mix the black and white wool together, and to separate the good from the bad or the coarse from the fine, while others are employed in carding and rolling. The spinning is done at leisure, sometimes a few females are collected to spin the wool. The wool is always greased before it is spun, 6 oz. of butter to grease a lb of wool. A dance generally concludes the web breaking.

Camps or Spinning Parties

It is not unusual for farmers to collect a number of females together with their wheels, to spin flax yarn for a warp when in a hurry to make up the rent. The girl who spins the most yarn is said to win the camp. There are many instances of girls spinning from 2 and a half to 3 hanks in a day at those camps. The girl who wins the camp is called the bride. A dance generally concludes the camp also. The females are generally well treated, get plenty of tea to breakfast with oatbread and strong butter, to dinner plenty of bacon and cabbage, tea in the evening and sometimes a glass of whiskey. From John Moody and John Donald, farmers, dated 3rd February 1835.

Woollen Trade

A weaver will weave 6 yards per day of woollen cloth and receive for weaving 8d per yard.

Rundale

By the exertions of Sir James Bruce and Conolly Gage Esquire, this system is almost abolished.

Smuggling and Illicit Distillation

No smuggling in the parish.

Illicit distillation: this system is only practised by the lower order of cottiers who are expert in hiding, particularly those near the shore and rabbit warrens; method: by making holes in the sand

and putting the vessels which contain the whiskey into these holes, then covering them with sand. Cartwheels are drawn across to deceive the police, who have often come to the place and could not succeed in making the seizure. Mr Gage has almost succeeded in putting it down altogether on his estate. It is much on the decrease in Magilligan.

Emigration

Annually about 20 emigrants to America of the labouring class and poor, very few to England, very few to England and Scotland. Those who emigrate to England and Scotland generally return. Emigrants to America do not return. Seldom the head of a family goes.

Enclosures

Conacres are let at 8 pounds per acre. Enclosures very few; those enclosed are by drains in the flat or sandy ground, stone and clay ditches on the hilly and more mountainous parts. Fields are tolerably well shaped, square and oblong on the flat, not so well on the uplands. From the want of permanent fences, herds are kept constantly with the cattle in summer and harvest. The drains are dry in summer and harvest. The drains on the flats of Magilligan are dry in summer and harvest but almost impassable in winter. Drains are the only fences or mearings between each man's farm in the lowlands and from the sandy nature of the soil, it is almost impossible to make fences or keep them in repair.

In order to abolish this system, Sir James Bruce has sent a number of young men and others (from this part of his estate) to America, who had small farms and has enlarged the farms of others, who also had small farms. No lease on any of the churchlands in this parish; a want of lease is one of the greatest obstructions to improvement.

Carrying Crops to Market

The expense of carrying crops to market (Coleraine and Newtownlimavady) is about 3s per day for man, horse and cart. Farmers generally send their own horses, carts and men to market with their crops.

Sheep-walks

The rabbit warrens are the only sheep-walks in the parish.

Fuel

The fuel of Magilligan is cut turf of very good

description procured on the mountains and wholly consumed in the parish. No charge for turf cutting or lime burning.

Drainage

Drainage is extensively practised, is performed by making a drain about 7 feet wide and 3 and a half or 4 feet deep between each man's farm on the flat or marshy land. On the middle part French drains are made about 2 feet wide and 2 feet deep. Some [are] piped, covered with tough sods, rushes or straw with stone regularly laid at the bottom and flags on top, then filled up with earth. The pipe is about 1 foot wide when finished. Drainage in the upper part of the land is found unnecessary, as the fall is so rapid from the mountains. Dated 4th February 1835.

Carpenters

Carpenters generally procure their foreign timber at Newtownlimavady or Coleraine. Other smaller timber is purchased at Downhill and Bellarena and is used for roofing office houses and making implements of husbandry.

Trees

The trees which seem to thrive best are ash, beech, sycamore and timber sallow. Along the foot of the mountain, alder, fir, larch, spruce and [?] sycamore, very little oak except at Bellarena. Trees do not thrive well in sandy soil, for when the roots reach the sand, from want of nourishment they die away.

Manures

Sea sand is used as manure and drawn from 1 and a half miles to 2 miles distant, expense is the mere drawing. From 150 to 200 cartloads to the acre and about 15 square feet to the cartload; stable manure, 80 cartloads to the acre of 26 square feet per load; compost of sea sand, clay and moss from the mountain, 100 to 150 cartloads per acre, about 21 square feet per acre; ashes from 100 to 140 cartloads per acre and drawn sometimes from 2 and a half to 3 miles distant, cost from 4d to 6d per load of about 15 square feet per load.

Kelp

None in the parish. After a strong westerly storm, abundance of seaweed is driven onshore and gathered east by the poor for manure. The barilla <brilla> plant is not known in the parish.

Straw Weld

This weed grows spontaneously along the front of the rabbit warrens between the warrens and the arable ground; is used by the poor for dyeing yellow, would grow if cultivated.

Netting Sea Fowl

Method of taking: poles are erected along the shore from 6 to 8 feet high. Nets are suspended from these poles. The barnacle, wild duck, widgeon and teal in their nocturnal flight are taken in these nets and are sold in Derry, Newtownlimavady and Coleraine, the barnacle from 1s to 1s 8d each, widgeon and teal from 8d to 10d each with feathers. Information obtained from John McCurdy, John Forsythe and John Moody, farmers. Dated 5th February 1835.

Fisheries

The fish are whitefish or cod, flounder, fluke, turbot and sand eel. The shellfish are oysters <oisters>, giggans, mussels <muscles>, cockles, limpets and whelks <wilks>. Method of taking codfish: a number of large hooks are tied to a line and about 6 feet asunder. Flounder and turbot are taken the same way as codfish. The bait for codfish is a piece of herring put to the hook. A sand eel is the best bait for a turbot. A piece of a fresh herring, a lugworm or a fish called a cowhorn inhabiting a spiral shell are all good baits for a codfish or fluke. The lugworm is found in great abundance along the Fore Strand in the sand. Cockles are taken in May and June at the reflex of the tide on a calm day. The codfish are taken at Inishowen from November to January, flounders are taken in summer. Very larger oysters are along the strand in Magilligan but very scarce. Whelks are taken at the Fore Strand. Giggans from November to July taken at the Back Strand in great abundance, taken after a storm and used by the poor, sometimes to excess, which has brought on diarrhoea. Giggans are sold at six a penny. Cockles are picked up at the Fore Strand and from the mouth of the River Roe to Magilligan Point; are found about an inch under the sand. Generally girls are employed or children who cannot work at agriculture.

The oysters are taken by a drag which is placed after the boat. About 4 or 500 per day of the large oysters are taken and are sold to carriers (who take them to Newtownlimavady) at 3 pounds per cartload of 31 hundred. 30 hundred is the regular load, the odd hundred for the support of the carriers. Cockles are found at the Fore Strand, where 20 quarts per day can be picked in the season, generally by females who take them to Newtownlimavady where they are sold at 1d per quart, at the strand for ha'penny per quart. Kerrywherries, a small shellfish found at the Back Strand, when used by the poor generally brings on vomiting; not so much used now. Information obtained from John McCurdy, John Moody and John Forsythe, farmers. Dated 6th February 1835.

Settlers

The settlers of Magilligan (English) are Connolly Gage Esquire, Renolds, Cust, Church, Luke, Lane. These are the descendants of the settlers, some of whom are at this day reduced to extreme poverty.

The Irish settlers or Roman Catholics came over from Inishowen in the capacity of herds and servants, some of whom are at this day independent farmers.

Drainage

The flats of Magilligan have been brought to their present state of dryness by the exertion and good example of Mr Bacon, an officer of Queen Anne's <Ann's> army, who adopted the system of drainage he had seen in the Netherlands. Mr Bacon purchased the townlands of Ballymaclary, Drummons and Upper Doaghs. Method: by making open drains from 6 to 8 feet wide and 4 feet deep. Mr Bacon also introduced drags (the claws are of iron, the handle of wood) for the purpose of clearing off the tough sods and keeping the drains open. [Marginal diagram of a drag with claws]. Dated 11th February 1835.

Tailors

There are 19 tailors in the parish of Magilligan, including journeymen and apprentices. Charge for making a frieze <frize> coat at the farmer's house 2s 2d, for making breeches or trousers 1s per pair, for making a waistcoat 1s.

Flax: Method and Expense of Cultivation

For preparing the ground for an acre of flax, twice ploughing and twice harrowing with 2 horses in the plough and 2 horses in the harrow, 1 pound 1s; 3 bushels of America seed to sow the acre, 2 pounds; 4 persons to weed the acre, 4s; pulling an acre with 10 women, 6s; binding and stooking with 2 men, 2s; drawing to the water (if convenient) and steeping, 2 men with 1 horse and cart, 6s;

taking it out of the water and spreading, 6s; lifting it off the spread and bringing it home, 4s; drying and attending the kiln, 5s; rolling at flax mill 7s 6d; milling i.e. the use of the mill, 1 pound 7s 6d; 3 persons to attend at the mill, 3s; drawing to the mill and bringing home, 5s; total to prepare it for market 6 pounds 17s. From John Moody and William Park, dated 11th February 1835.

Other expenses are as follows: cleaving <cloving> 4d per score; hackling 10d per score; spinning one spangle of 6 hank yarn 10d, 43 hanks of 3 hank yarn to the warp of a web of 52 yards, 44 hanks of 6 hank yarn to weft. The weaver is paid according to the price the cloth sells at market. If a web of 52 yards sells at 1s 6d per yard, the weaver receives 18s for weaving the web. There are 4 kinds of tow: the 2 coarse are mixed together and the 2 fine are also mixed together. The coarse used to make sacks and the fine for shirting. The coarse tow is sold from 3d to 4d ha'penny per lb, the fine at 4d per lb. From William Park and John Moody, dated 12th February 1835.

Lime and Manure

For the lower part of the parish, on Sir James Bruce's estate, the lime is procured at Woodtown, quarried for 8d per ton of 7 barrels. The expense[s] on a ton of lime are as follows: drawing from the quarry to the townland of Tircorran 1s 3d, breakins 1s, turf to burn the limestone 2s 6d, price of the stones 8d, attendance at the kiln 8d, total for the ton 6s. About 40 carts of manure, farmyard, would manure an acre of ground for potatoes.

Curious Harness and Other Equipment

About 50 years ago there were in use rush suggans made of straw twisted as thick as the cable of a ship, used for drawing. The back suggans are also of straw and placed on the horse's back to carry sacks full of corn. Log wheel cars (unshod) with gudgers of wood were also in use. Branks i.e. 2 pieces of wood suspended as a substitute for a halter, the pieces of wood as a noseband, used principally to tie horses on the grass.

The Big Drain

Mr Bacon <Beacon> laid out all the drains in the flats of Magilligan, the Big Drain commencing at Tircreevin burn and separates Clooney from the following townlands viz. Lower Ballyleighry, Duncrun, Margymonaghan and Ballymulholland, which last it separates in the end of its course from Drumahorragan.

Orthographical and Etymological Notes on Duncruthen by John O'Donovan

MEMOIR WRITING: NATURAL STATE AND ANTIQUITIES

Duncruthen: Authorities on Place-name

Colgan thinks the name signified "fort of the Crutheni" and conjectures that it was the same as Dunboe <Dunbo>. That this is the present Duncruin may be inferred from the following authorities. In the *Life of St Patrick* we are told that "our apostle departed from Inishowen and crossing the straits <streights> at the north end of Lough Foyle, proceeded to Duncruthen where he placed a bishop of the name of Beatus."

Lanigan adds that Colgan threw out a conjecture that Duncruthen was the same as the present Dunboe, and that he has been followed by Archdall that it is probable that Duncruthen was situated elsewhere, and quotes an old life of St Patrick stating that it was "in regione Kennacta."

The Monasticon states as fact what Colgan, who is quoted as authority, conjectures in one part of his work and corrects a subsequent part. An old life of St Patrick places it "in regione Kennactae", which show it can be no other than the present Duncrun in the parish of Magilligan, the barony of Kenaght. Colgan in *Tr[iadis] Th[aumaturgae]* postively asserts that it is not Dunboe, as he conjectured in another place, but the shrine of St Columbkille in Ardmic-Giollagan.

Notes on Orthography and Derivation of Benyevenagh by J. O'Donovan, T.A. Larcom and others, 1832

MEMOIR WRITING

Queries on Name of Benyevenagh

[J. O'Donovan] Benyevenagh, Sampson memoir; Benyevnagh, Sampson's map; Benevenagh, fair plan of Magilligan; Benyevenagh, Dubourdieu's *Statistical Survey of the County Antrim*.

Is this pronounced Ben or Beny by the natives? [Signed] by T.A. Larcom, 2nd March 1832. [Answer] It is pronounced Ben-ye-ve-nagh "the frightful precipice", [signed] William Lancey, Lieutenant Royal Engineers, 9th March 1832.

I have always observed it was called Ben, [signed] M. Waters, Captain Royal Engineers, 10th March 1832.

[Query] My Dear Fenwick, is the mountain called Ben-ye-ve-nagh or Ben-e-venagh; is the y sounded? Ever yours T.A. Larcom, 12th March 1832. [Answer] My dear Larcom, I believe the y is sounded: Ben-ye-venagh, [signed] R. Fenwick, 13th March 1832.

Letter from Lieutenant R. Fenwick to Lieutenant T. Larcom, 26th November 1831

MEMOIR WRITING: ANCIENT TOPOGRAPHY

Abbey in Duncrun

My Dear Larcom,

I hasten to reply to yours of the 25th inst. respecting the ecclesiastical ruins in the parish of Magilligan, but I fear you will be much disappointed in the results.

The abbey in Duncrun townland is levelled with the ground: indeed the grass grows over the foundations which are barely visible. They are composed of basalt, rudely hammered and cemented with lime mortar. I imagine that the building was in the form of a cross, as the ruins may be traced according to the accompanying hand sketch [ground plan, main dimensions 30 by 30 feet, "T" shape]. These dimensions are about the thing but I cannot be quite sure of them. At [position marked by a dot within a circle] is a slab lying, about 4 feet by 2, on which a cross has been sculptured. It is now so much worn from the effects of the weather as to be nearly effaced. I need not add that there are no doors etc. visible. It is said that the dwellings (of which the above was the church) were at the foot of the hill. There is not a vestige now remaining of them. The abbey was called St Columb's Throne, was plundered by the Danes in 1203 by Dermit Hua Lochluin, who was pursued and killed by the chieftains of the country *Archdall's Monasticon*. The refectory, dormitory were at the foot of the hill on which the church stood, and a precipitous way along the side of the hill is still called the Canon's Field.

Skreen Church

Skreen church is about 30 feet by 15, the foundations alone are visible. They are composed also of hammered basalt and cemented with lime. It is supposed that a separate parish has existed here and that it was the old parish church. This is the only tradition relating to it.

Tamlaghtard Old Church

Tamlaghtard old church was lately used as a

Romish place of worship (I think its ground plan dimensions are in the field books). It is roofed and has one long, narrow window about 6 feet high by 2 wide at the eastern end. The door is about 6 feet high and 4 wide and at the western end. There is no sculpture or inscription to be found about it. At the east end is an old grave covered with rudely-hewn stone and said to be that of St Aidan (I know not on what authority save Rev. John Graham's), who is said to have retired here in his old age. A short distance from this, and under the brow of a precipice is a well called Tubber-Aspug-Aidan; and on a hill which overhangs the churchyard is a rock from whence the saint is said to have preached. The old church is also cemented.

Old Castle

I [?] mention the site of an old castle, I think in Craig townland; there is not an atom of it now remaining. Tradition gives it to Fion-mac-coul. I forgot to mention that a castle is said to have existed in Duncrun but where, I could never find out. A set of stone weights from 1 to 30 lbs were dug out of the abbey ruins some years back.

I think I have now mentioned all I know about these buildings. However, if my letter be still unsatisfactory, pray let me hear from you again and I will cause enquiries to be made on the spot; but indeed the pursuit of antiquarian lore is a most uphill work as we rarely meet with anyone who can give us information. You shall have the best descriptions I can give you of the rest of my work as far as I can go, and so far from considering your queries a bore I am most anxious to give my work out of hand in the most complete manner possible. Believe me faithfully yours, [signed] R. Fenwick, 26 November 1831.

Queries and Answers on Orthography of Place-names by T.A. Larcom, R. Fenwick and others, 1831

<small>MEMOIR WRITING: NATURAL STATE</small>

Correspondence on Place-name: Drummons

[Query by T. Larcom] Drummonds in Magilligan, very obviously from Drumans "little hills or hill-ocks"; the sand hills bear this out. Would it be objectionable to spell them (there are 3 townlands) Drumans or Drummans instead of the family name Drummonds, which would point to a different origin? [Answer by R. Fenwick] I think Drummonds the true name. The townlands have

been called by it upwards of 60 years. I never heard of Drumans being used. It may be as well to remark that Magilligan was a Scotch settlement and which may account for the name.

[T. Larcom, 27th July 1831] Drummonds the best perhaps, as it has been so called 60 years; but it is Drummans on the Down Survey. What written document of 60 years date has Lieutenant Fenwick seen in which they are 'called Drummonds? [Answer] I have not seen any written document to prove this, nor do I think there is one in existence. A gentleman who was born in the townland and who is upwards of 60 years old said it never had any other name but Drummonds. I am very certain that if any person were to ask for Drumans, he would not be understood. However, it must be remarked that the names in this county are so corrupted that their original spelling is at best but a mere guess. I recollect 5 different spellings given of Kenaght (the barony in which Magilligan is situated). [Signed] R. Fenwick, Lieutenant Royal Engineers, 1st August; referred to Lieutenant Vicars.

If the spelling of the Down Survey is to super-sede that given by the division officers obtained on the best authority in their power to report, it is to be regretted that they have not the names given them as written on the Down Survey when the orthography of the parishes is under considera-tion. I should think in this case the Down Survey shows that the townlands were called after the "little hillocks" (drumins) and not from the Scotch family name Drummonds, unless the letter d has since been taken into the word Drummons as a modern and fashionable addition. [Signed] M. Waters, Captain Royal Engineers, 2nd August 1831.

Who is the lessee under the see of Derry? He would probably inform you how it was spelt in his old leases. [Signed] Thomas A. Larcom, 8th August 1831.

Lieutenant Fenwick is requested to make fur-ther enquiries and report the result. [Signed] M. Waters, Captain Royal Engineers, 10th August 1831.

[Covering note]: Sir James Bruce's letter dated 16 August is forwarded. [Signed] R. Fenwick, Lieutenant Royal Engineers, 18 August 1831. Sent to the Ordnance Survey Office 18th August 1831, [signed] M.M. Waters, Captain Royal En-gineers.

[Letter from Sir James Bruce] Downhill, 16th August 1831. Sir, I fear I cannot give you any satisfactory information as to the orthography of the townland of Drummonds, which I find in some leases spelt as above, in others Drummons and Sampson's map makes it Drumans. All my late leases are Drummonds, those that I can find prior to 1804, Drummons. I regret I cannot give you more satisfaction on this subject and remain, Sir, your obedient servant J.R. Bruce.

[Final note by T. Larcom] It was for an answer on Drummans I wrote this down the last time. I think Drummans is decidedly the best spelling. There be not very high written authority for Drummonds. The Down Survey is sufficient to decide for Drummans.

Correspondence on Place-name: Crook Dooish

Crook Dooish is a very doubtful word if it be pronounced Crookdooish and is "a round topped hill." This would be a very fair way of spelling it. Craigdooish seems violent and Cnoc Duais scarcely less so, [signed] Thomas A. Larcom, 13 July 1831. [Answer by Lieutenant Vicars] Craigdhuish or Craigdouish (rock, blackish) is most probably the correct mode of spelling this mountain. It is a round-topped hill, and when this name was given to it, no doubt, quite uncultivated. It is still so for some distance from its summit, [signed] Edward Vicars.

[T. Larcom] As Lieutenant Vicars twice states, now and 14 September 1830, that it is Craig Dooish, I suppose Craig must be adopted; but I cannot help thinking from his own statement that "it is a round-topped hill" crook would be more proper: cruac is a round-topped hill, and to the best of my recollection it is called crook in the country. It is very unusual to call a hill craig, but crook, croagh, croghan are very common. [Answer] I have made further enquiries respecting the best mode of spelling this name and learn from Mr Ogilby, a gentleman well acquainted with the Irish language and residing in Upper Cumber, that Cruacdooish is the best he gives as the probable meaning and derivation: cruit "a small lump or mound", dubhis "upon a greater hill" (as in this case); but states from the great corruption that has taken place much doubt and uncertainty exists in tracing the original meaning. [Signed] Edward Vicars, Lieutenant Royal Engineers, 25th July 1831.

[Diagram of shape of Crookdoish by Captain M. Waters]. [Query] Do you not object to Crook Dooish as a doubtful word? The hill is round and flat on its top. [Signed] M. Waters, Captain Royal Engineers, 29th July 1831. [Answer] Look at my note of 13th and 21st July and you will see that this is exactly the form to which crook would apply,

and because I recollected that this was the shape, I resisted Lieutenant Vicars' wish to spell it Craig, which would be wholly inapplicable. Cruach is literally "a large haystack" and figuratively a hill of similar form. [Signed] Thomas A. Larcom, 30th July 1831.

Letter from James Boyle to George Petrie, 20 October 1833

Letter from James Boyle to George Petrie

Newton, October 20 1833. My Dear Sir, Want of time has alone prevented my replying to your letter and giving you the information you requested in it before this, but I now commence doing so; and anything defective in my present communication shall be supplied in my next. I send you accompanying this a very rough sketch of the stone which lies horizontally in the centre of the foundations of the abbey of Duncrun. It is, however, a true sketch. The foundations of the abbey are so insignificant to all appearance as not to be worth drawing: there is merely a small square of about 16 by 14 feet.

The copy of the farthing (which was found near where the weights you got were) I also send on. One side bears some letters round the edge, which are illegible. The silver coin (of which I send you the impressions) was found at the foot of the rock with 7 others, not long since. As you may perceive, it is of the reign of Henry VIII.

I send you the ground plan of the foundations of a castle under the precipices opposite the abbey. It is on the summit of a steep land 100 feet high and about 150 yards from the foot of the rock. There is no tradition whatever concerning it, and it is almost entirely unknown, though the foundations are very visible. It is in the townland of Duncrun. I shall (if you wish) send you a drawing of it and the adjacent ground, as I am sure it must have been a place of great strength.

The tradition regarding Duncrun is that it was the favourite abbey of St Columb. It was called St Columb's Throne. The entire tract of country called Mac Gil Eogan (as the lands on the opposite side of the Foyle were called Kinel Eogan) were granted by the family of O'Cahan to support this abbey, and from the abbots the property was transferred to the bishops long prior to the Reformation, after which it devolved to the Protestant see of Derry. This abbey was plundered AD 1203 by Derrick McLochlin, vide Archdall's *Monasticon*. In the year 1185 Ambrose O'Coffey, Bishop of Kineleagan, died in this abbey, from whence his body was conveyed to Derry and buried in St Columb's Church (*Ware's Bishops*). Magilligan therefore differs from other church property in not having been granted to the church by the Crown.

Scrine, called in Colgan's *Thaumaturgae* <*Thaumatourgon*> "Scrinium olium monasterium ditissimum": schreen being the Irish for "a book", tradition sanctions a belief that here and at the church of Ballinascreen, in the other extremity of the county, there were ecclesiastical libraries in the middle ages. The foundations of a chapel still remain on the site of this abbey. The surrounding burial ground, being long since disused as such, is cultivated to the very walls, the interior of which is used for the burial of unbaptised infants and shipwrecked mariners. In the visitation book of the diocese of Derry for the year 1718 is the following record: "This parish (Magilligan) being divided by a great bog, so that some of the inhabitants cannot come to church in winter, hereupon Bishop King with the rector and parishioners repaired the old chapel of Scrine farther distant from the church, where the incumbent is obliged sometimes to officiate, the benefice being too small to support him and a curate." There is not a single inscription. No foundations of a castle exist, though here alleged heaps of stones fallen from the rocks have given rise to the tradition.

NATURAL HISTORY AND SOCIAL ECONOMY

Wildlife and Occupations

Eagles sometimes, tho' seldom, visit this mountain. There is a rock (called the Eagle rock) on the precipice near the sea. Hawks of many descriptions abound in Binevenagh <Bennyevenagh>. There are a few foxes and badgers in the townland of Craig; they are rarely seen; for half of the last century rewards were offered at the Easter vestries for those who brought their skins.

The population is employed in agriculture, catching rabbits, making bent matting, fishing; and a manufacture of a sort of grey woollen frieze is carried on to a small extent. The people here are I think on the whole rather comfortable than otherwise: their holdings area small as to arable land, but a large tract of rabbit warren is attached to each farm.

So far I can go at present, I have set Mr Graham to work for you. He is really competent to assist you. I am not, but what I can I will gladly do for you. I shall be glad to hear from you and remain very truly yours, [signed] James Boyle.

PS Solomon's is in the parish of Dunboe <Dunbo> and not in any district. I think it likely Mr Ligar sketched it. HMS [His Majesty's Service] [to] George Petrie Esquire, 21 Great Church Street, Mountjoy Square, Dublin. Newtown, October 20th 1833.